Fundamentals of Reasoning

FUNDAMENTALS OF REASONING

Stephen P. Schwartz
Ithaca College

Macmillan Publishing Company
New York

Maxwell Macmillan Canada
Toronto

To my parents,
Margery and Sidney Schwartz

Editor: Maggie Barbieri
Production Supervisor: Katherine Evancie
Production Manager: Paul Smolenski
Text Designer: Angela Foote
Cover Designer: Robert Vega
Cover Illustration: Reginald Wickham

This book was set in Helvetica and Garamond by Carlisle Communications, Ltd., and was printed and bound by Book Press, Inc. The cover was printed by Phoenix Color Corp.

Macmillan Publishing Company
866 Third Avenue, New York, New York 10022

Macmillan Publishing Company is part of the Maxwell Communication Group of Companies.

Maxwell Macmillan Canada, Inc.
1200 Eglinton Avenue East
Suite 200
Don Mills, Ontario M3C 3N1

Printing: 1 2 3 4 5 6 7   Year: 4 5 6 7 8 9 0

Library of Congress Cataloging-in-Publication Data
Schwartz, Stephen P.
    Fundamentals of reasoning / Stephen P. Schwartz.
        p.   cm.
    Includes index.
    ISBN 0-02-407785-2 (pbk.)
    1. Reasoning—Problems, exercises, etc.
    I. Title.
    BC177.S347 1994
    160—dc20   93-9443
                                            CIP

Acknowledgments

Sidney Harris. *Newsweek*. February 7, 1983. Cartoon caption reprinted with permission of the author.

Darrell Huff and Irving Geis. *How to Lie with Statistics*. 1954. Graphs on pp. 62–63. Reproduced from *How to Lie with Statistics* by Darrell Huff, pictures by Irving Geis, by permission of W. W. Norton and Co., Inc. Copyright 1954 by Darrell Huff and Irving Geis; © renewed 1982 by Darrell Huff and Irving Geis.

Elizabeth Kristol. *Violence and Videos*. November 16, 1989. © The Washington Post. Reprinted with permission.

James Rachels. *The Elements of Moral Philosophy*. 1986. McGraw-Hill, Inc. Reprinted with the permission of McGraw-Hill, Inc.

Ayn Rand. *Capitalism: The Unknown Ideal*. Copyright © 1962, 1963, 1964, 1965, 1966 by Ayn Rand. Used by permission of New American Library, a division of Penguin Books USA Inc.

Jeff Riggenbach. *USA Today*. December 28, 1990. "New Laws Not Needed; They Are Ineffective." Reprinted by permission of the author.

PREFACE

This text is intended for students in an introductory course in reasoning or informal logic and is designed to enhance reasoning skills. Reasoning and logic are the study of arguments with the purpose of determining which are successful and which are unsuccessful. Such a study requires close and detailed attention to language and how people use it to justify their ideas or convince others of their beliefs. Learning to reason, like learning a language, involves being able to understand others and being able to make ourselves understood.

As in learning a language, one learns reasoning as much by practice and exercise as by explanation. Explanations play an important role, but by themselves they are difficult to understand and apply. We need examples and exercises in order to understand fully the explanations. This book relies on many examples and exercises to enhance the explanations. The exercises should be used not just to sharpen skills, but to help develop the understanding of key concepts and techniques.

Generally, the exercises are arranged to proceed from easier to harder. There are "confidence builders" at the beginning of each set of exercises and some really challenging ones at the end.

Each chapter begins with explanations and discussion, but the explanations depend on the exercises for illumination. The exercises are to be worked with a view toward a better understanding of the explanations. Solutions to selected exercises (indicated by a ★) are provided in the appendix. The text plus the examples and exercises constitute a complete introductory course in reasoning, including the rudiments of formal logic.

One of the presuppositions of this book is that we can go a long way in judging the success or failure of ordinary arguments by using our common sense and background knowledge. Very little in the way of special formal knowledge is necessary for good reasoning. What is necessary is to use the common sense and knowledge we already have in a focused, careful, and directed way. The goal of this text is to help students develop these skills.

Chapter 1 sets out basic concepts and introduces many of the topics developed in detail in Chapters 2 through 8. These chapters are mainly concerned with understanding arguments and the notions of logical validity and soundness. Chapter 3, "Logic Puzzles," introduces formal material such as truth tables for "not," "and,"

and "or." This chapter is valuable because it forces students to argue validly before the notion of valid argument is formally defined in Chapter 4. Chapters 9 through 13 are mainly focused on premise evaluation and nondeductive reasoning. Many topics that are vital for understanding and evaluating the sorts of semitechnical reasoning that we find daily in the media are introduced in these chapters. These topics include causal, analogical, and statistical reasoning. Chapters 14 and 15 are primarily concerned with informal fallacies and persuasive abuses of language that interfere with good reasoning. Finally, Chapter 16 deals with extended passages in which all the skills and techniques of reasoning are brought to bear.

I wish to thank many people for help and encouragement in preparing this text. I am particularly indebted to my colleague, Frederik Kaufman, for reading drafts of the manuscript and making many criticisms and suggestions. His help has been invaluable. Linda Finlay and Robert Klee, also of Ithaca College, read large parts of the work, and I am grateful for their suggestions and encouragement. I would also like to thank Eric Pearson of Berea College for reading and commenting on an earlier version of the text; George Casella of Cornell University for help with statistics; and Maggie Barbieri, Katherine Evancie, and Nadine Grange of Macmillan Publishing Company for their help, guidance, and diligence in seeing this project through the many stages to publication. Thanks are due to Ithaca College for research grants and reassigned time from some course work so that I could devote more energies to writing. Finally, I would like to thank my students in Reasoning 14–151 for helping me to refine much of the material in the text and for providing many of the examples.

S.P.S.

CONTENTS

RECOGNIZING ARGUMENTS

This chapter is an introduction to the material in the next seven chapters. Many topics that will be taken up in much more detail later are introduced briefly here.

KEY TERMS AND HEADINGS

Discourse	The Principle of Charity
Argument	Conjunction
Premise	Disjunction
Conclusion	Conditional Statement
Argument Indicator	Explanation
Premise Indicator	Suppressed Premise
Conclusion Indicator	Suppressed Conclusion

A **discourse** is any sentence or group of sentences. In reasoning we are especially interested in a particular kind of discourse called an **argument.** An argument is any discourse in which someone attempts to support a claim by giving reasons. The reasons that are given as supporting the claim are called the **premises** of the argument, and the claim that is to be supported is called the **conclusion** of the argument. Often discourses that contain arguments are quite complex affairs in which premises and conclusions are strung together sequentially. Thus a conclusion from some premise could be a premise for some further conclusion. Frequently two or more premises may combine to support a conclusion.

Our best and most important guides to figuring out arguments are **argument indicators.** Argument indicators are words such as "therefore" and "because" that indicate that an argument is being given. Argument indicators are either **premise indicators** or **conclusion indicators.** Premise indicators precede or occur in premises, and conclusion indicators precede or occur in conclusions. We use argument indicators to detect the presence of an argument and to determine which of its statements are premises and which are conclusions.

The following is a list of some important premise indicators:

since	as	because
inasmuch as	for	follows from
firstly	secondly	in addition
being as	seeing that	

The following is a list of some important conclusion indicators:

therefore	thus	so
hence	accordingly	implies that
proves that	consequently	entails that
then (but not "if . . ., then . . .")		

For example, consider the following argument:

> Politicians have no incentive to protect
> children's rights since children cannot vote.
>
> Robert E. Schell and Elizabeth Hall,
> *Developmental Psychology Today,*
> 4th ed. (slightly adapted)

The reason being given in support of the claim that politicians have no incentive to protect children's rights is that children cannot vote. "Children cannot vote" is the premise, and this is indicated by the word "since," which comes in front of it. (This is an *argument,* but it may not be a *good* argument. The premise "Children cannot vote," although true, may not imply the conclusion "Politicians have no incentive to protect children's rights." For a discourse to be an argument the reason given need not be a good reason. The subject of argument evaluation is taken up in detail in later chapters.)

Here is an example of an argument using a conclusion indicator:

> Computers cannot do logic. I can do
> logic. Therefore, I am not a computer.
>
> Sidney Harris, *Newsweek,* February 7, 1983
> (A cartoon in which the argument is
> being given by a computer!)

The word "therefore" is a conclusion indicator and indicates that "I am not a computer" is the conclusion. The first two sentences are the premises. (Again, this is an argument, but of course it may not be a good argument either. Although the premises imply the conclusion, they may not be true, since computers *can* do logic to some extent.) These two arguments illustrate that the order of the statements is no indicator of which is the conclusion. Sometimes the conclusion comes last and sometimes it comes first (and at other times it can come in the middle).

To recognize and understand arguments effectively, we must learn and understand the words on the two lists of indicators, but we should also keep in mind that these lists are by no means complete and that many of the words on these lists have other uses (e.g., "since" in "I have been a Dodger fan since last June"). Often a discourse contains a word or phrase that is not a standard argument indicator but that in the context serves to definitely establish that an argument is present.

> The fact that the graduates of Paigetown
> University do not repay their student loans
> shows that they haven't learned anything in
> their ethics classes.

Here the expression "shows that" is being used as a conclusion indicator.

On the other hand, many arguments contain no argument indicators. A person often makes a claim and gives reasons for it without using any special argument indicator words. In such cases we rely on the context or our understanding of the relations among the statements made (for example, that some are likely to be used to support others) to determine that an argument is being given. In practice, however, determining whether a particular discourse is an argument is sometimes difficult. Of course, if there are argument indicators being used in their standard senses, then it is an argument; but when there are no argument indicators difficulties mount.

In determining whether a discourse without argument indicators is an argument (as well as in determining which of its statements are premises and which are conclusions) we must use **the principle of charity.** The principle of charity says "Always interpret a discourse in the way that makes the most sense given the information that we have." If the discourse makes more sense interpreted as an argument, then interpret it as an argument. The principle of charity does not eliminate the difficulties. It is at best a loose and vague (but indispensable) guide. It at least tells us this: Given two possible interpretations one of which makes more sense of the discourse than the other (given all the information that we have), choose the one that makes the most sense. Although we use the principle of charity all the time and it is essential for communication, we must use judgment to determine what makes the most sense, and disagreements in interpretation are possible. As we shall see in the chapter on informal fallacies (Chapter 14), the principle of charity is sometimes willfully violated.

SOME POINTS TO KEEP IN MIND

1. The words "and," "or," "unless," "but," "however," "although," "nevertheless," and "yet" are not argument indicators. "And," "but," "however," "although," "nevertheless," and "yet" are **conjunctions;** "or" and "unless" are **disjunctions.**[1] (For the logic of disjunctions and conjunctions, see Chapter 3.) "But," "however," "although," and "nevertheless" affirm the conjunction of two facts and indicate that

---

[1] Grammatically "or" is a conjunction as are "because" and "therefore." We are making distinctions here that can be ignored by the grammarian.

there is something surprising about this conjunction. For example, "Joan is very bright, but she does not get good grades." "And" asserts the conjunction of two facts without any suggestion of surprise.

2. Many expressions such as "I think that" and "I believe that" are attitude or confidence indicators and are *not* argument indicators. The phrase "I think that" in the statement "I think that Hot Trot will win the race" does not indicate that any reasoning is going on; rather it indicates the speaker's weak degree of confidence. Such an expression as "I know that" would indicate a higher degree of confidence. "I guess that" would indicate an even lower degree of confidence than "I think that." The words "must" and "cannot" are sometimes argument indicators, but often they are used to express degree of confidence. Oddly enough, "must" can indicate a low degree of confidence. Typically a sentence such as "He must have gone to the store" indicates that his going to the store is the most likely possibility given the evidence but confidence is low. (For more on attitude indicators, see the section on parenthetical elements in Chapter 16.)

3. The expression "If . . ., then . . ." is not an argument indicator. An if/then statement is a **conditional statement.** Conditional statements can occur as premises or conclusions of arguments but are not themselves arguments. (For more about the logic of conditional statements, see Chapter 6.)

4. Some argument indicator words, such as "because," are often used in explanations as well as arguments. An **explanation** is an attempt to say why something happened or why some statement is true rather than an attempt to support a statement with reasons for believing it. The distinction between explanations and arguments is not at all sharp and, indeed, many logicians treat explanations as a type of argument. The distinction is perhaps clearest if we consider that a statement "*A* because *B*" often makes as much sense as the statement "*B* because *A*." For example:

> The Wombats are the best team because
> they won the championship.

makes as much sense as

> The Wombats won the championship
> because they are the best team.

This can be confusing unless we keep in mind that the first is an argument in which a reason is given for believing the claim that the Wombats are the best team, but the second is an explanation of why they won (it was not luck, or fixed, and so on).

Many explanations are causal in nature (see Chapter 12 on causal reasoning). Sometimes such a causal explanation can itself be the conclusion of an argument. At times statements such as "*A* results in *B*," "*A* brings about *B*," or "*A* causes *B*" are themselves not separate arguments but can be parts of arguments or explanations.

As already mentioned, explanations can be treated as arguments and that is the way we will proceed here, although we must be aware of the distinction when ignoring it would clearly lead to confusion or misunderstanding.

5. Arguments often contain **suppressed premises** and occasionally contain **suppressed conclusions.** A suppressed premise (or conclusion) is one that is presupposed by the arguer but is not explicitly stated. Arguments often take place against a background of shared agreements and presuppositions. Such agreements and presuppositions need not be explicitly stated, indeed perhaps ought not to be in the interest of brevity, but are nonetheless part of the argument. For example, if someone argues "We can't go skating today on the pond because it is 50° outside," we understand the connection between the premise and the conclusion without being told that ponds melt at temperatures above 32°, that melting ponds are unsafe for skating, and so forth. The practice of using suppressed premises can be abused and leads to important complexities in understanding arguments. These topics are taken up in more detail in Chapter 9.

EXERCISE 1.1

For each of the following discourses indicate whether or not it contains an argument. Circle any argument indicators. If the passage contains an argument, state the conclusion. Some of these passages contain more than one conclusion.

★ 1. If there is increased industrial growth, there will be increased pollution. Pollution is bad for the environment and for us. So industrial growth must be slowed.

   2. Middle-aged people have more experience than the young because they have lived longer.

   Donald Hall, *Writing Well,* 4th ed.

   3. The boiler blew up because the main plate had a crack in it.

   4. Since trials are often characterized by extensive court delays, going to trial is both costly and time consuming.

   West's Business Law

★ 5. Because they originally exercised in the nude, Greek olympians probably never envisioned winter games.

   Time, February 15, 1988

   6. Everybody has needs. She didn't fill mine. So I split.

   7. Boil noodles in salted water 5 min. Drain and keep warm. Heat oil, brown onion and add Chinese cabbage. Add crab meat, stock, seasoning and simmer 5 min. Add cornstarch dissolved in cold water. Stir until thickened. Add chopped water cress, soy sauce and serve over hot noodles.

   Chinese Wok Cookbook

8. If there were no class divisions in American society, or if people were not assorted into a complex society of religious ethnic groups, occupations, and race, if, in short, Americans were a homogeneous people with no differences in situation, minds, interests, and demands—then the background of decision-makers would make no practical difference. Since such is obviously not the case, it is of more than passing interest that the vast majority of political decision-makers in the United States come from an exceedingly narrow, powerful, and privileged slice of American society.

Edward S. Greenberg, *The American Political System: A Radical Approach*

9. A boat is steered by means of a rudder against which pressure is exerted by a stream of water flowing past it. This stream of water is usually the result of the forward motion of the boat. If the tiller is moved to starboard, the rudder is moved to port; the stream of water flowing past the boat presses against the rudder and pushes the stern to starboard.

H. A. Calahan, *Sailing Technique*

★ 10. In its broadest sense logic is the study of the structure and principles of reasoning or of sound argument. Hence it is also a study of those relations in virtue of which one thing may be said to follow from . . . another.

Antony Flew, *A Dictionary of Philosophy*

11. Because it is in electronic format, it is easy to edit the document by making changes and corrections to the text. Therefore, the word processor is more efficient than the conventional typewriter.

Thomas J. Cashman, Gary B. Shelly, and Gloria A. Waggoner, *Computer Concepts with Microcomputer Applications*

12. I haven't seen a movie I liked since *Lawrence of Arabia*.

13. Skipping is not as stressful as running, because you often have both feet on the ground at the same time. Therefore, the pressure of pounding is diffused.

Superfit Magazine, Fall 1986

★ 14. The complexity of bacteria is not alone in arguing against their evolution. The very proteins that help make up bacteria, and other living things, show evolution to be hopelessly improbable.

Awake

★ 15. If we take eternity to mean not infinite temporal duration but timelessness, then eternal life belongs to those who live in the present.

Ludwig Wittgenstein, *Tractatus Logico-Philosophicus*

16. Man is to be free, and government is to be limited, because man has been created in the image and likeness of God, and hence has inherent dignity and worth.

National Review, July 4, 1986

17. Geneticists may consider that information flow is the principal life function and accordingly view viruses as alive because they are able to store and use genetic information to specify their own reproduction. Physiologists, on the other hand, may consider viruses as nonliving entities because of their inability to carry out physiological functions, such as ATP generation. Thus the perspective of an individual can bias the opinion on whether viruses should be viewed as living or not.

Ronald M. Atlas, *Microbiology*

18. There is no technique currently available to examine or count neurons in the living brain. Thus counts must be undertaken upon autopsy and can be done at only one point in the life of the individual. Since there is variability in the number of cells in human brains, it is difficult to estimate how much has been lost when an accurate count of what was present in earlier years is simply not available.

Diana Woodruff-Pak, *Psychology and Aging*

19. I hope that someday we can abolish sport and trophy hunting. Remember, 90 percent of us are non-hunters, therefore I'm assuming that all or most of our 90 percent respects wildlife. Being the majority, I feel we must have some power over the minority of hunters.

Ithaca Journal, November 1988

20. Unfortunately ears can't shut out noise the way eyes can shut out light because man was not born with ear lids, and therefore the ear is one of the more vulnerable parts of the body.

Richard Connell, *An Introduction to Systematic Learning*

CHAPTER 2

ARGUMENT DIAGRAMMING

In this chapter a simple method of representing the structure of arguments is introduced.

KEY TERMS AND HEADINGS

Argument Diagram	Basic Premise
Linked Premises	Final Conclusion
Intermediate Conclusion	Checking Your Work
Serial Argument	

To display the structure of an argument we will use an **argument diagram.** When diagramming an argument, we circle the argument indicators, bracket and number the statements, and use arrows to indicate the direction of the reasoning. An arrow points from a premise to a conclusion. In the diagram, the premises and conclusions are represented by numbers. The numbers themselves do not indicate which statements are premises or conclusions, but only the order in which the statements come in the discourse. To show which statements are premises and which are conclusions we need to use arrows.

EXAMPLE

ARGUMENT

Politicians have no incentive to protect children's rights since children cannot vote.

BRACKETING AND NUMBERING

<Politicians have no incentive to protect children's rights> since <children cannot vote.>

DIAGRAM

Often two or more premises combine to support a conclusion. We use a "+" between premises and a line under them when their combination is supposed to support a conclusion. We say that such premises are **linked premises.** The diagram of an argument in which the first two statements are linked premises supporting the third would look like this:

There are many ways that premises can combine to support a conclusion. The most important is logical combination. In the well-known example

All men are mortals. Socrates is a man.
Therefore Socrates is a mortal.

the first two statements combine to support the conclusion. This is a simple example of logical combination. (A great deal more will be said later, especially in Chapters 4 through 8, about how premises logically combine to support a conclusion.)

BRACKETING AND NUMBERING

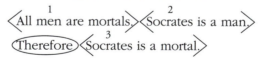

DIAGRAM

Another way that premises can combine to support a conclusion is by combining evidence. For example:

> The road is wet. The trees are dripping.
> The sky is dark. The air is moist. So it must
> have just rained.

Again this argument would be diagrammed and linked as follows:

BRACKETING AND NUMBERING

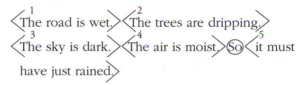

have just rained.

DIAGRAM

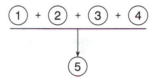

Here is another example of a linked argument fully diagrammed:

ARGUMENT

> Computers cannot do logic. I can do logic.
> Therefore, I am not a computer.

BRACKETING AND NUMBERING

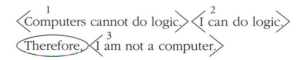

DIAGRAM

In this case the premises are linked by logical combination.

In a complex argument a particular statement may be both a premise and a conclusion. Such a statement is called an **intermediate conclusion.** In an argument diagram an intermediate conclusion has an arrow pointing to it *and* an arrow pointing away from it. An argument with an intermediate conclusion is called a **serial argument.**

Besides intermediate conclusions, serial arguments also contain **basic premises** and **final conclusions.** A basic premise is a premise that is unsupported in the argument. It has arrows pointing away from it in the diagram but no arrows pointing to it. A final conclusion is supported by premises in the argument but does not itself support anything else. In an argument diagram, a final conclusion has arrows pointing to it but no arrows pointing away from it. We can also speak of the premises of a simple argument as basic (they are not intermediate) and the conclusion as final (it is likewise not intermediate).

The following is an example of a serial argument fully diagrammed.

ARGUMENT

Since we all have different personal histories, we
may all interpret the same event differently.
Therefore, a serious stressor for one individual may
have no effect on someone else.

Roger J. Allen, *Human Stress,*
Its Nature and Control

BRACKETING AND NUMBERING

(Since) ⟨we all have different personal histories,⟩¹ ⟨we
may all interpret the same event differently.⟩²
(Therefore,) ⟨a serious stressor for one individual may³
have no effect on someone else.⟩

DIAGRAM

In the preceding argument, statement 1 is a basic premise, statement 2 is an intermediate conclusion, and statement 3 is the final conclusion.

More complex arguments can contain several premises and conclusions all connected in complex ways. The point is to show, using numbers and arrows, which statements are being used to support which statements and how they may combine to support those statements. Here is an example of a more complex argument fully diagrammed:

ARGUMENT

Trails in wilderness areas ought to be unmarked or marked as minimally as possible. Trail marking involves painting marks on rocks and trees, and such painting of rocks and trees is a form of defacement. So trail markers are a form of defacement in wilderness areas.

BRACKETING AND NUMBERING

⟨¹Trails in wilderness areas ought to be unmarked or marked as minimally as possible.⟩ ⟨²Trail marking involves painting marks on rocks and trees,⟩ and ⟨³such painting of rocks and trees is a form of defacement.⟩ (So) ⟨⁴trail markers are a form of defacement in wilderness areas.⟩

DIAGRAM

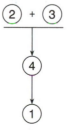

(For more discussion of this example, in particular of how we know that statement 1 is the final conclusion, see "Checking Your Work," p. 20.)

SOME POINTS TO KEEP IN MIND

1. Argument diagramming, especially when there are no argument indicators present, requires interpretation of discourses. When interpreting a discourse, we always use the principle of charity. The principle of charity (to repeat) says "Always interpret a discourse in the way that makes the most sense given all the information we have." What "makes the most sense" is a matter of judgment and people can disagree about it. But, of course, not anything goes. Some judgments are more plausible than others.

2. When a conclusion indicator is used, at least some of the premises are earlier in the discourse.

3. When the premise indicators "since" or "because" are used, the conclusion usually is another clause of the same sentence. There are two standard formats.

Format a: <conclusion> because <premise>.
Format b: Because <premise>, <conclusion>.

I use "because" for convenience but the same formats hold for "since." There is no difference in meaning between format a and format b. The same argument can be expressed either way.

EXAMPLES

Format a: Physical education should be required because physical activity is healthful.

Format b: Because physical activity is healthful, physical education should be required.

No matter how many premises there are they will occur together in one of the two formats.[1] In such cases the premises are linked.

Format a: <conclusion> because <premise 1>, <premise 2>, <premise 3>.
Format b: Because <premise 1>, <premise 2>, <premise 3>, <conclusion>.

EXAMPLES

Format a: It does not yet seem like football season because the weather is warm and humid, classes have barely started, and they are still playing baseball.

Format b: Because classes have barely started, the weather is warm and humid, and they are still playing baseball, it does not yet seem like football season.

---

[1] This rule, as just about any other involving natural language reasoning, has exceptions. In particular, when more than one indicator word is used, things get more complicated as in "Since Socrates is a man, he is a mortal, because all men are mortals." Also the premises and conclusion *can* be separated by periods as in "Socrates is a mortal. Why? Because he is a man and all men are mortals."

The diagrams of formats a and b would be different. In the preceding discourse expressed as format a, number 1 would be the conclusion. Expressed as format b, the conclusion would be number 4. In each case the conclusion is the same statement "It does not yet seem like football season," but it gets a different number because of where it occurs in the discourse.

4. Sentences of the form "If *P*, then *Q*" and "When *P*, *Q*" are bracketed as a single unit. Do not split apart an if/then sentence. Other sentences that should not be split apart are any of the form "*P* or *Q*" and "*P* unless *Q*."

5. Occasionally, argument indicators and especially conclusion indicators occur inside of, instead of in front of, statements.

> The Wombats won the championship. They are,
> therefore, the best team.

6. Quite often when an argument contains no argument indicators, the first statement is the conclusion. A common way to organize a paragraph is for the first sentence to be some claim that is then supported in the rest of the paragraph. As long as it is clear that the sentences after the first one are being given as reasons for the first one no argument indicator is needed. For example:

> Neighborhood watch programs are a mixed blessing.
> They promise too much for too little. They create the
> illusion that crime can be controlled on the cheap.
> They lack police professionalism. And they raise the
> specter of vigilante justice.
>
> Alan M. Dershowitz, *USA Today*,
> February 17, 1984

7. Explanations can be diagrammed exactly like other arguments and in general that is what we will do. A discourse such as

> *A* because *B*

can be diagrammed as

without having to decide whether it is an explanation. Such a decision is often difficult or impossible to make out of context in any case. Sometimes, however, it is necessary to diagram a statement such as "*A* causes *B*" or "*A* results in *B*" as a single unit, since it itself is a premise or conclusion of an argument.

8. If two statements say the same thing, then give them the same number in the diagram. If a statement is neither a premise nor a conclusion (if it is a definition or explanation of a key term used elsewhere in the discourse, for example), leave it out.

Another minor technical point is that often premises and conclusions are expressed as questions, commands, or noun phrases. There is nothing wrong with this in writing, but officially in reasoning and logic each premise and conclusion must be a statement. In practice it is too tedious to transform each question, command, or noun phrase into a statement. We should keep in mind, though, that a bracketed and numbered noun phrase, question, or command is really the statement it stands for in the argument. Likewise, officially again, every pronoun should be replaced by its antecedent. Unofficially we skip this in most cases, but we should be able to supply on demand the antecedent of any pronoun in an argument.

EXAMPLE

ARGUMENT

Of course the Wombats are the best team.
Didn't they win the championship?

BRACKETING AND NUMBERING

Of course ⟨the Wombats are the best team.⟩¹
⟨Didn't they win the championship?⟩²

DIAGRAM

The premise is "The Wombats won the championship"; the conclusion is "The Wombats are the best team." The premise as given is "Didn't they win the championship?" Officially we replace the question with a statement (because that is its intent) and the pronoun "they" with its antecedent. (It also would not hurt to say *what* championship, if that is known.)

9. Some discourses contain reports of arguments. Often an author will give a summary of someone else's argument in order to question or criticize it. When an argument is reported in a discourse, the argument should not be attributed to the author of the discourse.

For example, Fred says: "Sally says we can't go to the party tonight because it is only for seniors. But I heard that it was open to juniors too." The argument "We can't go to the party tonight because it is only for seniors" is Sally's argument not Fred's. Fred is reporting Sally's argument in order to question it. (For more on reports of arguments, see the section on reported arguments in Chapter 16.)

ONE FURTHER POINT ABOUT ARGUMENT DIAGRAMMING

To be done well, argument diagramming requires the *opposite* of speed reading. In other words, it requires slow and careful reading because it involves very careful, detailed attention to the passages. The diagramming of a moderately complex discourse often involves a great deal of poring and puzzling. Skilled argument diagrammers will sometimes disagree adamantly about the correct diagram of a particular, not very deep, argument. Speed reading may be appropriate for some kinds of prose, but it is definitely not appropriate for argumentative discourses. Readers must learn to slow down, reread, ponder. Oddly enough I think that most people need to learn slow reading more than they need to learn speed reading, at least for reading technical writing such as textbooks, editorials, and academic articles. In my opinion, many people read these kinds of works too fast. Circling argument indicators, bracketing statements, and trying to sort out premises and conclusions will help you to slow down and give you stopping places and things to ponder. It will also help to improve your own thinking, speaking, and writing.

CHECKING YOUR WORK

Although argument diagramming requires interpretation, certain basic checks can be used to verify parts of a diagram. If a numbered statement in the discourse is preceded by a *premise indicator,* then in the diagram *that number must have an arrow pointing away from it.* If that number does not have an arrow pointing away from it, then the diagram is wrong. It may also have an arrow pointing to it, in which case it is an intermediate conclusion, but it must at least have one arrow pointing away from it. If in the bracketing you have ". . . because <^{2} >," then check to see that in your diagram you have

or

Likewise, if a numbered statement is preceded by a *conclusion indicator,* then that number *must have an arrow pointing to it.* If that number does not have an arrow pointing to it, then the diagram is wrong. It may also have an arrow pointing away from it, in which case it is an intermediate conclusion, but it must have at least one arrow pointing to it. If in bracketing you have "Thus < ³ >," then in the diagram you must have

If in your diagram there is an arrow pointing from one number to another, ask yourself if the one with the arrow pointing away really could plausibly be taken to be a reason for the one the arrow is pointing toward. If it could not, then your diagram is probably wrong. This is especially important where there are no argument indicators. For example, in the diagram of the trail marking discourse, statement 4 ("Trail markers are a form of defacement in wilderness areas") is given as a premise for statement 1 ("Trails in wilderness areas ought to be unmarked or marked as minimally as possible") even though this is not determined by the argument indicators. It is implausible that the reason trail markers are a form of defacement is that trails ought to be unmarked or marked as minimally as possible. It does not make any sense that way. Thus we know that

cannot be right. Indeed it has got to be the other way around.

ARGUMENT DIAGRAMMING EXERCISES

General directions: Each set of exercises in this chapter contains a number of discourses. Most are from actual sources but others are made up. A few are clear and straightforward, others are unclear, and some contain poor writing and mistakes in punctuation. I leave these uncorrected. This is what we have to deal with in reading actual texts.

For each passage: (1) circle all the argument indicators, (2) bracket and number the statements, and (3) construct a diagram of the argument in which arrows point from premises to conclusions. A few examples are done here to help you get started.

EXAMPLE A

ᐸPaigetown University obviously does not teach its students ethicsᐳ ⟨since⟩ ᐸmany of them do not repay their loans.ᐳ

DIAGRAM

②
↓
①

EXAMPLE B

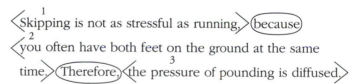
ᐸSkipping is not as stressful as running,ᐳ ⟨because⟩ ᐸyou often have both feet on the ground at the same time.ᐳ ⟨Therefore,⟩ ᐸthe pressure of pounding is diffused.ᐳ

DIAGRAM

②
↓
③
↓
①

EXERCISE 2.1

For each of the passages: (1) circle all the argument indicators, (2) bracket and number the statements, and (3) construct a diagram of the argument.

★   1.   Marijuana is classified as an hallucinogen because in sufficient dosages its active ingredient, THC, causes hallucinations.

John P. Dworetzky, Psychology

2.   In the Army Reserve what you won't find yourself doing is getting bored because this isn't ordinary part-time work.

Advertisement

3.   Since allergies can be treated but not yet cured, the most effective and obvious form of treatment is to avoid the offending substance.

Joanne Silberner, "Allergy Warfare," U.S. News
& World Report, February 20, 1989

4.   We ought to protect the environment because it's valuable to us.

Ann S. Causey, Environmental Action Guide

★ 5. Because people with AIDS can become incapacitated without warning, they expose themselves to possible disappointment whenever they make long—or even short—range plans.

Rose Weitz, *Sociology of Health and Illness*

6. Communication skills are important because it is through communication that we gain and offer the information we need to make successful decisions. . . .

Cheryl Hamilton, *Communicating for Results*

7. Lecturing is a commonly used teaching technique because it is efficient, it can be used with groups or entire classes rather than just with individuals, it gives the teacher control over the content, and it is easily combined with other methods and adjustable to fit the available time, the physical setting, and other situational constraints.

Thomas J. Good and Jere E. Brophy,
Educational Psychology

8. Because we know that classrooms, schools, and school districts can work, and we know how to make them work, it is not unreasonable to conclude that the continued "plight" of the urban public schools must reflect an unwillingness to make the fundamental political decision about whether a permanent under-class is acceptable and necessary.

Constance Clayton, "We Can Educate
Our Children," *The Nation*, July 24, 1989

9. Since a prince cannot use this virtue of liberality in such a way as to become known for it unless he harms his own security, he won't mind, if he judges prudently of things, being known as a miser.

Niccolò Machiavelli, *The Prince*

★ 10. Because pain and suffering are undesirable, and because both human and nonhuman animals are capable of pain and suffering, there is at least a *prima facie* case for treating all animals (both human and nonhuman) similarly when the infliction of pain and suffering is involved.

Tom L. Beauchamp, "Problems in
Justifying Research on Animals," in
Contemporary Issues in Bioethics

11. Many women who do paid work also work in the house. Because women have, in effect, two jobs, part-time work is often their only option in the labor market.

Bureau of Labor Statistics, U.S.
Department of Labor, August 29, 1985

12. Because it is harder for older people to see and hear, they often have trouble getting instructions and actually doing tasks.

Diane E. Papalia and Sally Wendkos Olds,
Human Development, 4th ed.
(slightly adapted)

EXERCISE 2.2

For each of the passages: (1) circle all the argument indicators, (2) bracket and number the statements, and (3) construct a diagram of the argument.

★ 1. It is important to save the earth. It is the only one we've got.

2. Overwhelming policy considerations weigh against imposing a duty on psychotherapists to warn a potential victim against harm. While offering virtually no benefit to society, such a duty will frustrate psychiatric treatment, invade fundamental patient rights and increase violence.

> California Supreme Court, "Tarasoff v.
> Regents of the University of California," cited
> in *Contemporary Issues in Bioethics*

3. The United Nations cannot be regarded as a perfect or problem-free organization. It has a cumbersome and sometimes irresponsible assembly; its bureaucratic structure slows progress; and it faces financial problems.

> Keeley Hanson, "The United Nations,"
> *The Humanist,* March/April 1990

4. Chances of being lonely are greater if you're poor. . . . Money makes it possible to entertain, to travel, to telephone, to exchange gifts, to provide others with aid.

> Catherine Houck, "How to Defeat
> Loneliness," *Cosmopolitan,* September 1989
> (slightly adapted)

★ 5. In many ways, the Supreme Court is the worst place to win a human rights case—even when an Earl Warren is sitting as Chief Justice. It takes a large amount of money and a long time to get a case to the Court. Even when a party wins, he may not come out with a clear victory. The decisions are seldom unanimous, and a five-to-four or six-to-three split tends to weaken the impact of a majority opinion. A Supreme Court decision may have a tremendous effect in the long run, but it seldom brings about immediate major changes.

Barron's How to Prepare for the LSAT

6. Our genes and our environment control our destinies. The idea of conscious choice is ridiculous. Yes, prisons should be designed to protect society, but they should not punish the poor slobs who were headed for jail from birth.

Time, October 4, 1982

7. New York is . . . the most charitable city in the world. Nowhere is there so eager a readiness to help, when it is known that help is worthily wanted; nowhere are such armies of devoted workers, nowhere such abundance of means ready to the hand of those who know the need and how rightly to supply it.

Jacob Riis, *How the Other Half Lives,* 1890

8. Concentration has increasingly characterized the brewing industry. In the last several decades the number of beer firms dropped from 900 to 50. The small local and regional brewers just could not match the economies of scale of the big brewers, nor could they match their aggressive marketing efforts. In eight years, the combined market share of the five largest brewers increased from 49% to 74% of total industry sales.

Robert F. Hartley, *Marketing Mistakes*

9. Moving toward inclusive language is a small, but absolutely necessary step in encouraging the full human development of both sexes. And the payoffs are enormous: we assure justice and equal treatment to all in a country that at least nominally prizes equality; we clarify fuzzy, illogical, and unrealistic thinking; and our writing becomes more sharply expressive and dynamic.

Rosalie Maggio, *The Nonsexist Word Finder*

EXERCISE 2.3

For each of the passages: (1) circle all the argument indicators, (2) bracket and number the statements, (3) construct a diagram of the argument, and (4) answer any questions that are asked about the discourse.

★   1.   Since three-syllable words are harder to read than one- or two-syllable words, and since simple ideas are more easily transferred from one human being to another than complex ideas, advertising copy tends to use ever simpler language all the time.

> Charles A. O'Neill, "The
> Language of Advertising," in
> *The Contemporary Reader*

2.   With love's light wings did I o'erperch these walls;
For stony limits cannot hold love out,
And what love can do, that dares love attempt.
Therefore thy kinsmen are no stop to me.

> William Shakespeare, *Romeo
> and Juliet* (Romeo speaking to Juliet)

3.   The engine is the most important part of the car because unless the engine is working, the other parts of the car are useless.

4.   If a woman doesn't know where a man is vulnerable, then she can't ever use that knowledge against him. So men bolster their control of a relationship by sealing off parts of their identity, and by refusing to reveal their doubts or fears.

> Robert Masello, "Intimacy: How to
> Get it, How to Give it," *Glamour,*
> January 1987

★ 5. Aerobic exercise is an integral part of the Pritikin program. This continuous, submaximal exercise (at training heart rate) aids in weight control because it enables you to burn an increased number of calories during exercise.

Holly Brubach, "The Pritikin
Promise," *Vogue*, February 1987

What is the antecedent of "it"?

6. Since an individual left to himself cannot realize all the good things that he might otherwise obtain, he must live and work with others. But society is not possible without sympathy and love; therefore the primary virtue which it is the duty of every one to develop is love for mankind.

M. M. Sharif, *Muslim Thought*

7. Man is to be free, and government is to be limited, because man has been created in the image and likeness of God, and hence has inherent dignity and worth.

National Review, July 4, 1986

8. With all the emphasis on heart disease recently, we often forget that other parts of the body—such as the brain, the legs, and the kidneys—can be starved for blood because of arterial blockages. Since the consequences of such problems can be devastating, it's important to know just how these conditions come about—and how they can be successfully treated.

Harvey Wolinsky, M.D., and Edward
Fisher, M.D., "Not Just an Affair
of the Heart," *Newsweek*, February 10, 1992

9. Brezhnev argues that since the Soviet Union has not sent in the tanks they should not be punished, for they have "acted with restraint despite provocation."

Ithaca Journal, January 21, 1982

(Leave "Brezhnev argues that" out of your diagram. The *Ithaca Journal* is reporting Brezhnev's argument.)

What is the antecedent of "they"?

How do you know that it is not "the tanks"?

★ 10. Very small babies suffer from many potentially fatal complications. Because they have less fat to insulate them and to generate heat, they have more trouble maintaining normal body temperature. . . . Because their immune systems are not fully developed, they are more vulnerable to infections. Their reflexes are not mature enough to perform functions basic to survival; they may, for example, be unable to suck and have to be fed intravenously.

Diane E. Papalia and Sally Wendkos Olds,
Human Development, 4th ed.

What is the antecedent of "they" and "their"?

EXERCISE 2.4

For each of the passages: (1) circle all the argument indicators, (2) bracket and number the statements, (3) construct a diagram of the argument, and (4) answer any questions that are asked about the discourse.

★ 1. Since trials are often characterized by extensive court delays, going to trial is both costly and time consuming.

West's Business Law

2. The electoral rules of most democratic countries create a multi-idea party system, for they have a parliamentary rather than a presidential structure. Because the Prime Minister is selected by the legislature from among its members after the election, there is less pressure toward two preelectoral coalitions, thus making the existence of several issue-oriented parties possible.

G. William Domhoff, *The Powers That Be*

3. The Palestinian people themselves have varying views as to how the conflict with Israel should be settled. Roughly 60 percent of the world's 3.5 million Palestinians live in Jordan and the Israeli-occupied West Bank and Gaza Strip, and because they face the reality of Israel they are more apt to seek a negotiated compromise. Others, particularly those living in teeming refugee camps in Lebanon and Syria, still harbor desperate dreams of returning to their homes in what was once Palestine but is now Israel.

Newsweek, 1979 (adapted from Stephen N. Thomas, *Practical Reasoning*)

What is the antecedent of "they"?

4.   Warfare in the nuclear age is a no-win proposition. Since I cannot say "Deal me out," I am going to join those who are working to freeze, and eventually reduce, nuclear warheads.

Time, February 21, 1983

★   5.   The morally right thing to do, on any occasion, is whatever would bring about the greatest balance of happiness over unhappiness. Therefore, on at least some occasions, mercy killing may be morally right.

James Rachels, *The Elements of Moral Philosophy* (Rachels is reporting an argument.)

6.   Personality change follows change in behavior. Since we are what we do, if we want to change what we are we must begin by changing what we do, must undertake a new mode of action. Since the import of such action is change, it will run afoul of existing entrenched forces which will protest and resist. It may be undertaken lightly but can be sustained only by considerable effort of will. Change will occur only if such action is maintained over a long period of time.

Allen Wheelis, *How People Change*

7.   Every person has a right to life. So the fetus has a right to life. No doubt the mother has a right to decide what shall happen in and to her body, everyone would grant that. But surely a person's right to life is stronger and more stringent than the mother's right to decide what happens in and to her body and so outweighs it. So the fetus may not be killed; an abortion may not be performed.

Judith Jarvis Thomson, "A Defense of Abortion" (Thomson is paraphrasing an argument that she will subject to criticism.)

8. Because the computer does not process general information in the same subconscious manner as human commanders, and because errors are incredibly costly, computer technology forces an immense clarification of thought and a precision of action in preparing computer inputs.

David F. Schuman, *A Preface to Politics*

EXERCISE 2.5

For each of the passages: (1) circle all the argument indicators, (2) bracket and number the statements, (3) construct a diagram of the argument, and (4) answer any questions that are asked about the discourse.

★   1.   We need not be ashamed of our defense mechanisms. They are a part of our nature, they are necessary to our survival; and there is no one who is completely free of them. We do not have to be "defensive" about our defense mechanisms. We all have them.

> Terry O'Banion and April O'Connor,
> *The Shared Journey: An Introduction*
> *to Encounter*

2.   Because so many Americans are sedentary, however, lack of exercise poses a major risk to the health of the nation as a whole.

> *University of California, Berkeley Wellness*
> *Letter,* February 1989

3.   Since labor in capitalism is a commodity to be bought when needed and discarded when no longer required, and since this market relationship leads to highly disproportionate power in the workplace, capitalism is continuously beset by serious tensions at the point of production.

> Edward S. Greenberg, *The American*
> *Political System: A Radical*
> *Approach*

4.   If we cannot control the arms race, then there will be a nuclear war, and a nuclear war, you can be sure, would end life as we know it. So we must control the arms race.

★ 5. Women (who perform household labor, including child care) are a group who work outside the money economy. Their work is not worth money, is therefore valueless, is therefore not even real work. And then women themselves who do this valueless work can hardly be expected to be worth as much as men who work for money.

Margaret Benston, "The Rise of Women's Lib,"
Ramparts, 1969

What is the antecedent of "their"?

6. Climbing is one of the fastest and most efficient ways to burn calories and lose weight. This is because you're using many muscles at once, thus burning more calories more quickly than in most other activities.

Shape Magazine, October 1987

7. We see things which lack knowledge, such as natural bodies, act for an end, and this is evident from their acting always, or nearly always, in the same way, so as to obtain the best result. Hence it is plain that they achieve their end, not fortuitously, but designedly. Now whatever lacks knowledge cannot move towards an end unless it be directed by some being endowed with knowledge and intelligence; as the arrow is directed by the archer. Therefore some intelligent being exists by whom all natural things are directed to their end; and this being we call God.

St. Thomas Aquinas,
Summa Theologica

8. Since happiness consists in peace of mind, and since durable peace of mind depends on the confidence we have in the future, and since that confidence is based on the knowledge we should have of the nature of God and the soul, it follows that knowledge is necessary for true happiness.

    G. W. F. Leibniz,
    The General Science

9. Although a true allergy to tobacco smoke has not been demonstrated, the smoke can be particularly irritating to people with hay fever or other allergies. It may also aggravate the symptoms of people who experience chest pain (angina) from coronary disease and of those who suffer from asthma or other chronic respiratory diseases. Accordingly, even if passive exposure is not found to cause disease in healthy people, it can be a nuisance to many and a possible risk to some people with chronic illness.

    "The Many Hazards of Secondhand Smoke,"
    Consumer Reports, February 1985

★ 10. Since I know now that my nature is very weak and limited, but that the nature of God is immense, incomprehensible, and infinite, therefore, I also know with sufficient evidence that he can make innumerable things whose causes escape me.

    René Descartes, *Meditations*

CHAPTER 3

LOGIC PUZZLES

Some important logical concepts are introduced using
logic puzzles.

KEY TERMS AND HEADINGS

Knight and Knave Puzzles
When Can Answers Be
 Determined?
Disjunctions and
 Conjunctions in Knight and
 Knave Puzzles
Conjunctive Sentence
Conjunct
Truth-Table

Truth-Value
Disjunctive Sentence
Disjunct
Negation
Applications to Knight and
 Knave Puzzles
Knights, Knaves, and
 Normals

Logic and reasoning can be used to solve puzzles as well as to analyze and evaluate arguments. There is a long tradition of puzzles that can be solved by pure reasoning. Sometimes the puzzles are illuminating and often they are surprising and diverting. In this chapter are puzzles to be solved and some suggestions about how to solve these puzzles. These puzzles are valuable because they can be used to illustrate key concepts of logic and reasoning.[1]

Most logic puzzles give several pieces of information, from which another piece of information that answers an indicated question can be derived by pure reasoning. Generally the puzzle can be solved by making an assumption and deducing consequences from the assumption. If a conflict occurs with the given information or a contradiction results, then the assumption cannot be correct. In these puzzles only a limited number of assumptions are possible, usually two or three. If all the assumptions are eliminated but one, then the remaining one is the answer.

---

[1] These logic puzzles are based on the work of the logician and author Raymond Smullyan. See his book *What Is the Name of This Book?* (New York: Simon and Schuster, 1978) for many more puzzles and many more different types of logic puzzles.

Usually people are able to solve these puzzles using their intuitive reasoning abilities, but these abilities must be used carefully and sharply. The following suggestions may seem obvious, but it helps to keep them in mind: (1) Use all the information given, (2) try to make some sort of visual representation of the puzzle (I give suggestions below), and (3) work carefully and neatly, taking small steps of reasoning if necessary.

KNIGHT AND KNAVE PUZZLES

These puzzles have two kinds of characters, knights and knaves. Knights always tell the truth and knaves always lie. Everything a knight says is true and everything a knave says is false. Generally you are asked to determine from what the individuals say what type they themselves, or others they talk about, are.

There are two ways of proceeding in solving these puzzles: (1) If you know that what an individual is saying is false, then you know that he is a knave. If you know that what an individual is saying is true, then the individual is a knight. (2) Given a type and what is said, use it as information. If you are told or have deduced that an individual is a knight, then you know that what he says is true and that it can be used as further information. If the individual is a knave, then negate what he says and use the negation as further information (see p. 46 for a discussion of negation). So if an individual says "2 + 2 = 4," then you know that he is a knight. If you know that A is a knave and he says that B is a knave, then you know that B is a knight.

Alas, it is not always so easy. Often it is possible to get started when one of the characters says something about herself or her associates that determines what type she is. For example, if A says "At least one of us is a knave," then we know that A is a knight. The reasoning is as follows: If A is a knave, then what she says is true—at least one of them is a knave (namely A herself)—but knaves cannot speak the truth. So A is a knight (that she is a knave is contradictory given what she says, as we have just seen) and she is speaking the truth (knights always speak the truth). So at least one of them is a knave. This is just one example of the kind of steps of reasoning we go through in solving knight and knave puzzles.

EXERCISE 3.1

The following puzzles take place on the Island of Knights and Knaves. Each inhabitant is either a knight or a knave. Knights only tell the truth and knaves only lie. Although A, B, and C are used in each puzzle, each puzzle is independent and separate. When one of the characters says "we" or "us," he or she is referring to the characters in that problem. Read each problem and answer the questions following it.

1.   I once met three characters on the Island of Knights and Knaves.

    A said: At least one of us is a knave.[2]

    B said: A is a knight.

    C said: B is a knave.

What is A? _____ What is B? _____ What is C? _____
We have already done most of the work on this one. We know that A is a knight (see p. 38). So at least one of them is a knave because that is what A says. But B says that A is a knight. B is telling the truth, so B is a knight too. But then C is lying. C is a knave. And there we have it.
To make a visual representation of this reasoning, start with what you know: namely that A is either a knight or a knave. Put a ☆ under a path that ends in a contradiction.

CASE 1		CASE 2
A is a knight	(or)	A is a knave
↓		☆
B is a knight	(or)	B is a knave
↓		☆
C is a knight	(or)	C is a knave
☆		

2.   This puzzle has three characters—A, B, and C—each of whom is either a knight or a knave.

    A said: We are all knights.

    B said: At least one of us is a knave.

    C said: B is a knight.

What is A? _____ What is B? _____ What is C? _____

3.   This puzzle has three characters—A, B, and C—each of whom is either a knight or a knave.

[2] "At least one" means "one or more."

A said: We are all knaves.

B said: A is a knight.

C says nothing.

What is A? _____ What is B? _____ What is C? _____
Explain briefly how you know that A is a _____.

4.   This puzzle has three characters—A, B, and C—each of whom is either a knight or a knave.

A said: We are all knaves.

B said: At most one of us is a knight.[3]

C says nothing.

What is A? _____ What is B? _____ What is C? _____
Explain briefly how you know that B is a _____.

★ 5.   This puzzle has three characters—A, B, and C—each of whom is either a knight or a knave.

A said: B is a knave.

B said: At most two of us are knights.

C said: A is a knight.

What is A? _____ What is B? _____ What is C? _____
Explain briefly how you know that B is a _____.

[3] "At most one" means "zero or one."

6. This puzzle has three characters—A, B, and C—each of whom is either a knight or a knave.

   A said: At least one of us a knight.

   B said: At most one of us is a knight.

   C says nothing.

   What is A? _____ What is B? _____ What is C? _____

7. This puzzle has only two characters— A and B. Let us say that two characters are of *the same type* if they are both knights or both knaves. Knights are one type, knaves are the other.

   A said: I am of the same type as B.

   B said: A is a knight.

   What is A? _____ What is B? _____

WHEN CAN ANSWERS BE DETERMINED?

So far all the answers could be determined. That is, each case had enough information to definitely answer the question about what type the character is. This need not always be the case, however. Sometimes a character's type cannot be determined. For example, if we are given only the information that A said "I am a knight," then we cannot determine what type A is. A could be a knight telling the truth or A could be a knave lying. This illustrates why we cannot simply tell what type a character is by asking him "What type are you?" A knight will tell the truth and say "I am a knight." A knave will lie and say "I am a knight." On the other hand, a question that *will* separate the knights from the knaves is easy to formulate, if you know a little arithmetic. Just ask any character "Does 2+2 equal 5?" Unfortunately, on the Island of Knights and Knaves you are rarely allowed to ask just any question you want.

Sometimes a problem has enough information to determine one character but not the others. We recall that two characters are of the same type if they are both knights or both knaves. Consider the following puzzle:

A said: I am of the same type as B.

B said: I am a knight.

We cannot determine what type B is from what B says alone. However, consider what A says. There are two possibilities.

Case 1:   A is a knight. Then B is a knight (because what A says is true, so they are of the same type).

Case 2:   A is a knave. Then B is a knight (because what A says is false, so A and B are different).

In this puzzle we never get a contradiction, but it is important that there are only two cases. In one case A is a knight, in the other A is a knave. So there is not enough information to determine what type A is. However, B is a knight because she is a knight in both cases—and there are only two. We can determine that B is a knight regardless of what A is. If A is a knight, then B is a knight. If A is a knave, then B is a knight. But A is either a knight or a knave. So B is a knight.

Let us say that a combination of types for the characters is *live* if there is no contradiction given the information we have. A character's type can be determined if it is the same in every live combination. In the problem we just did there are two live combinations—cases 1 and 2—and in each B's type is the same. So B's type can be determined. On the other hand, A's type is a knight in one live combination (case 1) and a knave in the other (case 2). So A's type cannot be determined.

EXERCISE 3.2

The following puzzles take place on the Island of Knights and Knaves. Read each problem and answer the questions following it.

★ 1. Recall that two characters are of the same type if they are both knaves or both knights. This puzzle has two characters—A and B—each of whom is a knight or a knave.

A said: I am of a different type than B.

B said: I am a knight.

Can it be determined what type A is? _____ If so, what type? _____
Can it be determined what type B is? _____ If so, what type? _____

2. This puzzle has two characters—A and B—each of whom is a knight or a knave.

A said: I am of the same type as B.

B said: I am of a different type than A.

Can it be determined what type A is? _____ If so, what type? _____
Can it be determined what type B is? _____ If so, what type? _____

3. Here we have three characters—A, B, and C—each of whom is a knight or a knave.

A said: B and C are of the same type.

B said: A is a knave.

We then ask B "Are A and C of the same type?"
What does B answer? _____ (Note the question.) Can it be determined what type B is? _____
Can it be determined what types A and C are? _____
If so, what types? _____

4. Once again there are three characters, each of whom is either a knight or a knave.

A said: All of us are knaves.

B said: C is a knave.

C said nothing.

Can it be determined what type A is? _____ If so, what type? _____
Can it be determined what type B is? _____ If so, what type? _____
Can it be determined what type C is? _____ If so, what type? _____
Suppose someone were to ask C "Is B a knight?" Can it be determined how C would answer? _____ If so, how would C answer? _____ (C must answer either "yes" or "no.")

DISJUNCTIONS AND CONJUNCTIONS
IN KNIGHT AND KNAVE PUZZLES

Many reasoners get confused as soon as knight and knave puzzles involve the words "or" and "and." The following are several points about the logic of "and" and "or" that are essential for solving knight and knave puzzles.

Conjunction

The word "and" is a conjunction. If P is some statement and Q is some statement (e.g., P might be "Ralph is in Chicago" and Q might be "Brenda is in Detroit"), then the sentence formed by putting "and" between P and Q is a **conjunctive sentence.** P is one **conjunct** and Q is the other. The logical meaning of "and" can be set out very explicitly in the form of a **truth table.**

Truth table for "and"

P	Q	P and Q
T	T	T
T	F	F
F	T	F
F	F	F

What this truth table says is that "P and Q" is true just when P is true and Q is true. If P is false or Q is false, then "P and Q" is false. In the table above we have set out all the combinations of true and false for P, Q. T stands for true, F for false (true and false are the two **truth-values**).

There are many other conjunctions besides "and." "However," "yet," "although," "nevertheless," and "but" are all conjunctions. As far as logic is concerned they are all treated the same as "and" and get the same truth table.

Disjunction

The word "or" is called a disjunction. The sentence formed by putting "or" between P and Q is a **disjunctive sentence.** P is one **disjunct,** Q is the other.

Truth table for "or"

P	Q	P or Q
T	T	T
T	F	T
F	T	T
F	F	F

This table says that "*P* or *Q*" is true if either *P* is true or *Q* is true or they are both true. Other ways to express "*P* or *Q*" are "Either *P* or *Q*" and "*P* or else *Q*." These mean the same as "*P* or *Q*" and get the same truth table.

EXAMPLES

"Ralph is in Chicago and Brenda is in Detroit" is a conjunctive sentence.
"Ralph is in Chicago or Brenda is in Detroit" is a disjunctive sentence.

The truth tables for "and" and "or" apply only when these words occur between statements. When they or the other conjunctions and disjunctions occur in lists or elsewhere, they may mean something different. For example, "Bob and Alice are married" does not mean just that Bob is married and Alice is married, because presumably they are married to each other. Likewise, "Jim is taller than either Harry or Nate" can be used to state that Jim is taller than Harry *and* Jim is taller than Nate.

Negation

The **negation** of a statement is another statement that must have the opposite truth-value. If *P* is some statement, then *it is not the case that P* (usually expressed as simply *not P*) is its negation. Care must be taken not to treat a statement that merely disagrees with a statement as its negation. For example, "There are exactly ten planets" is *not* the negation of "There are exactly nine planets." "There are exactly ten planets" and "There are exactly nine planets" do not have to have opposite truth-values—they might both be false (although they cannot both be true). One way to express the negation of "There are exactly nine planets" is "There are not exactly nine planets."

Truth table for "not"

P	not *P*
T	F
F	T

It is not always obvious what the negation of some statement is. In particular negating conjunctions and disjunctions can be tricky. The following may be helpful:

Not (*P* and *Q*)   =   Not *P* or not *Q*
Not (*P* or *Q*)   =   Not *P* and not *Q*

"Not *P* and not *Q*" is often expressed as "Neither *P* nor *Q*." So "Neither *P* nor *Q*" is the negation of "*P* or *Q*." In fact, we can prove both

Not (*P* and *Q*)   =   Not *P* or not *Q*

and

$$\text{Not } (P \text{ or } Q) \quad = \quad \text{Not } P \text{ and not } Q$$

by constructing truth tables. When constructing truth tables of complex statements, we proceed in a stepwise fashion. For example, in constructing the truth table for "Not P or not Q," we start with the values for P and Q. From them we compute the values for "Not P" and "Not Q,"; then from those we compute the values for "Not P or not Q." The numbers show the order in which we proceed:

$$2 \quad 1 \quad 3 \quad 2 \quad 1$$
$$\text{not } P \text{ or not } Q$$

Now consider "Not $(P \text{ and } Q)$" and "Not P or not Q." The values in the "2" columns are computed from those in the "1" columns, and the values in the "3" columns are computed from the values in the "2" columns.

1	1	2	2	2	3	3
P	Q	not P	not Q	P and Q	not $(P$ and $Q)$	not P or not Q
T	T	F	F	T	F	F
T	F	F	T	F	T	T
F	T	T	F	F	T	T
F	F	T	T	F	T	T

This shows that "Not $(P \text{ and } Q)$" always has the same truth-value as "Not P or Not Q." We can do the same for "Not $(P \text{ or } Q)$" and "Not P and not Q."

1	1	2	2	2	3	3
P	Q	not P	not Q	P or Q	not $(P$ or $Q)$	not P and not Q
T	T	F	F	T	F	F
T	F	F	T	T	F	F
F	T	T	F	T	F	F
F	F	T	T	F	T	T

EXAMPLES

The negation of "Either Ralph is in Chicago or he is in Detroit" is "Ralph is neither in Chicago nor in Detroit."

The negation of "Ralph is in Chicago and Brenda is in Detroit" is "Either Ralph is not in Chicago or Brenda is not in Detroit."

APPLICATIONS TO KNIGHT AND KNAVE PUZZLES

Knights always tell the truth, but this does not mean that every part of every sentence a knight utters has to be true. Likewise, knaves always lie, but this does not mean that every part of every sentence a knave utters has to be false. The rule is this: *Every conjunctive sentence and every disjunctive sentence uttered by a knight will be true. Every conjunctive sentence and every disjunctive sentence uttered by a knave will be false.* But remember that a conjunctive sentence can be false and still have a true conjunct (e.g., "I am male and I am female"). Remember also that a true disjunctive sentence can have a false disjunct (e.g., "I am male or I am female").

For example, someone on the Island of Knights and Knaves says "I am a knight and I am a knave." What type is she? We can deduce that she is a knave because what she says is false. She says that she is both a knight and a knave, but no one is *both* a knight and a knave. (But note that one of the conjuncts—"I am a knave"—is true.) Now someone else on the Island of Knights and Knaves says "I am a knight or I am a knave." What type is he? We can deduce that he is a knight because what he says is true. He *is* a knight *or* a knave, since every inhabitant of the island is a knight or a knave.

EXERCISE 3.3

Circle the correct answer—true or false—for each of the following sentences. You may assume standard facts of arithmetic and astronomy.

★   1.   2 + 2 = 4 or the earth has two natural moons.   True   False

2.   2 + 2 = 4 and the earth has two natural moons.   True   False

3.   My car is red or my car is not red.   True   False

4.   2 + 2 = 0   or   2 + 2 = 1   or   2 + 2 = 2   or
2 + 2 = 3   or   2 + 2 = 4   True   False

★   5.   (Change all the or's in question 4 to and's.)   True   False

6.   Everyone in this class is either male or female.   True   False

7.   Everyone in this class is male or everyone in this
class is female.   True   False

8.   My car is red and my car is not red.   True   False

9.   2 + 2 = 4 or 2 + 2 = 5 and the earth has two natural
moons.   True   False

★ 10.   Give the negation of "My car is red or my car is
green."

11.   Give the negation of "My car is purple and Ralph's car is red."

12.   Give several different (but equivalent) ways of negating "There are at least two
planets."

13.   Give several different (but equivalent) ways of negating "There are at most two
planets."

EXERCISE 3.4

Answer each of the following questions based on the truth tables for "and," "or" and "not."

★ 1.   Suppose you know that "*P* and *Q*" is false and that *P* is true. Can the truth-value of *Q* be determined just on the basis of this information alone? . If so, what is it? _____

2.   Suppose you know that "*P* or *Q*" is true but that *P* is false. Can the truth-value of *Q* be determined just on the basis of this information alone? _____. If so, what is it? _____

3.   Suppose you know that "*P* and *Q*" is false and that *P* is false. Can the truth-value of *Q* be determined just on the basis of this information alone? . If so, what is it? _____

4.   Suppose you know that "*P* or *Q*" is true and that *P* is true. Can the truth-value of *Q* be determined just on the basis of this information alone? _____. If so, what is it? _____

★ 5.   Suppose you know that "Neither *P* nor *Q*" is true. Can the truth-value of *P* be determined just on the basis of this information alone? _____. If so, what is it? _____

6.   Suppose you know that "Neither *P* nor *Q*" is false. Can the truth-value of *P* be determined just on the basis of this information alone? _____. If so, what is it? _____

EXERCISE 3.5

The following puzzles take place on the Island of Knights and Knaves. Each inhabitant is either a knight or a knave. Knights only tell the truth, knaves only lie. Read each problem and answer the questions.

★ 1.   Here we have three characters, each of whom is a knight or a knave.

A said: I am a knave and at least one of us is a knight.

B said: A is a knight.

C said nothing.

What is A? _____ What is B? _____ What is C? _____

2.   Here again we have three characters, each of whom is a knight or a knave.

A said: I am a knave or at least one of us is a knight.

B said: A is a knight.

C said nothing.

This puzzle is just like the previous one except that A says *or* instead of *and*.)

Can it be determined what type A is? _____ If so, what type? _____.
Can it be determined what type B is? _____ If so, what type? _____.
Can it be determined what type C is? _____ If so, what type? _____.

3.   Here we have two characters, each of whom is a knight or a knave.

A said: I am knave or B is a knight.

B said nothing.

What is A? _____ What is B? _____

4.   Here again we have only two inhabitants of the Island of Knights and Knaves.

A said: I am a knave and B is a knight.

B said nothing.

What is A? _____ What is B? _____

★ 5.   In this puzzle we have three inhabitants.

A said: All of us are knights or all of us are knaves.

B said: C is a knight.

C said nothing.

Can it be determined what type A is? _____ If so, what type? _____.
Can it be determined what type B is? _____ If so, what type? _____.
Can it be determined what type C is? _____ If so, what type? _____.

6. In this puzzle there are three inhabitants of the Island of Knights and Knaves.

A said: C is a knight.

B said nothing.

C said: A is a knave and B is a knave.

Can it be determined what type A is? _____ If so, what type? _____.
Can it be determined what type B is? _____ If so, what type? _____.
Can it be determined what type C is? _____ If so, what type? _____.

7. This puzzle has three characters, each of whom is either a knight or a knave.

A said: C is a knight.

B said: A is a knave or C is a knight.

C said nothing.

Can it be determined what type A is? _____ If so, what type? _____.
Can it be determined what type B is? _____ If so, what type? _____.
Can it be determined what type C is? _____ If so, what type? _____.

KNIGHTS, KNAVES, AND NORMALS

On the Island of Knights, Knaves, and Normals some of the inhabitants are knights. They always tell the truth. Some of the inhabitants are knaves. They always lie. But some of the inhabitants are normals. Normals sometimes lie and sometimes tell the truth.

EXERCISE 3.6

The following exercises take place on the Island of Knights, Knaves, and Normals. Read each of the problems and answer the questions.

★ 1.   This problem involves three inhabitants—A, B, and C—of the Island of Knights, Knaves, and Normals. It is known that exactly one of A, B, and C is a normal. (Be sure to use this piece of information in solving the problem.)

    A said: I am a knight.

    B said: I am a normal.

    C said: I am a knave.

Can it be determined what type A is? _____ If so, what type? _____.
Can it be determined what type B is? _____ If so, what type? _____.
Can it be determined what type C is? _____ If so, what type? _____.

2.   In this problem there is one knight, one knave, and one normal, but not necessarily in that order.

    A said: I am not a knight.

    B said: I am not a normal.

    C said: I am not a knave.

Can it be determined what type A is? _____ If so, what type? _____.
Can it be determined what type B is? _____ If so, what type? _____.
Can it be determined what type C is? _____ If so, what type? _____.

3.   On the Island of Knights, Knaves, and Normals, knights are highest rank, normals are middle rank, and knaves are lowest rank. Again, in this problem there is one knight, one knave, and one normal, but not necessarily in that order.

A said: I am lower in rank than B.

B said: I am higher in rank than C.

C said: I am higher in rank than A or lower in rank than B.

Can it be determined what type A is? _____ If so, what type? _____.
Can it be determined what type B is? _____ If so, what type? _____.
Can it be determined what type C is? _____ If so, what type? _____.

4.   In this problem there is one knight, one normal, and one knave, but not necessarily in that order. It is also known that the knight is married to the knave.

A said: I am a bachelor.

B said: I am married to A or I am married to C.

C said: I am not married to A.

Can it be determined what type A is? _____ If so, what type? _____.
Can it be determined what type B is? _____ If so, what type? _____.
Can it be determined what type C is? _____ If so, what type? _____.

★ 5.   In this problem there are three people—A, B, and C—one of whom is a knight, one of whom is a normal, and one of whom is a knave, but not necessarily in that order.

A said: I am a knave or C is a normal.

B said: I am a knight and I am a knave.

C said: I am knave or I am a normal.

Can it be determined what type A is? _____ If so, what type? _____.
Can it be determined what type B is? _____ If so, what type? _____.
Can it be determined what type C is? _____ If so, what type? _____.

CHAPTER 4

VALIDITY AND SOUNDNESS OF ARGUMENTS

The main concepts of argument evaluation are introduced in this chapter.

KEY TERMS AND HEADINGS

Validity
Valid Argument
Invalid Argument
Soundness
Sound Argument

Unsound Argument
Determining Validity and
    Invalidity
Logic Puzzles and Validity

VALIDITY

In reasoning we want to be able to determine which arguments are valid and which invalid. A **valid argument** is an argument in which the premises imply the conclusion. An **invalid argument** is one in which the premises do not imply the conclusion. Unless you know what it is for premises to imply a conclusion, however, this will not be much help.

The most accurate and careful definition of valid and invalid arguments is the following: A valid argument is an argument where it is *impossible* for the premises to be true and the conclusion false, and an invalid argument is one where it is *possible* for the premises to be true and the conclusion false.

Given this definition, the crucial question for determining validity is: Is IT IMPOSSIBLE FOR THE PREMISES TO BE TRUE AND THE CONCLUSION FALSE? If the answer is yes, then the argument is valid. If the answer is no, then the argument is invalid.

This is not just a technical distinction. Determining whether an argument is valid or invalid is an important first step in evaluating it. The premises of a valid argument guarantee its conclusion. If the premises of a valid argument are true, then the conclusion is guaranteed to be true. Valid reasoning is truth preserving in the sense that only truths can validly be deduced from truths. Falsehoods can never be validly deduced from truths. On the other hand, the premises of an invalid argument do not guarantee its conclusion. If, as in an invalid argument, the premises could be true and the conclusion false, then the premises by themselves are not enough to completely establish the conclusion. Something must be known or assumed beyond the premises in order to be sure of the conclusion. However, despite this not all invalid arguments should be summarily rejected. For one thing, some arguments are not intended to establish their conclusions with a 100% guarantee. Arguments that use statistics (see Chapter 11) or causal or analogical reasoning (see Chapters 12 and 13) are often only intended to establish their conclusions with a degree of probability. For another, many superficially invalid arguments have suppressed premises (see Chapter 8), which if stated explicitly would make them valid.

A WORD OF CAUTION

The word "valid" is used in ordinary language as a general word of praise. In logic the word "valid" is a technical term and has a special meaning. Some people confuse the ordinary meaning of "valid" with its technical sense in logic. *To be valid* (as the term is used in logic) *an argument need not have true premises*. A valid argument is not automatically a good argument (and as was mentioned above an invalid argument is not automatically a bad one). In doing logic, when we say that an argument is valid we are saying that something is impossible but what is impossible is a conjunction of conditions. Namely it is impossible that the premises be true and the conclusion false, but an argument can meet this condition and not have true premises.

EXAMPLE[1]

New York City is the capital city of the United States.

The United States has exactly one capital city.

Washington, D.C., is not New York City.

_____

Therefore Washington, D.C., is not the capital city of the United States.

This argument has one false premise and a false conclusion; nevertheless it is valid, because it is impossible for the premises to be true and the conclusion false. The premises imply the conclusion; but the premises are not all true.

---

[1] In setting out arguments for study, a line will be used to separate premises from conclusions. The premises are above the line and the conclusion below. In such arguments the premises are always linked. To help indicate the conclusion, a conclusion indicator will often be used, but it should be understood that the conclusion indicators are not part of the conclusions.

SOUNDNESS

Not all valid arguments are good arguments. A valid argument that has a false premise is not a good argument. A valid argument with a false premise could have a false conclusion. All that is guaranteed is that a valid argument with true premises has a true conclusion. Given a valid argument with a false premise, we know that the premises imply the conclusion, but we cannot tell from the argument whether the conclusion is true. A valid argument whose premises are true is a **sound argument**. An argument that is either invalid or has at least one false premise is an **unsound argument.**

A sound argument actually proves its conclusion in the sense that if we agree that an argument is sound, then we are committed to accepting its conclusion. Merely agreeing that an argument is valid does not yet commit us to accepting its conclusion. Agreeing that an argument is sound does commit us to the conclusion. If all that is demanded of an argument in order to be a good argument is that it prove its conclusion, then all sound arguments are good arguments.

SUMMARY

Valid Argument: Premises imply conclusion.

Invalid Argument: Premises do not imply conclusion.

Sound Argument: Premises imply conclusion and all premises are true.

Unsound Argument: Premises do not imply conclusion or at least one premise is false.

DETERMINING VALIDITY AND INVALIDITY

Logicians do not proceed by considering each argument individually. The validity or invalidity of an argument depends on its form, and its form in turn depends on the occurrence in it of such words as "all," "are," "are not," "no," "or," "and," "if . . . , then . . . "—the so-called logical words. Logicians classify arguments as valid or invalid by their forms. If an argument is of a valid argument form, then it is valid.

To see how this works consider a valid argument.

All zebras are mammals.
All mammals are animals.

_____

Therefore all zebras are animals.

Everybody is able to see immediately that this is a valid argument. If they had trouble, we could draw circles for them.

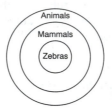

(This drawing indicates that the class of zebras is entirely contained in the class of mammals, and the class of mammals in that of animals.)

This also happens to be a sound argument but the truth of the premises depends not on logic but on facts of biology. If somebody disputed these biological facts, merely drawing circles would not help. They would have to look up the facts in a zoology text. In any case, the validity of the argument does not depend on these biological facts. It does not depend on the content of the argument at all. In fact, any argument of the same form is also valid. The form of the argument is given as follows:

All *A* are *B*.
All *B* are *C*.
———————————
Therefore all *A* are *C*.

Any argument of the same form as this is valid, and we can say that this is a valid argument form. By "any argument of the same form" we mean any argument gotten from this form by substituting terms (such as "animal" or "zebra") for the italicized letters, being sure not to substitute different terms for the same letter. For example, if we substitute "zebra" for *A*, then we must substitute "zebra" (and no other term) for *A* every place *A* occurs. Any time we substitute terms for letters in an argument form we get a substitution instance of that argument form.

MORE ABOUT DETERMINING VALIDITY AND INVALIDITY

Every argument of the form

All *A* are *B*.
All *B* are *C*.
———————————
Therefore all *A* are *C*.

is valid. That means that it is impossible to find a substitution instance such that the premises are true and the conclusion false. If an argument form is invalid, then there are substitution instances where the premises are true and the conclusion false.

For example, consider the following argument form.

All *A* are *B*.

All *C* are *B*.

_____

Therefore all *A* are *C*.

This is an invalid argument form. This means that there are substitution instances where the premises are true and the conclusion false. For example:

$$\text{All} \quad \underset{A}{\textbf{boys}} \quad \text{are} \quad \underset{B}{\textbf{humans}}.$$

$$\text{All} \quad \underset{C}{\textbf{girls}} \quad \text{are} \quad \underset{B}{\textbf{humans}}.$$

_____

$$\text{Therefore all} \quad \underset{A}{\textbf{boys}} \quad \text{are} \quad \underset{C}{\textbf{girls}}.$$

We can also show that this form is invalid by drawing circles. If we can draw circles in such a way that we picture the premises without automatically picturing the conclusion, then the argument form is invalid. This can easily be done.

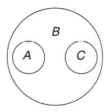

The first premise says that the *A* circle is inside the *B* circle, and the second premise says that the *C* circle is also inside the *B* circle. But clearly the *A* circle and *C* circle can both be inside the *B* circle without the *A* circle overlapping (or even touching) the *C* circle (as in the drawing).

We show that an argument form is invalid by finding substitution instances of the form in which the premises are true and the conclusion false or by drawing circles in which we picture the premises without picturing the conclusion. What this shows is that the premises of an invalid argument do not, by themselves, guarantee the conclusion.

When looking for substitution instances, keep in mind and understand clearly that the only combination we are interested in for determining validity is true premises and false conclusion. That the premises are false and the conclusion false, for example, is irrelevant for determining validity because a valid argument can have false premises and a false conclusion. If the only information you have about an argument is that its premises are false, you cannot determine from that information alone whether the argument is valid or invalid. What a valid argument cannot have is true premises and a false conclusion.

When presented with an argument, we proceed as follows: Determine the form of the argument. Then determine whether the form is valid or invalid by searching for another argument of the same form with true premises and a false conclusion. If you find it, the argument is invalid. Of course, not finding an argument of the same form with true premises and a false conclusion does not prove that the argument is valid, because you may not have looked hard enough.

With drawings the argument is proved invalid by drawing circles representing the premises without automatically representing the conclusion. If you can draw the premises without thereby drawing the conclusion, the form of the argument is invalid. It is possible to get confused because with most invalid arguments making a drawing that pictures both the premises and the conclusion is easy. This is irrelevant to determining whether the form of the argument is invalid. For example, consider the invalid argument form:

All *A* are *B*.

All *C* are *B*.

_____

Therefore all *A* are *C*.

We can easily make a drawing that pictures the premises and the conclusion.

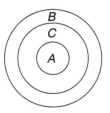

But this drawing gives us no information about the validity of the argument form. What does prove that the argument form is invalid is a drawing of the premises that does not picture the conclusion; and we saw that this can be done. So to show by drawings that an argument form is invalid, try to figure out a way to draw the premises without drawing the conclusion. If you can do it, the argument form is invalid. Again, not finding a way to draw the premises without drawing the conclusion does not prove that the argument form is valid because you may not find a way even though there is one. In practice, however, most people can correctly determine the validity or invalidity of simple arguments by doing circle drawings. After you try a bit to draw the premises without drawing the conclusion you either succeed or see that it cannot be done.

To show that an argument is invalid

1. Determine the form of the argument. Try to find another argument of the same form with true premises and a false conclusion. If you succeed, the argument is invalid.

or

2. Try to draw circles representing the premises without automatically representing the conclusion. If you can do it, the argument is invalid. That you can draw a picture representing the premises and the conclusion is irrelevant to validity or invalidity.

EXERCISE 4.1

Answer each of the following questions. (Note: To some the correct answer is "Nothing.")

★ 1. Suppose you are given the following information about an argument: (a) it is valid, (b) its conclusion is false. What can you tell about the truth or falsity of the premises of the argument on the basis of this information alone?

2. Suppose you are given the following information about an argument: (a) it is valid, (b) its conclusion is true. What can you tell about the truth or falsity of the premises of the argument on the basis of this information alone?

3. Suppose you are given the following information about an argument: (a) it is unsound, (b) it is valid. What can you tell about the truth or falsity of the premises of the argument on the basis of this information alone?

4. Suppose you are given the following information about an argument: (a) it is unsound, (b) it is invalid. What can you tell about the truth or falsity of the premises of the argument on the basis of this information alone?

★ 5. Suppose you are given the following information about an argument: (a) it is valid. What can you tell about the truth or falsity of the premises of the argument on the basis of this information alone?

6. Suppose you are given the following information about an argument: (a) it is sound. What can you tell about the truth or falsity of the premises of the argument on the basis of this information alone?

7. Suppose you are given the following information about an argument: (a) it is valid. What can you tell about the truth or falsity of the conclusion of the argument on the basis of this information alone?

8. Suppose you are given the following information about an argument: (a) it is sound. What can you tell about the truth or falsity of the conclusion of the argument on the basis of this information alone?

9. Suppose you are given the following information about an argument: (a) it is valid, (b) all of its premises are true. What can you tell about the truth or falsity of the conclusion of the argument on the basis of this information alone?

★ 10. Suppose you are given the following information about an argument: (a) it is invalid, (b) all of its premises are true. What can you tell about the truth or falsity of the conclusion of the argument on the basis of this information alone?

EXERCISE 4.2

For each of the following arguments: (1) state the form of the argument, (2) determine whether it is valid or invalid, (3) if it is invalid, show that it is invalid by finding substitutions in which the premises are true and the conclusion false, and (4) if it is invalid, demonstrate invalidity by drawing circles.

★   1.   All shrimps are toadstools.

No wallabies are shrimps.

Therefore no wallabies are toadstools.

2.   All careful trolls are worthy opponents.

All careful trolls are amusing chaps.

Therefore all worthy opponents are amusing chaps.

3. All shrimps are toadstools.
    No wallabies are toadstools.
    _____

    Therefore no wallabies are shrimps.

4. Some[2] Spanish olives are jumbo figs.
    No jumbo figs are dates.
    _____

    Therefore no Spanish olives are dates.

★   5. All careful trolls are worthy opponents.
    All worthy opponents are amusing chaps.
    _____

    Therefore all amusing chaps are careful trolls.

[2]"Some" means "at least one."

6. All restless cowboys are natural athletes.
    Some happy-go-lucky dudes are restless cowboys.
    _____

    Therefore some happy-go-lucky dudes are natural athletes.

7. No nacho fans from Detroit are true believers.
    No true believers are quaint princes.
    _____

    Therefore no nacho fans from Detroit are quaint princes.

8. All of grandma's cookies are lemon snaps.
    No lemon snaps are Fig Newtons.
    _____

    Therefore none of grandma's cookies are Fig Newtons.

9. All carnivorous lilies are edible.

    Some lilacs are not edible.
    _____

    Therefore some lilacs are not carnivorous lilies.

★ 10. No carnivorous lilies are pink.

    Some lilacs are not pink.
    _____

    Therefore some lilacs are not carnivorous lilies.

EXERCISE 4.3

For each of the following arguments determine whether it is valid or invalid. If it is invalid, attempt to articulate why. When determining validity, it is permissible to add premises that are obviously true and presupposed by the argument.

★   1.   He's happy all the time. Therefore he's happy in the evenings.

   2.   Bulgaria has no nuclear weapons. This proves that Bulgaria is a peaceful nation.

   3.   Nadine is married to Jim. A person can be married to only one person at a time. Therefore Nadine is not married to Ralph.

   4.   Harriet's printer won't print. So the ribbon must be all used up.

★   5.   Harriet's ribbon is all used up. So her printer won't print. (Note that argument 5 is just like argument 4 except that the premise and conclusion are reversed.)

   6.   Long-Life Batteries last and last. In fact Long-Life Batteries last up to twelve hours. Therefore each Long-Life Battery will last twelve hours.

7. Long-Life Batteries last and last. In fact Long-Life Batteries last up to twelve hours. Therefore some Long-Life Batteries will last twelve hours. (Note that argument 7 is just like argument 6 except that "each" is changed to "some.")

8. There were seventy-five cookies in this jar. The cookies were thoroughly stirred and mixed before sampling. The first seventy-four cookies that I removed, all of which were chosen at random, were all lemon snaps. Therefore, the last cookie in the jar is also a lemon snap.

9. He's guilty of the murder all right. Didn't he tell the police that he did it?

★ 10. Everyone in this room is either male or female. Therefore everyone in this room is male or everyone in this room is female.

11. It is not true that he is tall and handsome. Therefore he is not tall.

12. My roommate brushed his teeth every night so far this term. So he will brush his teeth tonight.

EXERCISE 4.4

For each of the following arguments determine whether it is valid or invalid. If it is invalid, attempt to articulate why. When determining validity, it is permissible to add premises that are obviously true and presupposed by the argument.

★   1.   Everyone who reads crisis romance novels is a silly dreamer. Calvin reads crisis romance novels. Therefore he's a silly dreamer.

2.   Jones is a devout Catholic. Therefore, Jones believes in the existence of God.

3.   All serious runners are in good physical condition. My physics teacher is in very good physical condition. So he must be a serious runner.

4.   My chance of winning the lottery is one in ten billion. Therefore I will not win the lottery.

★   5.   My chance of winning the lottery is one in ten billion. Therefore it is impossible for me to win the lottery.

6.   My chance of winning the lottery is one in ten billion. Therefore it is possible for me to win the lottery.

7. The chance of intelligent life occurring on earth by purely accidental natural processes is one in ten trillion. Therefore it is possible that intelligent life occurred on earth by purely accidental natural processes.

8. All octopuses have exactly eight legs. All crabs have exactly six legs. Therefore no octopus is a crab.

9. He jumped out of the plane over an hour ago. Therefore he's hit the ground by now.

★ 10. It takes me three seconds to load, aim, and fire my rifle. Consequently in a period of seven seconds it is impossible for me to get off more than two shots.

11. No one in the room is taller than Harry. So Harry is taller than everyone else in the room.

12. No aspirin gets into the bloodstream faster than Zonk aspirin. Hence Zonk aspirin gets into the bloodstream faster than any other aspirin.

13.   No one in Athens is wiser than Socrates (says the infallible oracle at Delphi). Therefore Socrates is wiser than anyone else in Athens.

14.   We here at Crucible Widgets are working and working to keep prices down. Our goal is to make Crucible widgets the best bargain on the market. Therefore Crucible widgets are (or will soon be) the best bargain on the market.

★ 15.   Last Monday the stock market had its biggest one-day gain in history. Hence last week the market was the highest it has ever been.

LOGIC PUZZLES AND VALIDITY

We have seen that in a valid argument it is impossible for the premises to be true and the conclusion false. Thus if we know two things about an argument—(1) that it is valid and (2) that its conclusion is false—then we know that at least one of the premises is false. This feature of valid arguments is often used in reasoning and in particular is used in solving knight and knave puzzles. In solving knight and knave puzzles we start with an assumption; for example, A is a knight. We then reason from that assumption. If we end up with a contradiction, then we know that A is not a knight. This procedure depends on the fact that a valid argument with a false conclusion has a false premise. In this case the premise in question is "A is a knight." (We use other premises, such as that knights only tell the truth, but these are given as true and are not in question.) It is important not to contaminate our procedure by having more than one questionable premise at a time; otherwise when we arrive at a contradiction, we will not know which of the questionable premises to reject.

What we do, then, is construct an argument with the premise "A is a knight." We must be sure that this is the only questionable premise, and we must be sure that each step in the argument is valid. If we arrive at a false conclusion (false because it violates given information or is a contradiction), then we know that the premise is false. A is not a knight. So remember, you have to be sure to test only one thing at a time and be sure to reason validly. If you arrive at a falsehood, then the one thing you tested is false.

If you begin with the questionable premise "A is a knight" and you do *not* arrive at a contradiction, that does not conclusively prove that A *is* a knight. You may not have enough information to determine what A is.

Reasoning about knights and knaves is not that different from much reasoning in ordinary life—just a bit more formal and fanciful. Your car is not working. Your mechanic reasons as follows: "Let's suppose it's the ignition that's broken." Then she deduces certain consequences from this assumption in conjunction with other premises about how cars work. Say she deduces that the spark plugs won't fire. If the conclusion is false (the spark plugs *do* fire), then it isn't the ignition (assuming now that the other premises are true and that she has reasoned validly). Of course, if the spark plugs do *not* fire that doesn't prove it *is* the ignition. It might be a dead battery or some other problem.

CHAPTER 5

CONDITIONAL RELATIONSHIPS

This chapter introduces the notions of sufficient conditions, necessary conditions, and conditional sentences. The explanations of logical relationships in the following chapters rely on the notions of necessary condition and sufficient condition. Besides being interesting and valuable in its own right, a discussion of necessary conditions and sufficient conditions is valuable for further work in studying reasoning.

KEY TERMS AND HEADINGS

Conditional Sentences	Biconditional Sentences
Converse	Definitions
Antecedent	Necessary and Sufficient
Consequent	Conditions
Sufficient Conditions	Class Inclusion Method
Necessary Conditions	Checking Your Answers

CONDITIONAL SENTENCES

The topic of conditional relationships requires a brief discussion of **conditional sentences** (usually just called "conditionals"). A conditional sentence is a sentence using the word "if" that expresses the claim that one condition is sufficient for another. For example, the sentence "If you detonate a lot of dynamite, then you cause an explosion" expresses the claim that your detonating a lot of dynamite is sufficient for your causing an explosion.

The logic of conditionals is difficult and somewhat controversial (see Chapter 6 for a discussion of the logic of conditionals and for different ways of expressing conditional relationships). A few features of conditionals should always be kept in mind, however. "If *P*, then *Q*" is *not* equivalent to "If *Q*, then *P*." "If *Q*, then *P*" is called the **converse** of "If *P*, then *Q*." The converse of "If you detonate a lot of dynamite, then you cause an explosion" is "If you cause an explosion, then you detonate a lot of dynamite" and is certainly not equivalent because there are other ways of causing explosions than detonating a lot of dynamite. A conditional and its converse are not in general equivalent. Conditionals are different from conjunctions and disjunctions in this respect. (Note that "P or Q" is equivalent to "Q or P" and that "P and Q" is equivalent to "Q and P.") With conditionals the order is all important. To keep track of this order we call the part of the conditional that comes between "if" and the comma the **antecedent** and the part that comes after the "then" the **consequent.**

> If *antecedent,* then *consequent.*

In the conditional "If you detonate a lot of dynamite, then you cause an explosion," "you detonate a lot of dynamite" is the antecedent. "You cause an explosion" is the consequent. What this conditional says is that the condition expressed by the antecedent is sufficient for the condition expressed by the consequent.

SUFFICIENT CONDITIONS

One way of thinking of sufficient conditions is in terms of class inclusion. If S is sufficient for $E,$ then you can think of the class of S (or S events) as being included in the class of E (or E events). So, for example, the class of events of detonating a lot of dynamite is entirely included in the class of events of causings of explosions (assuming, as we are, that detonating a lot of dynamite *is* in fact sufficient to cause an explosion). As we saw, this relation is expressed in the conditional "If you detonate a lot of dynamite, then you cause an explosion." Conditionals that express the claim that S is sufficient for E are equivalent to universal generalizations such as "All S is E" (see Chapter 6 on the logic of conditionals for more discussion of this equivalence). The conditional "If you detonate a lot of dynamite, then you cause an explosion" is true because the class indicated by its antecedent is entirely included in the class indicated by its consequent.

Consider another example: Being a hammer is a sufficient condition for being a tool. This relationship between being a hammer and being a tool is expressed by the sentence "If something is a hammer, then it is a tool." What this sentence says is that the condition expressed by its antecedent (being a hammer) is sufficient for the condition expressed by its consequent (being a tool), and it is true because the class of hammers is entirely included in the class of tools. In other words, all hammers are tools.

Contrast these examples with an example of a false conditional. "If you are a boy, then you are an athlete." This conditional is false because the class of boys is not entirely included in the class of athletes (a lot of boys are not athletes). Being a boy is not sufficient for being an athlete. Besides being a boy you have to participate in sports, be good at them, and so forth to be an athlete. (Nor is being a boy necessary for being an athlete.)

NECESSARY CONDITIONS

Necessary conditions can also be thought of in terms of class inclusion. For example, a necessary condition for being a bachelor is being unmarried. We can express this with a conditional by saying "If you are a bachelor, then you are unmarried." In general a conditional expresses the claim that its consequent is necessary for its antecedent (and also that its antecedent is sufficient for its consequent). Note that the class of bachelors is entirely included in the class of unmarried people. So if *N* is necessary for *E,* then the class *E* will be entirely included in the class *N.* Consider another example: A necessary condition for being a doe is being female. We can express this by saying "If it is a doe, then it is female." This sentence expresses the fact that being female is a necessary condition for being a doe (and also that being a doe is a sufficient condition for being female). It is true because the class of females entirely includes the class of does.

BICONDITIONAL SENTENCES

Sometimes, especially in technical writing, one comes across the claim that one condition is necessary *and* sufficient for another. A **biconditional sentence** (usually just called a "biconditional") is a sentence of the form "*P* if and only if *Q,*" which expresses the claim that one condition is necessary *and* sufficient for another. For example, the biconditional "The number four is even if and only if it is divisible by two without remainder" is a biconditional and expresses the claim that four's being divisible by two without remainder is necessary and sufficient for its being even. One of our best sources of true and interesting biconditionals are **definitions.** A good way to define a term is to give a specification of the necessary and sufficient conditions for falling under the term. For example, a bachelor is an unmarried man. Being an unmarried man is a necessary and sufficient condition for being a bachelor. Someone is a bachelor if and only if he is an unmarried man. (Here is another example that you should know by now: An argument is sound if and only if it is valid and has no false premises.) A biconditional (unlike a conditional) is always equivalent to its converse.

NECESSARY AND SUFFICIENT CONDITIONS

Again, a good way to think of conditions that are both necessary and sufficient is in terms of class inclusion. When *A* is both necessary *and* sufficient for *B, A* is entirely included in *B* and *B* is entirely included in *A.* In other words, *A* and *B* are really just the same class. For example, being a mare is necessary and sufficient for being a female horse. The class of mares and the class of female horses is the same class. This relation is expressed with the biconditional "Something is a mare if and only if it is a female horse."

CLASS INCLUSION METHOD

The intimate relation between class inclusion and necessary and sufficient conditions suggests a method that helps in answering questions about necessary and sufficient conditions. This method involves a way of visually representing necessary and sufficient conditions that greatly simplifies thinking about these conditions.

When one class is entirely included in another class (as is, for example, the class of horses in the class of animals), being a member of the smaller class is always a sufficient condition for being a member of the larger class. Likewise, being a member of the larger class is always a necessary condition for being a member of the smaller class.

It always works like this. If class *A* is entirely included in class *B,* then being an *A* is sufficient for being a *B* and being a *B* is necessary for being an *A*.

If the two classes *A* and *B* include each other (i.e., they are in the same class, such as mares = female horses), then *A* and *B* are necessary *and* sufficient for each other.

If *A* is entirely included in *B* and *B* is bigger than *A*, then *A* is sufficient but not necessary for *B* and *B* is necessary but not sufficient for *A*.

EXAMPLES

Being a horse is a sufficient condition, but not necessary, for being an animal.

Being a cow is also a sufficient condition, but not necessary, for being an animal.

Being an animal is a necessary condition, but not sufficient, for being a cow.

Being an animal is a necessary condition, but not sufficient, for being a horse.

Being a doe is a necessary and sufficient condition for being a female deer.

All of this can also be expressed in terms of sets.[1]

Being an *A* is sufficient for being a *B* means that the set of *A*s is a subset of the set of *B*s.

Being an *A* is necessary for being a *B* means that the set of *B*s is a subset of the set of *A*s.

Being an *A* is sufficient but not necessary for being a *B* means that the set of *A*s is a proper subset of the set of *B*s.

Being an *A* is necessary but not sufficient for being a *B* means that the set of *B*s is a proper subset of the set of *A*s.

Being an *A* is necessary and sufficient for being a *B* means that the set of *A*s and the set of *B*s is the same set.

On page 79 is a visual representation of the relations between conditions and class inclusion.

---

[1] If you are familiar with sets, this may be helpful. If not, skip it and go to the next page.

Classes can be related to each other in four ways.

The classes are related as in picture 1 means that being an *A* is sufficient but not necessary for being a *B* and being a *B* is necessary but not sufficient for being an *A*.

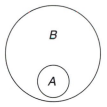

   1.   One is included in but not equal to the other.

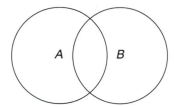

   2.   They overlap each other but neither includes the other.

The classes are related as in picture 2 or 3 means that neither is necessary nor sufficient for the other.

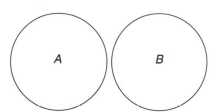

   3.   They are completely separate.

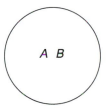

   4.   They are the same one class (with possibly more than one name).

The classes are related as in picture 4 means that *A* and *B* are necessary and sufficient for each other; in other words, *A* and *B* are just different designations for the same class.

EXAMPLES

1.   Being a boy is sufficient but not necessary for being a human.

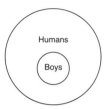

Note also that being a human is necessary but not sufficient for being a boy (same picture!).

2.   Being a boy is neither necessary nor sufficient for being an athlete.

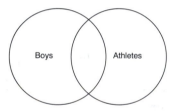

3.   Being a boy is neither necessary nor sufficient for being a horse.

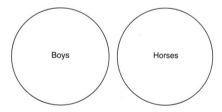

4.   Being a young male human is necessary and sufficient for being a boy.

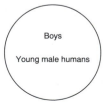

We have talked so far of being an *A* or being a *B,* but the same rules hold for touching an *A,* looking at . . . , eating . . . , owning . . . , killing . . . , kissing . . . , and so forth. For example, owning a horse is sufficient for owning an animal (but not necessary), because the class of horses is entirely included in the class of animals.

So now, if someone were to ask you to give a condition that is sufficient but not necessary for owning an animal, you can easily do it. Think of a class that is entirely included in the class of animals (e.g., horses) and state confidently: "Owning a horse is sufficient but not necessary for owning an animal." If someone were to ask you to give a condition that is necessary but not sufficient for kissing a boy, think of a class that includes all the boys (e.g., humans). So you can correctly say: "Kissing a human is necessary but not sufficient for kissing a boy."

EXERCISE 5.1

The following exercises involve questions about necessary and sufficient conditions. Answer them using the methods described in the text.

★ 1.   Give two different conditions that are each necessary but not sufficient for being a brother in the biological sense.

2.   Give a combination of conditions that is necessary and sufficient for being a brother in the biological sense.

A necessary and sufficient condition for being a brother in the biological sense is _____ and _____.

3.   Express your answer to question 2 in the form of a biconditional.

4.   Give two different conditions that are each necessary for being a wife.

A necessary condition for being a wife is having _____.
A necessary condition for being a wife is being _____.

5.   Give a condition that is sufficient but not necessary for eating cooked potatoes.

State what the item in column A is to the item in column B.

S = A is sufficient but not necessary for B.

N = A is necessary but not sufficient for B.

N & S = A is necessary and sufficient for B.

0 = A is neither necessary nor sufficient for B.

	Column A	Column B	Answer
★ 6.	Being a U.S. citizen	Being president of the United States	_____
7.	Eating an apple	Eating a piece of fruit	_____
8.	Loving an athlete	Loving a hockey star	_____
★ 9.	Knowing a boy	Knowing a human	_____
10.	Knowing a human	Knowing a boy	_____
11.	Owning a chair	Owning a piece of furniture	_____
12.	Owning a piece of furniture	Owning a chair	_____
13.	Being exactly six feet tall	Being at least five feet tall	_____

Explanation: The circle method can be used for problems involving numbers, which tend to be harder than the others. You just have to draw the circles more carefully.

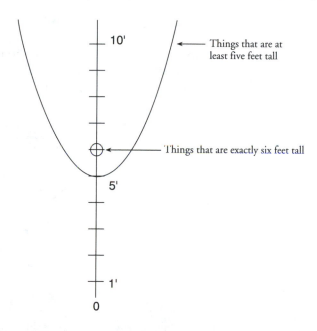

So the class of things that are exactly six feet tall is entirely included in the class of things that are at least five feet tall. Thus the correct answer to question 13 is S. We can also see how this works with conditionals. "If a thing is exactly six feet tall, then it is at least five feet tall" is definitely true, so being exactly six feet tall is sufficient for being at least five feet tall.

"If a thing is at least five feet tall, then it is exactly six feet tall" is certainly not in general true. So being exactly six feet tall is not necessary for being at least five feet tall.

		Column A	Column B	Answer
★	14.	Being greater than one-half	Being less than one-third	_____
	15.	Being an animal	Not being a plant	_____
	16.	Being an uncle	Having a nephew	_____
	17.	Being water	Being H_2O	_____
	18.	Being water	Being liquid	_____
★	19.	Having at least $100 in the bank	Having more than $150 in the bank	_____
	20.	Being later than ten o'clock on a given day	Being later than eleven o'clock on that day	_____

CHECKING YOUR ANSWERS

You can check your answers using conditionals in the following way. A conditional sentence of the form "If P, then Q" says that the condition expressed by P is sufficient for the condition expressed by Q and that the condition expressed by Q is necessary for that expressed by P. A biconditional of the form "P if and only if Q" says that P is necessary and sufficient for Q.

Consider the conditional sentence with blanks:

If _____, then _____.

Take any two conditions X and Y and plug them into the two blanks. If the conditional sentence

If X, then Y.

is definitely true, then X is sufficient for Y and Y is necessary for X.

EXAMPLE

If you are looking at a horse, then you are looking at an animal.

Further, if you switch the X and Y, and the sentence is no longer definitely true, then X is sufficient but not necessary for Y and Y is necessary but not sufficient for X.

EXAMPLE

If you are looking at an animal, then you are looking at a horse.

Your looking at a horse is sufficient but not necessary for your looking at an animal (you could look at a cow instead and still be looking at an animal), and your looking at an animal is necessary but not sufficient for your looking at a horse (you could be looking at an animal and be looking at a cow instead of a horse).

If both "If X, then Y" and "If Y, then X" are true, then X is necessary and sufficient for Y (and vice versa).

In using this method certain grammatical adjustments may be necessary. Looking at a horse is sufficient for looking at an animal, but we cannot say "If looking at a horse, then looking at an animal." Instead we must say "If you are looking at a horse, then you are looking at an animal." In most cases such grammatical adjustments are obvious and do not lead to any change in content.

EXERCISE 5.2

Complete the following exercises, which involve questions about necessary and sufficient conditions, using the methods described in the text.

1.   Give two conditions that are each necessary but not sufficient for being a grandmother.

2.   Combine the two necessary conditions you gave for being a grandmother and make one condition that is both necessary and sufficient for being a grandmother.

Express your answer to the above question in the form of a biconditional.

★ 3.   Give a condition that is sufficient but not necessary for owning a piece of furniture.

Express in a conditional sentence the relation between your answer and owning a piece of furniture.

What is the antecedent?

What is the consequent?

4.　Give a condition that is necessary but not sufficient for owning a chair.

Express in a conditional sentence the relation between your answer and owning a chair.

What is the antecedent?

What is the consequent?

5.　Give a condition that is necessary but not sufficient for living in Texas.

Express in a conditional sentence the relation between your answer and living in Texas.

What is the antecedent?

What is the consequent?

★ 6.   Give a condition that is sufficient but not necessary for being an uncle.

Express in a conditional sentence the relation between your answer and being an uncle.

7.   Give a condition that is necessary but not sufficient for being an uncle.

Express in a conditional sentence the relation between your answer and being an uncle.

8.   Give a condition that is necessary but not sufficient for weighing at least ten pounds.

Express in a conditional sentence the relation between your answer and weighing at least ten pounds.

9.   Give a condition that is sufficient but not necessary for weighing at least ten pounds.

Express in a conditional sentence the relation between your answer and weighing at least ten pounds.

10. Give a condition that is necessary and sufficient for weighing at least ten pounds. (Hint: There are sixteen ounces in a pound.)

Express in a biconditional sentence the relation between your answer and weighing at least ten pounds.

★ 11. Give a condition that is sufficient but not necessary for being later than 2:16 p.m., January 2, 1987.

Express in a conditional sentence the relation between your answer and being later than 2:16 p.m., January 2, 1987.

12. Give a condition that is necessary but not sufficient for being later than 2:16 p.m., January 2, 1987.

Express in a conditional sentence the relation between your answer and being later than 2:16 p.m., January 2, 1987.

EXERCISE 5.3

For each of the following try to give interesting necessary and sufficient conditions. It may not be possible but the attempt should be illuminating. If you run into problems, at least try to give interesting necessary conditions.

★ 1.   Being a knife. State your answer in the form: "Something is a knife if and only if it is . . . ."

2.   Murder. State your answer in the form: "X murdered Y if and only if . . . ."

3.   Stealing. State your answer in the form: "X stole Y from Z if and only if . . . ."

4.   Being a person. State your answer in the form: "X is a person if and only if . . . ."

5.   Being a work of art. State your answer in the form: "Something is a work of art if and only if . . . ."

★ 6.   Suicide. State your answer in the form: "X commits suicide if and only if . . . ."

EXERCISE 5.4

State what the item in column A is to the item in column B.

> S = A is sufficient but not necessary for B.
> N = A is necessary but not sufficient for B.
> N & S = A is necessary and sufficient for B.
> 0 = A is neither necessary nor sufficient for B.

		Column A	*Column B*	*Answer*
★	**1.**	Being an aunt	Having a niece	_____
	2.	Being a sound argument	Being a valid argument	_____
	3.	Being a zebra	Being an animal	_____
	4.	Being at least ten feet tall	Being at least eight feet tall	_____
★	**5.**	Weighing at least nine pounds	Weighing exactly twenty pounds	_____
	6.	Living in France	Learning French	_____
	7.	Having at least three legs	Being a normal horse	_____
	8.	Finding a mouse in the kitchen	Finding an animal in the kitchen	_____
★	**9.**	Being a copy of a book	Being found in the library	_____
	10.	Having a complete chess set	Having all the black pieces of a chess set	_____

EXERCISE 5.5

Answer each of the following questions about necessary and sufficient conditions using the methods described in the text.

1. Give a condition that is necessary but not sufficient for owning a house in California.

★ 2. Give a condition that is sufficient but not necessary for being a college student.

3. Give a condition that is necessary but not sufficient for being a college student.

4. Give a condition that is necessary but not sufficient for being a part of the human body.

★ 5. Give a condition that is sufficient but not necessary for owning something that will cut paper.

6. Give a condition that is necessary but not sufficient for owning something that will cut paper.

7.   Give a condition that is sufficient but not necessary for being a U.S. citizen.

8.   Give a condition that is necessary but not sufficient for being an oak tree.

9.   Give a condition that is sufficient but not necessary for being an athlete.

★ 10   Give a condition that is necessary and sufficient for being a grandfather.

CHAPTER 6

THE LOGIC OF CONDITIONALS

This chapter is a continuation of some of the topics discussed in the last chapter. Special emphasis is placed on alternative ways of expressing conditionals.

KEY TERMS AND HEADINGS

Brief Review
Truth Conditions for
 Conditionals

Alternative Ways of
 Expressing Conditionals
Biconditionals

BRIEF REVIEW

Conditionals were introduced in the last chapter to facilitate the discussion of necessary and sufficient conditions. A brief review is in order. A conditional sentence is a sentence using the word "if" that expresses the claim that one condition is sufficient (or necessary) for another. For example, the conditional sentence "If you own a horse, then you own an animal" expresses the true claim that your owning a horse is a sufficient condition for your owning an animal and your owning an animal is a necessary condition for your owning a horse.

In a conditional sentence, the part between the "if" and the "then" is called the antecedent, and the part between the "then" and the period is called the consequent. In the conditional sentence "If you own a horse, then you own an animal," "you own a horse" is the antecedent and "you own an animal" is the consequent. A conditional sentence says that the condition expressed by its antecedent is sufficient for that expressed by its consequent and that the condition expressed by its consequent is necessary for that expressed by its antecedent.

Biconditional sentences were also introduced in the last chapter. A biconditional sentence states that one condition is necessary *and* sufficient for another. The biconditional sentence "You own a mare if and only if you own a female horse" says that your owning a female horse is necessary and sufficient for your owning a mare.

A conditional sentence "If P, then Q" is *not* in general equivalent to its converse ("If Q, then P"). On the other hand, a biconditional sentence is always equivalent to its converse. "P if and only if Q" is equivalent to "Q if and only if P."

TRUTH CONDITIONS FOR CONDITIONALS

Much of the logic of conditionals in natural language is controversial; however, a few important things are widely accepted. Although we cannot give a truth table for "If P, then Q,"[1] we can give one row of the truth table.

P	Q	If P, then Q
T	F	F

In other words, "If P, then Q" is definitely false when its antecedent is true and its consequent is false. There may also be other ways for a conditional to be false, but at least this much is beyond controversy: If you can show that P is true and Q is false, then you have shown that "If P, then Q" is false. Having a true antecedent and a false consequent is a sufficient (but probably not necessary) condition for a conditional's being false.

This follows from the meaning of a conditional. A conditional says that its antecedent is sufficient for its consequent. But if the antecedent occurs or obtains (i.e., the antecedent is true) and the consequent does not (i.e., the consequent is false), then the antecedent could not be sufficient for the consequent. Likewise, a conditional says that its consequent is necessary for its antecedent, but if you could have the antecedent and not have consequent, then the consequent could not be necessary for the antecedent. In either case what the conditional says is definitely false.

Example of a false conditional

If 2 + 2 = 4, then 4 is an odd number.

This conditional is false because the antecedent is true but the consequent is false. In fact, being equal to 2 + 2 is a sufficient condition for 4 being *even*.

---

[1] But in formal logic a truth table for "If . . . , then . . ." is used.

P	Q	If P, then Q
T	T	T
T	F	F
F	T	T
F	F	T

In formal logic, "If P, then Q" is true whenever its antecedent is false or its consequent is true. It is generally felt that this does not reflect ordinary usage. "If today is Monday, then tomorrow is Sunday" is true, according to this interpretation, on every day of the week but Monday. Whereas most people would say that it is just plain false.

With biconditionals, two rows of the truth table are noncontroversial.[2]

P	Q	P if and only if Q
T	F	F
F	T	F

If P differs from Q in truth-value, "P if and only if Q" is false. We can show that P and Q are not necessary and sufficient for each other by showing that one (it does not matter which one) obtains but the other does not.

ALTERNATIVE WAYS OF EXPRESSING CONDITIONALS

There are a vast number of different but equivalent ways of expressing the claim that one condition is sufficient (or necessary) for another. Indeed any statement that makes a claim that one situation cannot or will not occur without another situation can be expressed as a conditional. So, for example, if I say "We cannot have peace without arms control," I am saying that arms control is a necessary condition for peace. I am not claiming that arms control is *sufficient* for peace; we may have arms control and still not have peace. But I am saying that without arms control peace is impossible. (You may disagree with the *content* of the example, but that is irrelevant. We are interested only in the *logic* of the claim.) We can express this claim—that without arms control peace is impossible—with a conditional: "If we have peace, then we have arms control." Granted, this conditional seems a bit odd as it stands, so in ordinary language we would dress it up a bit and it would come out, for example, as "If we are to have peace, then we must have arms control." The dressing up indicates that we do not have peace and that peace is desirable to the speaker. What we have seen, then, is that the claim "We cannot have peace without arms control" can equally well (as far as logic is concerned) be expressed as "If we are to have peace, then we must have arms control."

---

[2] Again in formal logic there is a complete truth table for the biconditional.

P	Q	P if and only if Q
T	T	T
T	F	F
F	T	F
F	F	T

Again, this seems not to reflect ordinary usage. According to the meaning of "P if and only if Q" in formal logic, any two conditions that actually obtain are necessary and sufficient for each other. And likewise any two conditions that both fail to obtain are necessary and sufficient for each other.

This same thought can be expressed in other ways. Each of the following sentences is equivalent to all the others.

We cannot have peace without arms control.

Peace is impossible without arms control.

We will not have peace without arms control.

We will not have peace unless we have arms control.

We will have peace only if we have arms control.

Arms control is a necessary condition for peace.

If we do not have arms control, then we will not have peace.

If we are to have peace, then we must have arms control.

Two other small but confusing points about conditionals are: (1) The "then" often is left out of the conditional sentence. The "if" is essential, but the "then" is dispensable. We can equally well say "If we are to have peace, we must have arms control." The "then" is gone and we hardly even miss it. (2) When the "then" is missing, we can put the "if" clause second without changing the meaning. "We must have arms control, if we are to have peace" means precisely the same as "If we are to have peace, then we must have arms control."

It will be helpful to state all these equivalencies formally.

If *P*, then *Q*

Each item in the following list is equivalent to "If *P*, then *Q*."

If *P*, *Q*.
Q, if *P*.
P only if *Q*.
Not *P* unless *Q*.
P is sufficient for *Q*.
Q is necessary for *P*.
If not *Q*, then not *P*.

SOME IMPORTANT POINTS TO KEEP IN MIND

1. In each item in the preceding list the order of *P* and *Q* is all important. If the order is changed, then the form is no longer equivalent. To repeat "If *P*, then *Q*" is not equivalent to "If *Q*, then *P*."

If *P*, then *Q*   If *Q*, then *P*

Likewise,

$$\text{If } P, \text{ then } Q \quad P, \text{ if } Q$$

but

$$\text{If } P, \text{ then } Q = Q, \text{ if } P$$

The same is true of the other items on the "If P, then Q" list. If you switch the order of P and Q, then it is no longer equivalent to "If P, then Q." Keep the order as given, and it is equivalent.

2. Some of the equivalences sound wrong sometimes. Consider "P only if Q." According to the "If P, then Q" list

$$\text{If } P, \text{ then } Q = P \text{ only if } Q$$

and

$$\text{If } P, \text{ then } Q \quad Q \text{ only if } P$$

This will seem right or wrong depending on the example chosen.

> If you own a horse, then you own an animal.

is true and is clearly equivalent to

> You own a horse only if you own an animal.

which is also true.[3]
On the other hand,

> If you heat water to 212°, then it will boil.

certainly does not sound equivalent to

> You heat water to 212° only if it boils.

---

[3] But

> If you own a horse, then you own an animal.

is clearly *not* equivalent to

> You own an animal only if you own a horse.

which is false.

But the "If P, then Q" list says it is and it is! You cannot heat water to 212° (under normal conditions) without its boiling.

The point to keep in mind is that the equivalence of "If P, then Q" with "P only if Q" sounds wrong when the Q is supposed to come after the P or be caused by the P. For the sake of unity of treatment, we will note this "sounding wrong" but nevertheless treat "P only if Q" as always equivalent to "If P, then Q." This "sounding wrong" is a feature of some of the other equivalencies. For example, it sounds wrong to say that boiling water is a necessary condition for heating it to 212°. But it is! So remember:

$$\text{If } P, \text{ then } Q = P \text{ only if } Q$$

but

$$\text{If } P, \text{ then } Q \quad Q \text{ only if } P$$

When going from the "If . . . , then . . ." way of expressing a conditional to the equivalent ". . . only if . . ." way (or vice versa), the order of the P and Q stays the same.

3. Sometimes in changing from one way of expressing "If P, then Q" to another we need to make minor changes or do some dressing up. For example, owning a horse is sufficient for owning an animal, but we cannot say "If owning a horse, then owning an animal." Instead we have to make some minor changes. So instead we say "If you own a horse, then you own an animal" or more formally "If one owns a horse, then one owns an animal." These changes should not alter the content of what is expressed and only allow for smoother reading.

4. The number of different ways of expressing the relation expressed by "If P, then Q" is probably limitless, but not everything that sounds like it is expressing a conditional relationship is. For example, "P implies that Q," "P entails that Q," or "Q follows from P" are not always equivalent to "If P, then Q." As we remember from Chapter 1, "implies that," "entails that," and "follows from" are argument indicators. "P implies that Q" can be used to state an argument in which P is the premise and Q is the conclusion. "If P, then Q" is not an argument, it is a single statement that claims that there is a certain relationship between P and Q. When someone says, for example, "If we are to have peace, then we must have arms control," he is not offering "we have arms control" as a conclusion that is supported by the claim that "we have peace." Thus, we also now see why "If P, then Q" is always bracketed as a single statement in doing an argument diagram.

5. Many sentences of the form "All A are B" can be expressed as conditionals, and many conditionals can be expressed in the form "All A are B." For example, we can express the statement "All zebras are animals" as "If something is a zebra, then it is an animal." Again there are many equivalent ways of expressing "All A are B." For example, "Zebras are animals," "Zebras are all animals," and "A zebra is an animal" are different ways of saying that "All zebras are animals." As with conditionals, the converse "All B are A" is not equivalent to "All A are B."

BICONDITIONALS

Biconditional sentences occur only in technical or semitechnical contexts, although they have an important role there. As with conditionals, biconditionals can be expressed in a number of different ways. A biconditional is really a conjunction of conditionals. The biconditional "*P* if and only if *Q*" is a conjunction of the conditionals "*P*, if *Q*" and "*P* only if *Q*." Expressed in the "if, then" form, the biconditional "*P* if and only if *Q*" is "If *P*, then *Q* and if *Q*, then *P*." This relationship between *P* and *Q* is expressed in different ways in technical writing. For example, in mathematics "*P* iff *Q*" means "*P* if and only if *Q*." Sometimes a wide double arrow is used: $P \Leftrightarrow Q$.

P if and only if Q

Each item in the following list is equivalent to "*P* if and only if *Q*."

> If *P*, then *Q* and if *Q*, then *P*.
> *P* is necessary and sufficient for *Q*.
> *P* iff *Q*.
> $P \Leftrightarrow Q$.

A conjunction implies each of its conjuncts (*A* and *B* implies *A*). Since a biconditional is a conjunction, it implies each of its conjuncts. Thus "*P* if and only if *Q*" implies "If *P*, then *Q*." But a conjunct does not imply the conjunction (*A* does not imply *A* and *B*). "If *P*, then *Q*" does not imply "*P* if and only if *Q*."

EXERCISE 6.1

The following are exercises involving different ways of expressing conditionals. Fill in the blanks or underline items as instructed.

★ 1.   Express "*S* is sufficient for *N*" in the equivalent "if, then" and "only if" forms.

   S is sufficient for *N* = If _____, then _____ = _____ only if _____.

2.   Express "*T* is necessary for *G*" in the equivalent "if, then" and "only if" forms.

   T is necessary for *G* = If _____ , then _____ = _____ only if _____

3.   Rewrite "If *R*, then *Q*" in the equivalent "only if" and "not . . . unless" forms.

   If *R*, then *Q* = _____ only if _____ = Not _____ unless _____.

4.   Rewrite "If *S*, then *N*" in the equivalent ". . . is a necessary condition for . . ." and ". . . is a sufficient condition for . . ." forms.

   If *S*, then *N* = _____ is a necessary condition for _____.

   If *S*, then *N* = _____ is a sufficient condition for _____.

5.   Underline just those items that are equivalent to "If *A*, then *B*." (Note: "Equivalent to" means "always has the same truth-value as.")

   a.   *A* only if *B*.
   b.   *B* only if *A*.
   c.   Not *A* unless *B*.
   d.   Not *B* unless *A*.
   e.   *A*, if *B*.
   f.   *B*, if *A*.

★ 6.   Underline just those items that are equivalent to "*S* only if *N*."

   a.   If *N*, then *S*.
   b.   *N*, if *S*.
   c.   If *S*, then *N*.
   d.   Not *S* unless *N*.
   e.   *S*, if *N*.
   f.   Not *N* unless *S*.

7.   Underline just those items that are equivalent to "Not *D* unless *E*."

    a.   *D*, if *E*.

    b.   *D* only if *E*.

    c.   If *D*, then *E*.

    d.   *E* only if *D*.

    e.   *E*, if *D*.

    f.   If *E*, then *D*.

8.   Underline just those items that are implied by "*G* if and only if *H*." (Note: This one is "implied by" not "equivalent to." "*P* is implied by *Q*" means that it is impossible for *Q* to be true and *P* false. In other words, *P* follows from *Q*. *P* is equivalent to *Q* means that each follows from the other. That you own exactly two horses implies that you own an even number of horses. But that you own an even number of horses does not, of course, imply that you own exactly two horses—you might own four. Owning exactly two horses is equivalent to, for example, owning more than one and fewer than three horses.) So, to repeat: Underline just those items in the following list that are *implied by* "*G* if and only if *H*."

    a.   If *H*, then *G*.

    b.   If *G*, then *H*.

    c.   *G* only if *H*.

    d.   *H* only if *G*.

    e.   *G*, if *H*.

    f.   *H*, if *G*.

    g.   Not *G* unless *H*.

    h.   Not *H* unless *G*.

    i.   *G* is sufficient for *H*.

    j.   *H* is necessary for *G*.

    k.   *G* is necessary for *H*.

    l.   *H* is sufficient for *G*.

    m.   *G* is necessary and sufficient for *H*.

★ 9.   Underline just those items in the following list that are equivalent to "*J* if and only if *K*." (Note: This one is "*equivalent to*" not "implied by.")

    a. If *K*, then *J*.

    b. If *J*, then *K*.

    c. *J* only if *K*.

    d. *K* only if *J*.

    e. *J*, if *K*.

    f. *K*, if *J*.

    g. Not *J* unless *K*.

    h. Not *K* unless *J*.

    i. *J* is sufficient for *K*.

    j. *K* is necessary for *J*.

    k. *J* is necessary for *K*.

    l. *K* is sufficient for *J*.

    m. *K* is necessary and sufficient for *J*.

EXERCISE 6.2

Following are additional exercises involving different ways of expressing conditionals.

★ 1.   Underline each item in the following list that is equivalent to

If something is a duck, then it is a bird.

a.   Something is a bird only if it is a duck.
b.   Something is a duck only if it is a bird.
c.   Something is not a duck unless it is a bird.
d.   Something is a bird, if it is a duck.
e.   Something is a duck if and only if it is a bird.

2.   Underline each item in the following list that is equivalent to

If you live in Chile, then you live in South America.

a.   Living in South America is a sufficient condition for living in Chile.
b.   You live in South America, if you live in Chile.
c.   If you do not live in South America, then you do not live in Chile.
d.   You live in South America if and only if you live in Chile.
e.   If you live in South America, then you live in Chile.

3.   Underline each item in the following list that is equivalent to

You can play hockey only if you can skate.

a.   If you can play hockey, then you can skate.
b.   Being able to skate is a sufficient condition for being able to play hockey.
c.   You cannot play hockey unless you can skate.
d.   You can play hockey, if you can skate.
e.   If you cannot skate, then you cannot play hockey.

4.   Underline each item in the following list that is equivalent to

You cannot twirl unless you can spin.

a.   If you can spin, then you can twirl.
b.   You can spin and you can twirl.
c.   You can twirl only if you can spin.
d.   You can twirl, if you can spin.
e.   You can spin if and only if you can twirl.

5.   Underline each item in the following list that is equivalent to
Penguins are found in Antarctica only if some birds are found in Antarctica.

a.   If some birds are found in Antarctica, then penguins are found in Antarctica.

b.   Some birds are found in Antarctica if and only if penguins are found in Antarctica.

c.   Penguins are not found in Antarctica unless some birds are found in Antarctica.

d.   Penguins are found in Antarctica or some birds are found in Antarctica.

e.   Some birds are found in Antarctica, if penguins are found in Antarctica.

★ 6.   Underline each item in the following list that is equivalent to

If you own a horse, then you own a dog.

a.   You own a horse only if you own a dog.

b.   You don't own a horse unless you own a dog.

c.   If you don't own a horse, then you don't own a dog.

d.   You own a dog and you own a horse.

e.   Owning a dog is a necessary condition for owning a horse.

7.   Underline each item in the following list that is equivalent to

You admire the works of Plato if and only if you are a philosopher.

a.   If you admire the works of Plato, then you are a philosopher.

b.   You are not a philosopher unless you admire the works of Plato.

c.   Being a philosopher is necessary and sufficient for admiring the works of Plato.

d.   You admire the works of Plato if you are a philosopher.

e.   If you are a philosopher, then you admire the works of Plato.

8.   Underline each item in the following list that is *implied by*

You admire the works of Plato if and only if you are a philosopher.

a.   If you admire the works of Plato, then you are a philosopher.

b.   You are not a philosopher unless you admire the works of Plato.

c.   Being a philosopher is necessary and sufficient for admiring the works of Plato.

d.   You admire the works of Plato if you are a philosopher.

e.   If you are a philosopher, then you admire the works of Plato.

CHAPTER **7**

PATTERNS OF INFERENCE

Various common patterns of argument are introduced in this chapter. Recognition of these patterns enables us to determine the validity of an argument.

KEY TERMS AND HEADINGS

Patterns of Inference
Inference
Immediate Inferences
Double Negation
Conversion
Transposition
Syllogisms
Modus Ponens
Mixed Hypothetical
   Syllogism

Fallacy of Affirming the
   Consequent
Modus Tollens
Fallacy of Denying the
   Antecedent
Pure Hypothetical Syllogism
Disjunctive Syllogism

This chapter discusses several important **patterns of inference** (an **inference** is the process of drawing a conclusion). The pattern of inference of an argument represents its form. Determining an argument's pattern of inference can be crucial to determining its validity or invalidity. We recall that an argument's validity depends on its form not on its content. These forms can be set out and studied as patterns of inference. Although we cannot possibly name and know all the infinite patterns of inference, many of these patterns are well known and have been given names that are widely used. Some of the common patterns of inference included in this chapter occur frequently and are crucial for reasoning.

The first several patterns of inferences are immediate inferences. An immediate inference is an argument with one premise and one conclusion. The rest of the patterns are syllogisms. A syllogism is an argument, more or less formally set out, with *two* premises and a conclusion.

IMMEDIATE INFERENCES

Double Negation (DN)

A moment's reflection on the truth table for "Not *P*' shows that "*P*' and "Not not *P*' will always have the same truth-value. So any argument of the following pattern is valid.

Not not *P*.
_____

P.

(In setting out patterns of inference, a line will be used to separate premises from conclusions. The premises are above the line and the conclusion below. Generally, no argument indicator will be used.)

Any argument of this pattern is called "double negation." Although not often explicitly included in ordinary arguments, double negation is an important pattern of inference. Saying "It is not the case that it is not the case that what you ask is possible" would be quite awkward, but if someone did, what he said would be equivalent to "What you ask is possible." Usually in ordinary speech the negations are included in the terms. So, for example, if someone said "What you ask is not impossible," you would understand that what she was saying is equivalent to "What you ask is possible." "Impossible" is the negation of "possible," so "not impossible" equals "possible." However, one must be careful and sensitive to the subtleties of language. For example, "unhappy" is not the negation of "happy," so "not unhappy" does not equal "happy." The problem is not with double negation. The problem is that not everyone is either happy or unhappy. Some people are neither happy nor unhappy—just neutral. As long as we are sure to stick to true negations, then double negation will always be valid.

Conversion (CON)

We have already seen that "If *P*, then *Q*" is *not* equivalent to "If *Q*, then *P*." "If *Q*, then *P*" is the converse of "If *P*, then *Q*." So the following is an invalid pattern of inference:

If *P*, then *Q*.
_____

If *Q*, then *P*.

When we say that this pattern of inference is invalid, we mean that not every argument of this pattern is guaranteed to be valid. In fact, virtually every argument of this pattern is invalid (although there are some technical exceptions). (We put an *X* over the pattern to indicate in a particularly graphic way that the pattern is not valid.)

We should recognize "All *A* are *B*" as the converse of "All *B* are *A*." And likewise the pattern of inference

$$\frac{\text{All } A \text{ are } B.}{\text{All } B \text{ are } A.}$$

is invalid. For example, "All boys are humans" is true, but its converse "All humans are boys" is not.[1]

Transposition (TRANS)

We form the **transpositive** of a conditional statement by switching its antecedent and consequent and negating each. A conditional is always equivalent to its transpositive. The pattern of inference

$$\frac{\text{If } P, \text{ then } Q.}{\text{If not } Q, \text{ then not } P.}$$

is valid.

We can understand the validity of transposition if we think of what the conditional says in terms of necessary and sufficient conditions. If Q is necessary for P (i.e., if P, then Q), then if you do not have Q, then you do not have P (i.e., if not Q, then not P).

When inferring transpositives, one can end up with a lot of *nots*. For example, the transpositive of "If P, then not Q" is "If not not Q, then not P." In practice we would simplify this further by double negation and replace "not not Q" with "Q." So the following pattern of inference is transposition and is valid.

$$\frac{\text{If } P, \text{ then not } Q.}{\text{If } Q, \text{ then not } P.}$$

Transposition requires two steps: (1) switch the antecedent and consequent and (2) negate each. If you only do one, then it is invalid (and not transposition). For example, the following is not transposition and is not valid.

$$\frac{\text{If } P, \text{ then } Q.}{\text{If not } P, \text{ then not } Q.}$$

(The antecedent and consequent have been negated but not switched.)

---

[1] As we have emphasized, a conditional is not in general equivalent to its converse, but some types of statements are equivalent to their converses. For example, a statement of the form "No P are Q" is always equivalent to its converse "No Q are P." Likewise a statement of the form "Some P are Q" is always equivalent to its converse "Some Q are P."

SYLLOGISMS

Modus Ponens (MP)

Several important patterns of inference involve both conditional and nonconditional premises. These are called **mixed hypothetical syllogisms.** They each start with the premise "If P, then Q," but they differ in the other premise and the conclusion.[2]

The following pattern of inference is valid and is called *modus ponens:*

> If P, then Q.
> P.
> _____
>
> Q.

The validity of this pattern of inference is easy to see. If P is sufficient for Q (which the conditional premise says) and you have P (which the other premise says), you must have Q. It is impossible for P to be sufficient for Q and to have P and yet not have Q. So a conditional premise plus the antecedent of that conditional premise always implies the consequent of the conditional premise. The following argument is an example of *modus ponens* and is valid.

> If you own a dog, then you own an animal.
> You own a dog.
> _____
>
> So you own an animal.

It does not matter how complicated the antecedent or consequent of the conditional premise are. A conditional plus the assertion of its antecedent implies the consequent of the conditional. For example, the following argument is *modus ponens:*

> If P or Q, then R and not S.
> P or Q.
> _____
>
> R and not S.

This holds for all the patterns: It does not matter how complicated the expressions are that replace the letters (as long as the replacement is uniform). The argument will still be of that pattern.

---

[2] Although we set out the syllogisms with the conditional premise first and speak of it as the first premise, the order in which the premises occur makes no difference to the validity of the argument or which pattern it is. This is true of all arguments.

Fallacy of Affirming the Consequent (FAC)

The following pattern of inference is invalid (thus it is called a fallacy), but it is so important that it requires separate treatment. The fallacy of affirming the consequent is

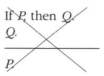

If P then Q.
Q.
_____
P.

Part of the problem is that it is so similar to *modus ponens*; another is that people do seem to have a psychological tendency to reason this way despite its obvious invalidity. To see the invalidity of this pattern, consider an example similar (but not identical) to the one for *modus ponens*:

> If you own a dog, then you own an animal.
> You own an animal.
> _____
> So you own a dog.

Clearly, you could own an animal and not own a dog—you could own a cat. The premises could easily be true and yet the conclusion false.

We can also think of the invalidity of affirming the consequent in terms of necessary and sufficient conditions. From the fact that, say, A is necessary for D and you have A it does not follow that you have D.

Modus Tollens (MT)

The following pattern of inference is valid and is called *modus tollens:*

> If P, then Q.
> Not Q.
> _____
> Not P.

Consider an example of *modus tollens:*

> If you own a dog, then you own an animal.
> You do not own an animal.
> _____
> So you do not own a dog.

The validity of *modus tollens* can easily be seen in terms of necessary and sufficient conditions. If Q is necessary for P (i.e., if P, then Q) and you do not have Q, then you cannot have P. If you did have P, that would be proof that either Q was not necessary for P or you did have Q.

Modus tollens is often used in doing knight and knave problems and in other reasoning. We reason, for example, in the following pattern:

If A is a knight, what he says is true.

What A says is false.

_____

So A is not a knight.

The first premise is true by the definition of "knight." The truth of the second premise would have to be determined independently, of course.

Again the complexity of the argument does not matter; as long as it is of the form where one premise is a conditional sentence, another is the negation of the consequent of the conditional premise, and the conclusion is the negation of the antecedent of the conditional it is *modus tollens*. So, for example, the following argument is a *modus tollens* and is valid:

If P, then not Q.

Q.

_____

Not P.

Fallacy of Denying the Antecedent (FDA)

The following pattern called fallacy of denying the antecedent is very similar to *modus tollens* but unlike *modus tollens* is invalid.

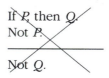

If P, then Q.

Not P.

_____

Not Q.

To see the invalidity of denying the antecedent, consider the following argument:

If you own a dog, then you own an animal.

You don't own a dog.

_____

So you don't own an animal.

Clearly the premises could be true (if you own a cat, say, instead of a dog), but the conclusion could be false. More generally, from the fact that P is a sufficient condition for Q and you do not have P it does not follow that you do not have Q. There could be many other sufficient conditions for Q besides P any of which could be fulfilled. So it is important not to confuse the fallacy of denying the antecedent with *modus tollens*.

Pure Hypothetical Syllogism (PHS)

Pure hypothetical syllogism is called "pure" because it involves only conditionals. It is always valid. The following pattern of inference is valid and is called pure hypothetical syllogism:

> If *P*, then *Q*.
> If *Q*, then *R*.
> ――――――――――
> If *P*, then *R*.

The validity of pure hypothetical syllogism is obvious, especially when we think of the conditionals in terms of necessary and sufficient conditions. If *P* is sufficient for *Q*, and *Q* is sufficient for *R*, then obviously *P* is sufficient for *R*. So for any argument of this pattern it is impossible for the premises to be true and the conclusion false. Consider the following example:

> If you own a dog, then you own a mammal.
> If you own a mammal, then you own an animal.
> ――――――――――――――――――――――
> So if you own a dog, then you own an animal.

If any of the conditionals in this pattern are replaced by its converse, the argument becomes invalid. So, for example, the following pattern is invalid and is not pure hypothetical syllogism:

> If *Q*, then *P*.
> If *Q*, then *R*.
> ――――――――――
> If *P*, then *R*.

There is a pattern of inference that is very similar to pure hypothetical syllogism and is also valid but does not involve conditionals. This pattern ought to be familiar since it is one of the patterns that we examined in the chapter on validity and soundness. The similarity of the following pattern of inference to pure hypothetical syllogism is evident.

> All *A* are *B*.
> All *B* are *C*.
> ――――――――
> All *A* are *C*.

In the Middle Ages various valid syllogisms were given names [that is where *modus ponens* (Latin for "affirming mode") and *modus tollens* (Latin for "denying mode") came from], and this one was called "barbara." The name "barbara" was part of an elaborate system devised to help students memorize a large number of valid syllogisms.

Disjunctive Syllogism (DS)

The following pattern of inference is called disjunctive syllogism because it involves a disjunction.

$$P \text{ or } Q.$$
$$\text{Not } P.$$
$$\overline{}$$
$$Q.$$

The validity of this pattern is evident from the truth table for disjunction. If "*P* or *Q*" is true and "*P*" is false (i.e., not *P*), then "*Q*" must be true. Note that it does not matter where the "not" occurs as long as one premise is a disjunction, the other premise is the negation of one of the disjuncts of that disjunction, and the conclusion is the other disjunct. So the following argument, for example, is a disjunctive syllogism and is valid:

$$\text{Not } P \text{ or } Q.$$
$$\text{Not } Q.$$
$$\overline{}$$
$$\text{Not } P.$$

SUMMARY

IMMEDIATE INFERENCES

DN (VALID)

Not not *P*

P.

CON (NOT VALID)

If *P*, then *Q*.
If *Q*, then *P.*

TRANS (VALID)

If *P*, then *Q*.
If not *Q*, then not *P.*

SYLLOGISMS

MP (VALID)

If *P*, then *Q*.
P.
_____

Q.

MT (VALID)

If *P*, then *Q*.
Not *Q*.
_____

Not *P*.

FAC (NOT VALID)

If *P*, then *Q*.
Q.
_____

P.

FDA (NOT VALID)

If *P*, then *Q*.
Not *P*.
_____

Not *Q*.

PHS (VALID)

If *P*, then *Q*.
If *Q*, then *R*.
_____

If *P*, then *R*.

BARBARA (VALID)

All *A* are *B*.
All *B* are *C*.
_____

All *A* are *C*.

DS (VALID)

P or *Q*.
Not *P*.
_____

Q.

EXERCISE 7.1

Diagram each of the following arguments using numbers and arrows. State which pattern of inference it is and whether the argument is valid or invalid.

★   1.   This computer can do word processing. And if it can do word processing, then it can probably do spread sheets. So this computer can probably do spread sheets.

   2.   Brenda is either in Phoenix or she is in Detroit. She is not in Detroit. So she is in Phoenix.

   3.   If Brenda is in Detroit or Harold is in Chicago, then Ralph is in Phoenix and Nate is in Boston. Brenda is in Detroit or Harold is in Chicago. So Ralph is in Phoenix and Nate is in Boston.

4. If this cookbook has a recipe for lasagna, then it has some recipes for Italian dishes. It has some recipes for Italian dishes. So it has a recipe for lasagna.

5. If Harry owns a dog, then Harry owns an animal. So if Harry does not own an animal, then Harry does not own a dog.

★ 6. If Harry owns a dog, then Harry owns an animal. Harry does not own an animal. So Harry does not own a dog.

7. Joanie has either a cold or a bad case of allergies. She doesn't have a cold. So she has a bad case of allergies.

8. [The following is a combination of two patterns of inference.]

    If my computer won't work, then either the hard drive has crashed or else the CPU is down. My computer won't work. Therefore either the hard drive has crashed or else the CPU is down. But the CPU isn't down. Therefore the hard drive has crashed.

9. If I've cooked this spaghetti for eleven minutes, then it is done. I have cooked it for eleven minutes. Therefore it is done.

10. All people who drive dangerous vehicles are likely to be in a serious accident. All people who ride motorcycles are people who drive dangerous vehicles. Therefore all people who ride motorcycles are likely to be in a serious accident.

EXERCISE 7.2

The following examples are from the files of my cousin, Sherlock Schwartz.

Diagram each of the following arguments using numbers and arrows. State which pattern of inference it is and whether the argument is valid or invalid.

★ 1.   [For the following argument, supply the conclusion yourself.]

We have previously established that it was either the butler or the duke. We now know it could not have been the butler.
Conclusion? _____

2.   [For the following argument, supply the conclusion yourself.]

If it was the butler, then the motive was revenge, but clearly the motive was not revenge.
Conclusion? _____

3.   If it was the duke, then the motive was fear. And we now know that the motive was fear. So it was the duke.

4. If the butler did it, then the chambermaid knew of it, and if the chambermaid knew of it, she would confide in the duchess. So if the butler did it, the chambermaid would confide in the duchess.

5. If the butler did it, the chambermaid would confide in the duchess. So if the chambermaid did not confide in the duchess, then the butler didn't do it.

★ 6. If an argument is sound, then it is valid. So if it is invalid, it's unsound.

7.   Argument 6 is not invalid. So it is valid.

8.   If the bald monkey of Anjou is missing, then the duke committed the murder. But the bald monkey of Anjou is not missing. So the duke did not commit the murder.

9.   If the butler committed the murder, then volume six of *Rosalie's Romance* would be missing from the library, but volume six of *Rosalie's Romance* is not missing from the library. So the butler did not commit the murder.

EXERCISE 7.3

Diagram each of the following arguments using numbers and arrows. State which pattern of inference it is and whether the argument is valid or invalid.

★   1.   Either the moon goes around the earth or the earth goes around the moon. The moon does not go around the earth. Hence the earth goes around the moon.

2.   If littering damages the environment, then we should outlaw it. Littering doesn't damage the environment. So we shouldn't outlaw it.

3.   If A is a knave, then A is lying. A is not lying. Consequently A is not a knave.

4. [Here is a longer argument that has embedded in it one of the patterns.]

    If there was a perfectly good, omniscient, and omnipotent god, then the world would not contain any more evil than the minimal amount necessary for the good that it contains. But the world contains more than the minimal amount of evil, since a great deal of the evil in the world is unnecessary and does not contribute to any good. For example, horrible birth defects that afflict innocent newborn babies cannot reasonably be thought to contribute to a greater good that could not be achieved without them. Therefore there is no perfectly good, omniscient, and omnipotent god.

★ 5. If I won the lottery, then I would have an obligation to donate some of my income to charity. I haven't won the lottery. So I have no obligation to donate some of my income to charity.

6. [The following argument is a combination of two patterns with a suppressed intermediate conclusion. Try supplying the suppressed intermediate conclusion, and then seeing which patterns are combined.]

    If my car won't start, then either it is out of gas or there is something wrong with it. But it isn't out of gas, and yet it still won't start. Therefore there is something wrong with it.

7. [This argument, likewise, is a combination of two patterns with a suppressed intermediate conclusion.]

    If the story told in *Genesis* about the origin and diversity of life is literally true (the view that it is literally true is called "creationism"), then all the animal and plant species were created at once and there has been no evolution. If all the animal and plant species were created at once and there has been no evolution, then there would be no fossil record of biological species coming into existence. But there is such a fossil record. In fact there is ample evidence in fossils of the appearance of some species long after the appearance and disappearance of other more primitive species. So creationism is false.

8. [Sometimes the conditional premises or conclusions are written in ways other than the "if . . ., then . . ." form. We should still be able to discern the patterns. If you have trouble, try rewriting the conditionals in the equivalent "if . . ., then . . ." form.]

    Joanie is home, because her lights are on, which they wouldn't be, if she weren't home.

9. Jed will not get the position unless he applies for it. He will apply for it. So he will get it.

★ 10.   Nancy will go to the party only if Zeke goes. Zeke is not going. So Nancy won't go.

11.   If she smokes, then I'm leaving. So if I'm staying, then she isn't smoking.

12.   Considering that Harry's fingerprints were found at the scene of the murder, and they would be found there if he is the murderer, we may conclude that Harry is the murderer.

13.   [Here is another argument with a suppressed intermediate conclusion.]
My boat is a sloop only if it does not have a mizzenmast. My boat either
has a mizzenmast or it is not a yawl. My boat is a sloop. So my boat is not a
yawl.

EXERCISE 7.4

Diagram each of the following arguments using numbers and arrows. State which pattern of inference it is and whether it is valid or invalid.

★   1.   [This argument is a combination of patterns with a suppressed intermediate conclusion.]

   If abortion is murder, then the fetus is a person. If the fetus is a person, then it has all the essential characteristics of persons. But the fetus does not have all the essential characteristics of persons. So abortion is not murder.

   2.   The Dandy Lions won only if Jethro scored eight goals. Jethro did not score eight goals unless the Wombat's goalie was a sieve. So if the Dandy Lions won, then the Wombat's goalie was a sieve.

3. [The following argument is a combination with a suppressed intermediate conclusion.]

    Ralph will not attend the rally unless his teacher lets class out early. His teacher will let class out early only if nobody asks any questions. Somebody will ask a question. Therefore Ralph will not attend the rally.

4. [Again, this argument is a combination with a suppressed intermediate conclusion.]

    The star k237 is visible. But if the star k237 were a black hole, then it would be invisible. And if k237 is not a black hole, then it is a red giant. So k237 is a red giant.

★   5. Dallas will make the playoffs only if Detroit loses or Buffalo wins. Pittsburgh is eliminated, if Detroit loses or Buffalo wins. So Dallas won't make the playoffs unless Pittsburgh is eliminated.

6. If either Brazil or Argentina join the alliance, then Chile will quit. Chile will quit the alliance. Consequently either Brazil or Argentina will join the alliance.

7. . . . [Art] doesn't seem to have any [moral effects] . . . . If it did, people who are constantly exposed to it, including all curators and critics, would be saints, and we are not.

> Robert Hughes, "Art, Morals,
> and Politics," *New York Review
> of Books,* April 23, 1992

[The following two examples are from sociology textbooks. Both present interesting problems in evaluation.]

8. If there were no class divisions in American society, or if people were not assorted into a complex society of religious ethnic groups, occupations, and race, if, in short, Americans were a homogeneous people with no differences in situation, minds, interests, and demands—then the background of decision-makers would make no practical difference. Since such is obviously not the case, it is of more than passing interest that the vast majority of political decision-makers in the United States come from an exceedingly narrow, powerful, and privileged slice of American society.

> Edward S. Greenberg, *The American
> Political System*

9. If all positions were equally important and required equal skill, it would then make little difference as to what individuals performed what jobs; but such is not the case. Thus, a society must offer rewards, as incentives to acquire the skill level needed to perform important jobs.

Charles E. Anderson, *Toward a New Sociology*

10. The existence of truth is self-evident. For whoever denies the existence of truth grants that truth does not exist: and, if truth does not exist, then the proposition *Truth does not exist* is true: and if there is anything true, there must be truth.

St. Thomas Aquinas, *Summa Theologica*

[The following two examples do not fit the patterns named in this chapter, but you should be able to use the patterns plus the methods of Chapter 4 to determine validity.]

★ 11. If something is worthy of desire, then it is good. If something is impossible to achieve, then it is unworthy of desire. So if something is good, then it is possible to achieve.

12.   [Supply the conclusion to this argument yourself.]

No good thing ever harms its owner. Wealth sometimes does harm its owner because wealthy people are the victims of kidnapers and thieves, not to mention the psychological harm that wealth can do.

Boethius, *The Consolation of Philosophy*
(Slightly adapted)

Conclusion? _____

CHAPTER 8

SUPPRESSED PREMISES

An essential step of argument evaluation, the adding of presupposed but not explicitly stated premises, is discussed in this chapter.

KEY TERMS AND HEADINGS

Suppressed Premise
Adding Suppressed Premises
Avoiding Purely Formal
  Suppressed Premises

Purely Formal Suppressed
  Premise
Finding the Correct
  Suppressed Premise

A **suppressed premise** of an argument is an unstated but implicit premise of the argument. To understand and evaluate arguments properly, we often need to make these suppressed premises explicit. In fact, it is rare for someone in an actual discourse to state explicitly all the premises of an argument. There is nothing wrong with using suppressed premises when arguing as long as the suppressed premises are common knowledge or would be accepted by everyone addressed by the arguer and are clearly presupposed by the argument. Although using suppressed premises is permissible when arguing, when *evaluating* arguments, we must make these suppressed premises explicit.

ADDING SUPPRESSED PREMISES

Making suppressed premises explicit is essential to argument evaluation for two main reasons: (1) Often an argument would appear very weak, much weaker than it actually is, without adding its suppressed premises. Many arguments appear to be invalid as explicitly stated but are easily made valid by adding an appropriate suppressed premise. Thus evaluating arguments without adding suppressed premises would lead to a very unsympathetic treatment of arguments. This is a violation of the principle of charity—an essential principle of argument analysis and evaluation. (2) Sometimes the most controversial premises of an argument will be left unstated. Although the motivation to do this is obvious and perhaps understandable, it is a cagey tactic that must be resisted. The best resistance is to force arguers (including ourselves) to make explicit, or at least be able to make explicit, these controversial suppressed premises.

Let us see how this works in an actual case. Consider the first two sentences of exercise 2.4, number 7.

Every person has a right to life. So the fetus has a right to life.

This was part of a much longer argument whose conclusion was that abortion cannot be allowed. Although the longer argument contained several other steps, the heart of it is right here, because once we grant that the fetus has a right to life it is much more difficult, and may even be impossible, to justify killing it.

Evaluating the argument simply as it is stated would be quite confusing.

Every person has a right to life.

So the fetus has a right to life.

What would we say? "After all it is surely invalid. The premise 'Every person has a right to life' doesn't even say anything about the fetus." Such a rejection of the argument is altogether too hasty, however.

The correct approach is to supply a suppressed premise that is clearly presupposed by the argument. In this case the suppressed premise is "The fetus is a person." The argument we should evaluate is the following:

[The fetus is a person.]
Every person has a right to life.

So the fetus has a right to life.

(The suppressed premise is put in brackets to indicate that it is an addition that was not present explicitly in the original.)

Clearly the argument is now valid. In fact, if we wanted to make the validity of the argument absolutely apparent, we could reconstruct it as a PHS or Barbara:

[If something is a human fetus, then it is a person.]
If something is a person, then it has a right to life.

So if something is a human fetus, then it has a right to life.

(In setting out the argument formally in this way, it does not hurt to state explicitly that it is the *human* fetus that is in question.) Expressed this way the argument is not as smooth, but its validity is evident. The first premise says that being a human fetus is a sufficient condition for being a person. The second says that being a person is a sufficient condition for having a right to life. And the conclusion says that being a human fetus is a sufficient condition for having a right to life.

Of course, just because the argument is valid does not mean that it is *sound*. We must now ask whether the premises are true. I will not attempt to answer this question here, but it should be noted that the most controversial premise of the argument was left suppressed—namely, that the human fetus is a person. Most of us would readily agree that all persons have a right to life.[1] That the human fetus is a person, on the other hand, is a highly controversial and doubtful claim. There would be something shady about leaving such a premise unstated.

By writing down the suppressed premise and explicitly adding it to the argument, we have made a great deal of progress and avoided confusion and wasteful detours. The original argument

> Every person has a right to life.
> So the fetus has a right to life.

really depends on the claim that the human fetus is a person, even though this is never explicitly stated in the argument. The validity of the (fully set out) argument is beyond question. All the controversy is focused on the suppressed premise, which is where it should be focused.

Whether a human fetus is a person is not something that is easy to determine and is not something all people are likely ever to agree about. (The next chapter includes a discussion of premise verification and falsification.) We should approach the question of whether the fetus is a person by trying to say what the necessary and sufficient conditions are for being a person (exercise 5.3, question 4) and seeing if the fetus meets those conditions.

When we consider the argument as fully set out, one lingering question may be: Was the suppressed premise "The fetus is a person" actually thought of by the arguer? In some sense it does not really matter. The argument needs that premise even to get off the ground. If the arguer declines to allow that premise (or one equivalent to it) to be added to the argument, then he or she runs the serious risk of simply being stuck with an invalid argument. Without the suppressed premise, the given premise is irrelevant to the conclusion. So, in any case, we can say that the argument requires or presupposes the premise that the human fetus is a person, and assessing this claim is crucial to the evaluation of the argument.

AVOIDING PURELY FORMAL SUPPRESSED PREMISES

When supplying suppressed premises, we are supplying the missing pieces of the reasoning, so we want to find a piece that "fits." When supplying a suppressed premise, we want to supply a premise that will make the argument valid. (If the argument is already valid, then it does not need a suppressed premise.)

---

[1] Some would claim that this right can be forfeited or lost by certain individuals (e.g., murderers).

Technically speaking, any invalid argument can be made valid by adding premises. Here is the proof: We know that *modus ponens* is a valid pattern of inference. Suppose that the argument

$$\frac{P}{C}$$

is invalid. We can make the argument valid by adding a conditional sentence "If P, then C" as a suppressed premise. The new argument has the form

$$\begin{array}{l} [\text{If P, then C}] \\ P \\ \hline C \end{array}$$

We now have an argument that is of the pattern *modus ponens* and is valid. Clearly this can be done for any argument. Here is a formula for constructing a suppressed premise that will make any argument valid: Construct the suppressed premise by forming a conditional with the given premise as the antecedent and the given conclusion as the consequent. If there is more than one premise, conjoin the premises and put the conjunction of the premises in the antecedent.

For any given invalid argument there are, in fact, infinitely many different premises we could add, each of which would make the argument valid. A serious question then is which premise should we add to the argument when evaluating it?

The problem with the premises gotten by the formula is that they are purely *formal* in the sense that they make the argument valid but may give us no insight into what is really going on with the argument. Consider again the fetus argument. If we add the premise "If every person has a right to life, then the fetus has a right to life," then the argument becomes valid but clearly this premise does not get to the heart of the matter in the way the premise "The fetus is a person" does. Let us call a premise that sheds no light on the argument and merely makes it valid in a purely formal way a **purely formal suppressed premise.**

What we want to do in supplying suppressed premises is to avoid supplying purely formal suppressed premises. We want to find suppressed premises that help us to see what is really going on with the arguments and help us to focus our evaluation of the arguments in a relevant way. In supplying a suppressed premise we want to find a suppressed premise that does this job. "The fetus is a person" is a suppressed premise that does this job for the fetus argument.

To help make clear what is meant, consider another argument:

> South Africa has a right to preserve
> apartheid, because apartheid is essential
> to the existence of South African society.

The given premise is: "Apartheid is essential to the existence of South African society." The given conclusion is "South Africa has a right to preserve apartheid." Clearly we need to supply a suppressed premise to evaluate this argument properly.

The premise "If apartheid is essential to the existence of South African society, then South Africa has a right to preserve apartheid" is a purely formal suppressed premise; it makes the argument valid but that is all that it does. It does not help us evaluate the argument. A much more interesting and relevant suppressed premise is "Any society has a right to preserve whatever is essential to its existence." This is a suppressed premise that gets to the heart of the matter. The argument we should evaluate is the following:

Apartheid is essential to the existence of South African society.

[Any society has a right to preserve whatever is essential to its existence.]

So South Africa has a right to preserve apartheid.

As in the fetus argument, the suppressed premise is very controversial. We should ask "Is it true that *any* society has a right to preserve *whatever* is essential to its existence?" What about evil societies? What about evil things that may be essential to good societies? And so on. These are questions that we would have to focus on to fully evaluate this argument. Making the suppressed premise "Any society has a right to preserve whatever is essential to its existence" explicit helps us to focus on these questions. A purely formal suppressed premise would not.

FINDING THE CORRECT SUPPRESSED PREMISE

1. People sometimes have difficulties finding a suppressed premise that does the job of really making explicit what is going on in the argument. Often such a suppressed premise will involve combining a term from the given premise and a term from the conclusion. For example, in the argument

All men are mortals. So Socrates is a mortal.

the conclusion does not mention men and the premise does not mention Socrates. What is needed to make the argument valid is a suppressed premise that connects the given premise and the conclusion. Avoid the purely formal suppressed premise "If all men are mortals, then Socrates is a mortal." In this case the suppressed premise we want is obviously "Socrates is a man." If you are having trouble formulating a suppressed premise, start by combining a key term that is mentioned in the premise (but is not mentioned in the conclusion) with a key term from the conclusion (that is not mentioned in the premise).

In the Socrates argument the given premise is a generalization and the suppressed premise is a specific statement about Socrates. In the South Africa argument both the premise and the conclusion are specific statements about South Africa and apartheid. When the premise and conclusion are both specific statements, a generalization is usually needed to connect them. Generalizations can be either wide or narrow. For example, "All African societies have a right to preserve whatever is essential to them" would make the apartheid argument valid but it is too narrow. It invites the question "Why just African societies?" "Anything has a right to anything" would also make the argument valid, but it is absurd because it is far too wide. What we want for the suppressed premise is a generalization that is as wide as possible without becoming absurd. The task is to find a suppressed premise with the right degree of generality. Of course, finding a suppressed premise with the right degree of generality can be a matter of interpretation and requires sensitivity and ingenuity. And again there will be more than just one way of stating the correct suppressed premise for a particular argument.

2. Another common problem with suppressed premises is that sometimes we are tempted to use the converse of the correct suppressed premise. The correct terms are there and it is the correct degree of generality, but the terms are in the wrong order. This can occur even in very simple arguments. For example, consider the following argument:

> The roof is leaking. So it must have snowed.

Someone might hastily offer the following as a suppressed premise for this argument: "The roof always leaks when it snows." Nevertheless, adding this premise to the argument does not make it valid. Indeed the argument with the added premise is of the pattern FAC. ("The roof always leaks when it snows" = "When it snows, then the roof leaks" = "If it snows, then the roof leaks.")

> [If it snows, then the roof leaks.]
> The roof is leaking.
> _____
> Therefore it snowed.

The premises do not imply the conclusion. "The roof leaks when it snows" and "The roof is now leaking" do not imply that it snowed, because the roof might also leak when it rains. It might be raining, not snowing.

In fact what is needed is the converse of the proposed suppressed premise: "If the roof is leaking, then it snowed." Now the argument becomes a version of *modus ponens*.

> [If the roof leaks, then it snowed.]
> The roof is leaking.
> _____
> Therefore it snowed.

This suppressed premise is a bit formalistic, but it helps us see that the suppressed premise we need for this argument is not "When it snows, the roof leaks" but rather "The *only* time the roof leaks is when it snows." In supplying suppressed premises we must be careful not to supply the converse of the correct suppressed premise.

3. Occasionally we may come across arguments that cannot be made valid in any simple, natural way (but, of course, they can be made valid by adding a purely formal suppressed premise). For example,

> Pupils may go on the trip only if they have a note from their parents.
> _____
> So Louise may go on the trip.

Adding the suppressed premise "Louise has a note from her parents" will not make the argument valid. The given premise says that having a parental note is a necessary condition for going on the trip. It does not say that it is sufficient.

The most charitable interpretation in a case such as this is to treat the given premise as a biconditional. People rarely, if ever, say "if and only if" in everyday discourse. We often say "only if" when we mean "if and only if," even though "only if" does not strictly and literally mean "if and only if." Usually our meaning is well understood. So, fully set out the argument would be as follows:

> Pupils may go on the trip [if and] only if they have a note from their parents.
> [Louise has a note from her parents.]
> _____
> So Louise may go on the trip.

Occasionally we must interpret a conditional premise as a biconditional in order to achieve a natural and charitable interpretation of the argument. Of course, such an argument will be sound only if the biconditional is true.

SUPPRESSED PREMISE EXERCISES

General directions: In each case supply a suppressed premise (or premises) that will make the argument valid. The suppressed premise should be different from the given premise and the conclusion and should work in logical combination with the given premise to imply the conclusion. Be sure to check that after the suppressed premise is added the argument is valid. The suppressed premise should not be a purely formal suppressed premise.

EXERCISE 8.1

For each argument supply a suppressed premise as described in the general directions. In this first set of exercises, all the examples are made up. However, some of these can be tricky.

★   1.   Whenever I go out, I come back late. So I'll come back late tonight.

2.   All hamsters are turtles. So all hamsters are reptiles.

3.   Either a Republican or a Democrat will be elected. So an independent won't be elected.

4.   Turtles are animals because they aren't plants.

★   5.   Children should have rights because children are people too.

6.   Children shouldn't have rights because they have no responsibilities.

7.   All the members of Phi Kappa Rho are seniors because every member of the football team is a senior.

8.   My computer just beeped. So I must have just typed a syntax error.

9.   Only students are allowed to park in lot Z. Therefore all philosophy majors are allowed to park in lot Z.

10.   Vertebrates are mammals. Gorillas are anthropoids. So gorillas are mammals.

11.   Good poets aren't good critics, because good poets aren't bitter.

★ 12.   Every member of the basketball team is an athlete. Therefore some English majors are not members of the basketball team.

EXERCISE 8.2

For each argument supply a suppressed premise as described in the general directions.

★ 1. Something can exist only if it is a material thing. So ghosts do not exist.

   2. Politicians have no incentive to protect children's rights since children cannot vote.

> Robert E. Schell and Elizabeth Hall,
> *Developmental Psychology Today,* 4th ed.
> (slightly adapted)

   3. The morally right thing to do, on any occasion, is whatever would bring about the greatest balance of happiness over unhappiness. Therefore, on at least some occasions, mercy killing may be morally right.

> James Rachels, *The Elements of Moral
> Philosophy* (Rachels is summarizing the
> utilitarian argument for mercy killing.)

   4. We need not be ashamed of our defense mechanisms. They are a part of our nature, they are necessary to our survival; and there is no one who is completely free of them.

> Terry O'Banion and April O'Connell, *The
> Shared Journey: An Introduction to
> Encounter*

★ 5. Because elementary school teachers work with the youngest children, they are the most important teachers of all.

> James W. Noll, *Taking Sides: Clashing Views
> on Controversial Education Issues*

6. It is essential in a democracy that individuals and groups be able to make their views known and fairly select their leaders and public officials. Hence, civil liberties are essential in a democracy.

Ira Katznelson and Mark Kesselman,
The Politics of Power

7. Susan: "You can't have it all ways babe. We are not children any more."

Michael Weller, *Loose Ends*

8. Because physical activity is healthful, physical education should be required.

9. Communism is opposed by reform liberals precisely because it violates individual freedom.

Kenneth Hooven, *Ideology and Political Life*

★ 10. Only doctors are authorized to prescribe medical treatment. Therefore Maynard is not a doctor.

11. Messing with Chris' women is trouble, so I know I'm in trouble now.

Edward Philips, *Sunday's Child*

12. A non-Christian [person living in Great Britian] is bound by [the Christian institution of marriage] . . . , not because it is part of Christianity but because, rightly or wrongly, it has been adopted by the society in which he lives.

Patrick Devlin, *The Enforcement of Morals*
(Lord Devlin was a British judge.)

13. We may not often find ourselves wondering, "Why do totally unselfish people suffer, people who never do anything wrong?" because we come to know very few such individuals.

    Harold S. Kushner, *When Bad Things Happen
    to Good People*

14. I don't know of any claims in my textbook that are wrong but there must be some, because I am a human being.

    Howard Kahane, *Logic and Contemporary
    Rhetoric* (slightly adapted)

15. Homosexuality is incompatible with military service. The presence of such members adversely affects the ability of the Armed Forces to maintain discipline, good order, and morale.

    "The Pentagon Papers," *Ithaca Journal,*
    November 1990

EXERCISE 8.3

For each argument supply a suppressed premise as described in the general directions.

1. We oppose censorship and classification by governments because they are alien to the American tradition of freedom.

   The Motion Picture Production Code

2. He was a Ninja. Therefore he was the only one with the highly special fighting skills needed to defeat the samurai.

   Ninja Magazine, April 1984

★ 3. I recognize that it is impossible for God ever to deceive me, since in all fraud and deception there is some kind of imperfection.

   Descartes, *Meditations*

4. Cross-country skiing is . . . an efficient cardiovascular exercise because it works the upper and lower body.

   Shape Magazine, September 1989

5. There is no question that legalization of marijuana is a risky business, since it may lead to an increase in the number of people who abuse drugs.

   The Playboy Forum, "Decriminalize Drugs Now," January 1989

6. If one tells falsehoods to a child who is wholly unable to perceive one's meaning, there is no lie involved, for one is equivalently talking to oneself.

   Edwin F. Healy, *Moral Guidance*

★ 7. The fetus is not socially perceived as human. It cannot communicate with others. Thus, both subjectively and objectively, it is not a member of society.

> John T. Noonan, "An Almost Absolute
> Value in History," in *Applying Ethics,*
> eds. Jeffrey Olen and Vincent Barry
> (Noonan is reporting the argument.)

8. I hope that someday we can abolish sport and trophy hunting. Remember, 90 percent of us are non-hunters, therefore I'm assuming that all or most of our 90 percent respects wildlife. Being the majority, I feel we must have some power over the minority of hunters.

> *Ithaca Journal,* November 1988

9. Lying is wrong. Cheating on your income tax involves telling falsehoods with intent to deceive. So cheating on your income tax is wrong.

10. [For this one give a suppressed intermediate conclusion and another suppressed premise.]

Every form of social deviation can be considered an illness. Criminal behavior is a form of social deviation. Thus, criminals are not to be condemned or punished but to be understood, treated, and cured.

> Howard D. Schwartz, ed., *Dominant Issues in
> Medical Sociology* (slightly adapted)

CHAPTER 9

PREMISE EVALUATION

Generalizations and Counterexamples

Premise evaluation is a crucial step in argument evaluation. This chapter and the next present methods for criticizing and evaluating claims that are made in an argument and suggestions for revising judgments in an organized manner. This chapter is concerned with the evaluation of general statements.

KEY TERMS AND HEADINGS

Generalizations

Counterexamples

Conceptual Versus Empirical
  Generalizations

Counterclaims

Revising Generalizations

Does the Exception Prove
  the Rule?

Vagueness and Ambiguity

So far in argument evaluation we have focused on the validity of arguments. To be sound, however, an argument, besides being valid, must have true premises. Premise evaluation means determining whether the premises of an argument are true or false. Thus premise evaluation is a key step in argument evaluation.

Clearly, however, premises can be about anything. Anyone who was able to determine the truth or falsity of every possible premise would know everything there is to know. This goes way beyond logic and reasoning and indeed is the point of all the sources of knowledge: science, philosophy, mathematics, religion, and so on. The truth-values of many claims that could be used as premises are unknown and perhaps will never be known. Many are highly controversial. The most that can be said here and in the next chapter are very general things about the steps that we as individual reasoners can take when confronted with the question of the truth or falsity of a premise.

Most of our knowledge other than of our immediate surroundings is gained communally or socially. This means that we rely on others for determining truth and falsity—in other words, if we have a question, we look up the answer or ask someone who knows. This does not mean, however, that we have to be passive. We can question, criticize, and doubt; but we question, criticize, and doubt as individual participants in the social enterprise of getting knowledge. Further we are all fallible and thus our judgments of truth or falsity are mostly provisional and subject to revision on the basis of new evidence.

GENERALIZATIONS

Most arguments contain at least one general premise, either explicitly or suppressed, and often these generalizations are the most controversial premises. Generalizations can be expressed in an almost limitless number of ways, but they all come down to claiming that every member of some class has some property.[1] With the generalization "Any society has a right to preserve whatever is essential to its existence," the class is societies and the property is having a right to preserve whatever is essential to its existence. The generalization states that every member of the class—societies—has the property—a right to preserve whatever is essential to its existence.

Sometimes statements that do not look like generalizations are in fact generalizations. For example, we saw that "The fetus is a person" was a key suppressed premise in the abortion argument. Even though the statement starts with "the" it is a general statement that claims that every member of some class—human fetuses—has some property—being a person. The following are some different ways that generalizations can be expressed. In this list C stands for the class and P for the property.

All C are P

Each item in the following list is equivalent to "All C are P."

Every C is a P.
Any C is a P.
If it is a C, then it is a P.
C are P.
C are all P.
No C are non-P.
Only P are C.

Furthermore the following types of statements can be used to make generalizations.

A C is a P.
The C is a P.

[1] Even negative generalizations of the form "No C are P" can be treated as saying that all the members of C have some property—namely the property of *not* having P. Note that statements such as "Most C are P" or "Many C are P" are not generalizations in the sense being used here.

We rely on the context to determine how they are being used. For example, the statement "A lion is a mammal" can be used to state that all lions are mammals. But the statement "A lion is in my living room" would not normally be taken to be a statement about all lions.

The process of premise evaluation begins by determining whether the premise is a generalization. If it is a generalization, then we should determine what the class is and what the property is.

COUNTEREXAMPLES

A generalization says that *all* the members of some class have some property. If an argument contains a general premise, then the argument cannot be sound unless the generalization is true—that is, unless every member of the class does have the property. To refute a generalization (and thus show that any argument using it as a premise is unsound) all that we need to do is find one member of the class that lacks the property. The member of the class (if there is such a one) that lacks the property being attributed to all the members of the class is called a **counterexample.** If the generalization is "All *C* are *P*," then a counterexample to this claim is a *C* that is *not* a *P*. Looking for counterexamples is an important method in evaluating generalizations (the next chapter contains a discussion of other methods).

Counterexamples serve as dramatic and powerful refutations, because only one is needed to refute the most sweeping generalization. A generalization that admits of even a single counterexample is false. On the other hand, a generalization that has no counterexamples is true. If the claim is that all *C* are *P* and there are no *C* that are not *P*, then it is true that all *C* are *P*. A key part of the process of determining the truth or falsity of a generalization is the search for counterexamples. If we find a counterexample, then the generalization is false. If we search for a counterexample and fail to find one, our confidence in the truth of the generalization grows.

CONCEPTUAL VERSUS EMPIRICAL GENERALIZATIONS

Some generalizations are *conceptual* and others are *empirical,* and these require different treatment. For example, the claim that all uncles are male is true because of the definition of "uncle." It is part of the concept of uncle that uncles are male. A generalization that is supposed to be true because *P* is part of the definition or concept of *C* is a conceptual generalization. On the other hand, the claim that all turtles are voiceless is empirical. It is based on research and observation. It is not part of the concept or definition of "turtle" that turtles are voiceless.

In practice determining whether a generalization is conceptual or empirical is not always easy, since the line between the two kinds of generalizations is not clear. There are lots of borderline and indeterminate cases.

The safest thing that can be said is that the kind of counterexample that is going to be relevant to a generalization will depend on the kind of generalization that it is. The more a generalization tends toward the conceptual the more relevant purely imaginary or conceptual counterexamples are going to be. For example, if someone claimed that all lies involve the telling of a falsehood, we might be able to imagine a story in which someone lies but states the truth (it is a lie perhaps because the person telling it thought it was false and meant to mislead the hearer).[2] That this story is purely fabricated is irrelevant. The claim that all lies involve falsehood is meant as a conceptual claim about lying. The claim is that being a falsehood is a necessary condition for being a lie because it is part of the concept of a lie. So if we can show that there could be a lie that is not a falsehood, then we have shown that being a falsehood is not a necessary condition for being a lie. The counterexample only needs to be possible in order to refute the claim. On the other hand, the fact that we can imagine a turtle that barks does not show that the claim that all turtles are voiceless is false. The claim that all turtles are voiceless is an empirical claim and would only be refuted by an actual turtle that barks (or makes some other kind of vocal sound).

COUNTERCLAIMS

The process of giving a counterexample is not the same as negating a generalization. And the negation of a generalization is *not* a counterexample, although it follows from a counterexample. The negation of "All *C* are *P*" is "Some *C* are not *P*" or "Not all *C* are *P*." These are other statements. A counterexample is *not* a statement. A counterexample is a member of the class *C* (one that lacks *P*).

If someone offers the generalization "All *C* are *P*," one does not give a counterexample to this by simply stating "Some *C* are not *P*" or "There is a *C* that is not *P*." If there is a counterexample to the claim that all *C* are *P*, then it is the case that some *C* are not *P*. But a counterexample is a *C* that is not *P*. So do not confuse counterexamples with **counterclaims.** To give a counterexample to a generalization is to prove that it is false. To give a counterclaim is just to deny it. Denying a claim and proving that it is false are two very different things.

For example, consider the false generalization that all U.S. presidents were born east of the Mississippi. We can simply deny this by making the counterclaim "Some U.S. presidents were born west of the Mississippi," but this denial does not show that the generalization "All U.S. presidents were born east of the Mississippi" is false. We show that it is false by giving a counterexample. This is an empirical

---

[2] Imagine the following case: A father hoping his kids will forget about a promised outing tells them "No picnic tomorrow. I've listened to the forecast. It's going to rain." Let us suppose that the forecast actually is for clear skies and he knows that but in fact unknown to him the forecast is wrong and it is going to rain. The father's idea is that the kids will forget the picnic, plan on something else to do—go to the movies, for example—and he will be off the hook and can play golf. I think that we would say that the father has lied; he has said something he believes to be false (but is actually true) with the intent to mislead.

generalization, so the counterexample must be real. And indeed there is such a counterexample—Richard Nixon (born in California). The counterexample to the claim that all U.S. presidents were born east of the Mississippi is Richard Nixon—that man himself. The claim that some U.S. presidents were born west of the Mississippi is *not* a counterexample.

REVISING GENERALIZATIONS

In actual dialogues, giving counterexamples often leads to revision rather than silence. When we are confronted with a counterexample to a premise we are using, we need not always throw up our hands and give up; we do have the option of revising the premise. If the generalization is "All *C* are *P*" and there is a *C* that is not a *P*, then of course it is not true that all *C* are *P* and we cannot continue to assert the generalization. There may, however, be ways to weaken or qualify the generalization so that it avoids the counterexample but still does the work we want it to do.

One option is simply to retreat from "All *C* are *P*" to "Most *C* are *P*." "Most *C* are *P*" is a weaker claim than "All *C* are *P*" in the sense that it does not claim as much and is thus harder to refute. "Most *C* are *P*" cannot be refuted by a counterexample. (This kind of claim is discussed in more detail in the next two chapters.) We must realize, however, that the claim "Most *C* are *P*" will not support the same conclusions that "All *C* are *P*" will. So in revising generalizations we should not weaken them to the point where they no longer do the work we want them to do.

For example, consider the argument

> Ralph is a lawyer.
>
> All lawyers are rich.
> _____
>
> Thus Ralph is rich.

This argument is valid but the claim that all lawyers are rich is false. My friend Dan is a lawyer and he is not rich. If we revise the claim that all lawyers are rich and make it "Most lawyers are rich," then the revision avoids the counterexample, but

> Ralph is a lawyer.
>
> Most lawyers are rich.
> _____
>
> Thus Ralph is rich.

is not a valid argument.

Another usually more promising possibility, when faced with a counterexample, is to qualify the generalization. Sometimes we can limit the class *C* in such a way that the counterexample can be avoided. For example, we saw that the generalization "All U.S. presidents were born east of the Mississippi" is false because Richard Nixon is a counterexample. We can, when faced with this counterexample, revise the generalization in many different ways. The revised generalization "All U.S.

presidents who served before 1920 were born east of the Mississippi" avoids the counterexample (and in fact is true). We have avoided the counterexample by qualifying the generalization. The class *C* was originally U.S. presidents. In the qualified generalization it is U.S. presidents who served before 1920. We can usually qualify a generalization in such a way as to avoid the offered counterexample. But again, when qualifying a generalization, we must make sure that the revised generalization will still do the work we want it to do.

DOES THE EXCEPTION PROVE THE RULE?

Most readers will be familiar with the old saying: "The exception proves the rule." This saying, which has the authority that comes from being often repeated, seems to conflict directly with what has been stated in this chapter. The "rule" in the saying is a generalization, the "exception" would seem to be a counterexample, and "proves" would seem to mean "shows to be true." Translated, the old saying seems to be asserting that "The counterexample shows the generalization to be true." This is directly contrary to the assertion of this chapter that the counterexample *disproves* the generalization.

Clearly, interpreted as asserting that a counterexample shows a generalization to be true, the old saying is just plain wrong. It is obvious that a counterexample disproves a generalization. To repeat: If the generalization is "All *A* are *B*," then an *A* that is not a *B* is a counterexample and the existence of such a counterexample disproves the generalization. It cannot be the case that all *A* are *B* if even one *A* is not a *B*. There can be no mistake about that. So if the old saying is asserting that the existence of a counterexample shows the generalization to be true, then it is a false saying and must be rejected.

On the other hand, there is a more charitable interpretation of the saying "The exception proves the rule" according to which it says something correct and useful. According to the dictionary, one of the meanings of "prove" is "put to the test" or just plain "test." If we replace "proves" with "tests," we get "The exception tests the rule." The saying is still not quite right, because a counterexample does not just test the generalization, it disproves it, in the sense of showing it to be false. But now we can interpret "exception" as "apparent counterexample" or "proposed counterexample." The old saying interpreted in this light becomes "A proposed or apparent counterexample tests a generalization." And, indeed, this is correct. One way we test a generalization is by considering proposed counterexamples. If apparent counterexamples can be shown not to be genuine counterexamples, if they can be explained away, then that tends to support the generalization. If they turn out to be genuine counterexamples, then they not only test but disprove the generalization. So the old saying according to this interpretation is asserting that we test generalizations by considering proposed or apparent counterexamples to them. This is useful to know and keep in mind. Naturally, I think that the more charitable interpretation is the correct one and that that is in fact what the old saying means. So, yes, "The exception does prove the rule" as long as this is properly understood as meaning that we test generalizations by considering proposed or apparent counterexamples to them.

VAGUENESS AND AMBIGUITY

Many expressions are either *vague* or *ambiguous* or both. Statements containing vague or ambiguous terms can be difficult to evaluate. A term is vague when it does not have sharp boundaries. For example, "tall person" is vague because there is no precise boundary for tallness. Certainly someone who is 6'5" is a tall person, but there are many people who are borderline. It just is not clear whether they are tall or not. (For example, someone who is 5'9".)

Ambiguity is to be distinguished from vagueness. A word or expression is ambiguous when it has more than one meaning. For example, the word "rose" is ambiguous. "Rose" can mean a kind of flower or it can mean the past tense of rise. The word "rose" has two distinct meanings. We have also just seen that the word "prove" is ambiguous. It can mean "show to be true with absolute certainty" or "put to the test," and "prove" has other related meanings as well.

Usually ambiguity can be resolved by attention to context. In the sentence "The sun rose at 6:14 A.M today," it is obvious that "rose" is being used as the past tense of "rise." In the sentence "There was a red rose in the vase on the table," it is obvious that "rose" is being used to refer to a flower.

Often vagueness can simply be noted and then ignored. The statement "Every great European painter was French" contains the vague and somewhat ambiguous term "great European painter." Clearly "great" is vague; there are no sharp dividing lines between great and nongreat, and different people will have different ideas about what is great and what is not great. Nevertheless without knowing precisely how "great European painter" is being used or what is meant by it, we can give a counterexample to the claim that every great European painter was French. For example, Rembrandt was a great European painter and he was not French (in fact, he was Dutch). Under any reasonable meaning of "great European painter" Rembrandt would be considered a great European painter. So we can give a counterexample to the claim that every great European painter was French even though "great European painter" is vague and we do not know precisely what is meant by it. Vagueness and ambiguity need not be insurmountable obstacles to evaluation. It may be that a vague or ambiguous statement comes out false (or true) under every reasonable interpretation of it, in which case we need not worry about which interpretation is meant.

If the ambiguity or vagueness is severe and cannot be resolved, it may make it impossible to evaluate the truth or falsity of the statement. On the other hand, a statement that is so ambiguous or vague that it cannot be evaluated is worthless for communicating ideas (although it may have emotional content). A local company claims in its ads that it supports each individual's right to "contribute their skills to society and earn a meaningful wage." We know well enough what "contribute their skills to society" means, but we have no clear idea what a "meaningful wage" is. The term "meaningful wage" is so vague in this context as to be useless for communicating an idea.

STEPS TO TAKE WITH GENERALIZATIONS AND COUNTEREXAMPLES

1. Determine if the premise is a generalization.
2. If it is, determine which is the class C and what is the property P that is being attributed to all members of C.
3. Determine whether the generalization is conceptual or empirical. Imaginary or merely possible counterexamples are relevant to conceptual generalizations.
4. Search for a counterexample. (Do not simply make a counterclaim.)
5. If a counterexample is found, see if the generalization can be revised in such a way as to avoid the counterexample and yet still do the intended work.

ONE FINAL POINT

When you are justifying or explaining a point that you are trying to make, you often use either explicit or suppressed generalizations for support. Consider, yourself, whether the generalizations that you are appealing to as premises have counterexamples. A moment's reflection may enable you to produce counterexamples to your own claim. People often make sweeping generalizations in discussions and arguments or in papers they are writing—generalizations that they themselves could refute with a bit of thought. This need not mean that you must give up the point you are trying to make. Perhaps a generalization that is not so sweeping would avoid the counterexamples and still support the point. Before you commit yourself to a generalization, take a moment to subject it to scrutiny.

EXERCISE 9.1

Rewrite each of the following in the equivalent "All *A* are *B*" form.

★   1. Basketball players are all tall.

2. Every computer in the school went down at 2 P.M.

3. If you own a dog, then you own a mammal.

4. Capital punishment is murder.

★   5. Poetry is always boring.

6. Pictures of naked people are never art.

7. A happy worker is a good worker.

8. The college teacher is an underpaid professional.

9. No women are combatants.

10. Only tame animals are kept at the petting zoo.

EXERCISE 9.2

For each of the following: (1) state what the class *C* is, (2) state what the property *P* is, and (3) give a counterexample. The first batch of examples should be easy to refute and are offered for practice. The later ones are more difficult and controversial. (The ones in quotes are from previous examples in the text.)

★   1.   Every state in the United States is on the North American mainland.

   2.   In all team sports the participants use a ball.

   3.   All mammals have legs.

   4.   Any picture that shows naked people is pornography not art.

   5.   Every European monarch is a man.

6. Every great European monarch was a man.

★ 7. Every great scientist was a man.

8. All potentially dangerous activities ought to be forbidden by the government.

9. [After giving a counterexample, revise the statement with a qualification.] Sticking other people with sharp metal objects is always wrong.

10. "People who have no responsibilities have no rights."

11. Any time someone kills someone else it is murder.

12. [Take this one *very* literally. Try to revise (by qualifying) this statement to avoid the initial counterexamples and then try to find counterexamples to the revised version.]
     People have a right to do whatever they want with their own body.

13. "In all fraud and deception there is some kind of imperfection."

                                                                      Rene Descartes

★ 14. "The morally right thing to do, on any occasion, is whatever would bring about the greatest balance of happiness over unhappiness."

15. All persons are human beings.

CHAPTER 10

PREMISE EVALUATION

Plausibility

In Chapter 9 the process of testing generalizations by counterexamples was discussed. In this chapter other methods of approaching the evaluation of claims are introduced.

KEY TERMS AND HEADINGS

Specific Claims	Explanations
Limited Claims	Revising Initial Plausibility
Initial Plausibility Rating	Ratings
Testimony	Disagreements

Although the search for counterexamples is an important part of the evaluation of general premises, there are other sorts of claims that cannot be dealt with by counterexamples. **Specific claims,** claims about an individual person, place, or thing (e.g., "Missouri is a state"), and **limited claims,** claims about some, a few, many, or most, of a class of things (e.g., "Most birds can fly"), cannot be refuted by counterexamples.

Once we have determined whether a premise is specific, limited, or general, then we must begin evaluation—the attempt to determine truth or falsity. If the premise is a general claim, then the search for a counterexample is appropriate.[1] If the premise is a specific or limited claim that we cannot verify or falsify by direct observation, we must begin our evaluation by making a determination of its initial plausibility.

---

[1] Actually this generalization requires minor revision. For example, the claim that all uncles are male, which was offered as an example of a conceptual generalization, is true by definition. This is an obviously true conceptual claim. There is no point in searching for a counterexample to the claim that all uncles are male, because we know in advance that we will not find one. Similarly, the claim that some uncles are female is false by definition. Anyone who knows the simple dictionary definition of "uncle" knows that it is not the case that some uncles are female. It would be more correct to say: "If the premise is a *nontrivial* generalization, then the search for a counterexample is appropriate."

PLAUSIBILITY

Each of us has background beliefs and a fair amount of common sense. We bring these to bear in evaluating claims. Many of our background beliefs are widely shared with others and can even be called background knowledge. Such claims as that Missouri is a state, knife blades are usually made of metal, the earth is not flat, most birds can fly, and so on, are not normally the subject of discussion and debate. Virtually everyone agrees. Other beliefs that form part of our background beliefs might be unique to ourselves or our families or to people of similar background and experience as ourselves. Each of us has a basic notion of how the world is, how it works, and what is going on. This notion forms the central core of our background beliefs.

The key step in evaluating a new claim is to judge it against our background beliefs. In this way we give the claim an **initial plausibility rating.** The better a new claim fits with our background beliefs and common sense, the more initially plausible it is. The more a claim conflicts with our background beliefs and common sense, the less initially plausible it is. It is not that each of our background beliefs is guaranteed to be true. On the contrary, it is one of our background beliefs that each of us is fallible in our beliefs. Although there is no guarantee that each of our background beliefs is true, we *begin* our evaluation by judging a claim against our background beliefs. The more a claim conflicts with our background beliefs, the more and firmer the evidence in favor of it needs to be in order for us to accept it. Furthermore, initial plausibility ratings can and often are revised in the light of new evidence and findings. This is why they are called "initial"!

Consider, for example, the claim that Hitler is still alive and living in South America.[2] This claim gets a very low initial plausibility rating for various reasons. For one thing, Hitler would be over one hundred years old now. This conflicts with our background belief that very few people live to be over one hundred. For another, there is a great deal of evidence that he in fact died in Berlin in 1945. There are eyewitness accounts, careful investigations by the allies, statements and expressions of intent to commit suicide to evade capture, and so on. Furthermore, Hitler would have had to escape from Berlin, which was surrounded by allied troops on the lookout for him, and evade detection in South America for over forty years. All this is extremely implausible.

However, it is not *impossible* that Hitler is alive and living in South America. Such an extraordinary man might live to be over one hundred; there might have been some error about his birth date and he is actually much younger; or perhaps the suicide was a cleverly planned hoax that fooled all of the allied investigators, and so on. But the fact that it is *possible* that Hitler is living in South America is no reason at all to think that he is. Possibility is not plausibility. Since the claim that he is alive conflicts with so many of our background beliefs, just on the face of it, there is no reason to believe that Hitler is still alive and a number of strong reasons to believe that he is not still alive and that he died in Berlin in 1945.

---

[2] A lead article in *Weekly World News* (May 12, 1992), a supermarket tabloid, claims that Hitler died in Argentina of a heart attack on April 14, 1992. The article has photos and also claims that President Bush has sent CIA experts to Buenos Aires to confirm the death. Unfortunately, this article came to my attention after having written the chapter.

To think that Hitler is still alive might be exciting, and we may even want it to be true—because then we could find him and punish him. Perhaps it gives us a thrill to think that he has been hiding in South America all these years. None of these are reasons for believing that he is still alive. When judging the plausibility of a claim, our wanting it to be true, for whatever reason no matter how noble or base, does not make it more plausible. When making judgments of plausibility, we must be on our guard against wishful thinking.

Plausibility ratings are relative not absolute, inexact not exact, revisable not fixed. For example, the claim that Elvis Presley is still alive has recently been made by many people. They claim to have seen him and some even claim to have talked with him. Certainly the claim that Elvis is still alive is implausible. But how implausible? It is not possible to give an exact determination here. The claim that Elvis is still alive is more plausible than the claim that Hitler is still alive, but we cannot say exactly how much more. Elvis would not be nearly as old as Hitler would be, and it might have been easier for Elvis to rig a hoax (he did not have the allied army after him). Still when judged against our background beliefs, it is implausible that Elvis is still alive.

Although a new claim is given a plausibility rating by comparing it to our background beliefs in a way that calls into play our conception of the way the world is and how it works, we should be able to defend our initial plausibility ratings by citing particular points. We should be able to say more than just "That is not how the world works" in defense of a low rating (or "That is how the world works" in defense of a high rating). For example, we are able to cite particular points in defense of our low rating of the claim that Hitler is still alive.

Two important ways in which our background beliefs come into play in evaluating claims is in making judgments about the testimony of others and the cogency of explanations.

TESTIMONY

Our judgment of a claim is going to depend partly on who is making it and why. We may be swayed to accept a claim that is initially implausible because we trust the person who is making it. On the other hand, we judge the reliability of others, especially those we do not know personally, by using our background beliefs and common sense. If the claim that Hitler is living in South America is made by a large group of reputable historians and researchers and is published in a reputable newspaper, then we would take it quite seriously (although we should still require extensive evidence to be convinced). It is part of our background beliefs that such groups of people are cautious in their claims and generally reliable. On the other hand, we know that people like to attract attention and raise a stir by making startling claims and that publishers want to sell newspapers. We rely on our background beliefs and common sense in judging the reliability of others who are making claims. In general, we trust experts making judgments in their field of expertise and eyewitnesses who have nothing to gain by lying. We should be leery of people who have a reason to be biased or are claiming to know something that they are in no position to know.

The mere fact that someone makes a claim or even claims to have witnessed something is some evidence in its favor but need not be conclusive. We must consider the qualifications of the person making the claim, the possibility of bias, and the possibilities of such things as simple error. The mere fact that someone claims to have personally seen and met Hitler recently in South America and even publishes this claim in a newspaper is not much evidence that Hitler is still alive. We want to know who the person making this claim is, how he or she is qualified to determine that the individual really is Hitler, and what motives that person might have for deceiving us. The fact that someone claims to have met Hitler recently in South America is far from "proving" that Hitler is still alive. (For more on the use of testimony, see the section on arguments from authority in Chapter 14.)

EXPLANATIONS

Many claims are offered not just as descriptions but as explanations. They attempt not just to tell us how things are but how they came to be the way they are. When a claim is offered as an explanation, it should be judged by how well it explains what it is intended to explain, how simple or complex it is, how well it fits with our background beliefs about how the world works, and how well competing explanations work.

There are always many different possible explanations for what is being explained. Some of these explanations will be initially more plausible than others. For example, suppose I am hiking and notice to my dismay that my compass needle is pointing in the direction of the setting sun. There are many possible alternative explanations for this happening. Here are four: (1) The earth and sun have shifted position so that the sun is now directly over the magnetic north pole. (2) The magnetic field of the earth has shifted so that the magnetic north pole is near the equator. (3) There is something in the area that is interfering with the operation of the compass. (4) The compass is broken. Each of these claims would explain the occurrence; however, explanation 1 is extremely unlikely. The earth has maintained its position relative to the sun for billions of years. Surely a shift of this magnitude would immediately create immense and noticeable havoc. No one would seriously entertain this as an explanation. Likewise for explanation 2. But note that a large part of the reason we would not seriously consider explanations 1 and 2 is that we have such simple alternatives, namely, explanations 3 and 4. In the absence of simple alternative explanations, a complex and difficult explanation would get a much higher plausibility rating. The plausibility of an explanation can only be judged in comparison with other competing explanations.

Explanation (more exactly, explanatory power) is another important factor in our judgment of the plausibility of a claim. The more a claim explains things in a way that makes sense to us given our notion of the way the world works, the more plausible it is. The more a claim leaves things unexplained or unexplainable, the less plausible it is. The claim that Hitler is alive in South America may explain certain things, but it leaves many more things unexplained, such as how such an apparent suicide and escape could have been perpetrated and how he could have evaded detection for so long. A claim that requires a long train of implausible explanations is going to be less initially plausible than one that explains things simply and easily.

REVISING INITIAL PLAUSIBILITY RATINGS

Plausibility ratings can always be revised upward or downward. After making an initial plausibility rating, if we are concerned to pursue the matter further, we should consider what would make us alter our rating. Once we have given a new claim an initial plausibility rating, we determine what are the tests or observations that we could make that would confirm or disconfirm it. Once we have made these tests or observations, our initial plausibility rating may change, and we can arrive at a revised plausibility rating that is higher or lower than the initial rating. In many cases the tests or observations will be simply looking something up or asking someone a relevant question. In other cases the tests would be complicated and difficult to perform.

For example, consider again the claim that someone has recently seen and talked to Hitler in South America. Initially this claim is extremely implausible, as we have seen. Nevertheless, there are various tests and observations that might cause us to revise our initial plausibility rating. We could travel to South America ourselves or hire experts to go there, take fingerprints, and so on. We could investigate the reliability and motives of the person making the claim. We could review even more carefully the evidence that Hitler died in Berlin in 1945. Most of these things would be difficult, expensive, or time consuming to do. In this case the claim is so initially implausible that we would not be motivated to conduct the further tests unless new evidence was produced in its favor. The point is that, besides making an initial plausibility judgment, we should at least be able to state what further tests or observations would be relevant to revising our initial plausibility judgment. Whether we are then interested in conducting those tests or making the observations is another matter. We should at least know what they are.

Another important method for revising our plausibility rating of a claim is to consider alternative claims. As we saw with explanations, a claim that is initially implausible may get a much higher rating if we come to realize that each of the competing claims is even less plausible. On the other hand, we should doubt a claim that has more plausible alternatives. For example, consider again the compass example. Explanations 1 and 2 were so unlikely as to be rejected out of hand, but explanations 3 and 4 are about equally plausible, at least initially. How can we test these claims? We might cast about for an even more plausible explanation, but we are unlikely to find one in this case. The claim that the compass is broken is difficult to test directly (I suppose) without special tools. We can, however, test the claim that something is interfering with the compass. We can move the compass to a different spot and see what happens, or we can put the compass on the ground away from pieces of metal. If we do this and the compass needle reorients itself properly, then the claim that something was interfering with the compass goes way up in plausibility and the claim that it is broken way down. On the other hand, if the needle continues to point away from the north even after moving the compass a distance, removing metal objects, and so on, then the likelihood that the compass is broken increases. The claim that the compass is broken becomes more plausible because the most plausible alternative—namely, that something is interfering with it—has become less plausible.

This procedure is very much like the way a doctor diagnoses a problem. Something is wrong. What is the explanation? Various claims are considered as explanations for what is wrong. These are rated by initial plausibility and then tested to arrive at revised ratings. The most plausible alternatives are tested first. As some explanations go down (or up) in plausibility their competitors go up (or down).[3]

DISAGREEMENTS

One fact of life is that people disagree with each other in some of their beliefs. Most disagreements in belief should be resolvable by the methods suggested here. Unfortunately some disagreements are very difficult to resolve rationally and may not even be resolvable at all. Different people operate with different background versions of how the world is and how it works. This makes some disagreements intractable. For example, consider the deep disagreements over the assassination of President Kennedy. Many people find it simply implausible that Oswald acted alone. These people are driven to seek other explanations of what happened than the official one. Many other people find it plausible that Oswald acted alone. They are content to accept the official version. This disagreement in rating the plausibility of the claim that Oswald acted alone is probably based on deep differences in background understandings of how people behave. Some view people as basically cunning and prone to engage in conspiracies. Others see people as capable of acting in bizarre and unpredictable ways for no good reason. Such differences in background beliefs will lead to differences in assessment of plausibility. Such disagreements are resolvable, if at all, only by digging deeper into our background beliefs until we find common ground, then proceeding from that common ground by careful reasoning and difficult and extensive research. Unfortunately, people do not always have the patience and will to engage in such a difficult process.

SUMMARY

We give a new claim an initial plausibility rating. We arrive at an initial plausibility rating by comparing the claim with our background beliefs and common sense. We compare the claim with our background beliefs and common sense by considering how well it fits with or conflicts with our notion of how the world is and how things work. We must consider the reliability of the person making the claim, and in the case of explanations, we must consider the plausibility of competing claims. That a claim is possible does not make it plausible. That we would like something to be true does not make it plausible.

Once we arrive at an initial plausibility rating, we consider what direct tests or observations would lead us to revise our rating. We also consider, especially in the case of explanations, what tests or observations would lead us to revise our ratings of competing explanations, testing the simplest and most plausible first.

---

[3] See also in this connection the note on logic puzzles and validity, Chapter 4, p. 73.

EXERCISE 10.1

For each of the following claims state whether it is specific, limited, or general. Many are from arguments previously quoted in the text. (If you are having difficulty deciding if a claim is general, consider whether it would be appropriate to search for a counterexample. If so, it is general.)

★   1.   Every person has a right to life.

   2.   Trials are often characterized by extensive court delays.

   3.   Everybody has needs.

   4.   Logic is the study of the structure and principles of reasoning.

   5.   Ninety percent of us are nonhunters.

★   6.   When skipping, you often have both feet on the ground at the same time.

   7.   Pain and suffering are undesirable.

   8.   Many women who do paid work also work in the house.

9. The United Nations faces financial problems.

10. In the last several decades the number of beer firms has dropped from nine hundred to fifty.

★ 11. It takes a large amount of money and a long time to get a case to the Supreme Court.

12. Ninjas are the only ones with the highly special fighting skills needed to defeat the samurai.

13. The United States is the world's biggest debtor.

14. Many Americans are sedentary.

EXERCISE 10.2

Give each of the following an initial plausibility rating. Cite specific items to defend your rating. You may also consider the reliability of testimony on those items where the source is given. Describe some reasonable tests or observations that would lead you to revise the initial plausibility rating.

★   1.   A local man suddenly died of heart failure after learning that he had won the lottery. (From a city newspaper.)

2.   A primitive tribe in Borneo worships airplanes and has built a crude airfield in the attempt to lure one to land. (From a chapter entitled "Cargo Cults" in a college anthropology text.)

3.   Some trees are capable of experiencing and feeling pain. (From someone who claims to be a scientist on a radio talk show.)

4.   Trials are often characterized by extensive court delays. (From a business law text.)

5.   Many Americans are sedentary. (From a health newsletter published by a university.)

6.   Use of tobacco is bad for your health. (From the Surgeon General.)

★   7.   Use of tobacco is not bad for your health. (From the cigarette companies.)

8.   We do not often find ourselves wondering about the lives of uncommon and rare individuals.

9.   These knives never need sharpening. (From a late-night television commercial for kitchen knives.)

10. Two out of three doctors surveyed recommended Blitz aspirin. (From an advertisement.)

11. There is a medical-government conspiracy to prevent the cure of AIDS. Actually it can be cured very easily but the establishment doesn't want it to be. (A claim by a caller to a radio talk show.)

12. This stain remover will remove virtually all stains—grass, oil, chemical, paint, even hard-to-remove blood stains—without damaging fabric or leaving a trace. (From a late-night television ad.)

★ 13. No other 100-watt light bulbs are brighter or last longer than GZ 100-watt bulbs. (From an advertisement.)

14. Anyone can lose ten, twenty, even fifty pounds painlessly by following the simple and easy FAST DIET. (From an ad in the back of a supermarket magazine.)

15. There are psychics who can exactly predict winning lottery numbers and the winners of horse races days before the event. (From an article in a supermarket tabloid.)

16. There is a tenth planet beyond the orbit of Pluto. (Claim made by an astronomer in a public lecture.)

EXERCISE 10.3

For each of the following consider the reliability of the testimony taking into account the nature of the source and the possibility of bias.

1. You take your car into a new garage in town for an oil change. The mechanic tells you that just by looking at your oil she knows your car needs a valve job even though it's been running fine.

2. Your roommate tells you that on the basis of his observations of his biology teacher's behavior in class that the teacher is a paranoid schizophrenic.

3. A member of the Abortion is Murder Coalition tells you that she has irrefutable proof that the fetus is capable of feeling pain right from the moment of conception.

★ 4. Your friend tells you that he saw the cute senior you've been dating walking downtown with someone else.

5.   On the television, the person giving the weather report says that this year so far has been just about average in temperature.

6.   You read an article in the paper in which an executive of GM claims that a recent series of reports about how much better Japanese cars are than American cars was backed by anti-American interests and is full of exaggerations and outright lies.

EXERCISE 10.4

For each of the following events give three or four possible explanations—some of the three or four should be plausible but they need not all be. Rank the explanations from 1 to 4 in order of plausibility (most plausible first). State some tests that would help you decide among the two most plausible explanations.

★ 1.   You are in an office downtown. You hear a low rumbling and the office begins to shake a little. A coffee cup on the desk rattles.

2.   Whenever you walk into the computer room at school, you begin to sneeze and your eyes water. As soon as you leave it stops. This happens over and over again.

3.   Your friend finds a wallet with quite a bit of money in it. You can tell by the identification that the owner is of the opposite sex and quite attractive. Your friend personally returns the wallet including all the money.

4.   You get a phone call one night. The caller says he is God (it is a long-distance call) and commands you to burn all your possessions and hitchhike around the country telling people about this miraculous event.

5.   You see a demonstration in which a scientist hooks some electrodes up to a tomato plant. Every time she brings a lighted match near the plant the dial goes crazy.

CHAPTER 11

NONDEDUCTIVE SUPPORT

Plausibility Arguments, Statistical Inferences, and Inductive Generalizations

In this chapter the distinction between deductive and nondeductive reasoning is introduced. Three kinds of nondeductive arguments are described.

KEY TERMS AND HEADINGS

Deductive Arguments

Nondeductive Arguments

Plausibility Arguments

Belief, Rationality, and
  Evidence

Statistical Arguments

Inductive Generalizations

Margins of Error

A Caution About Statistics

Deductive vs. Nondeductive
  Arguments

PLAUSIBILITY ARGUMENTS

Unlike **deductive arguments** that must be valid to be successful, **nondeductive arguments** need not be valid to be successful. For example, the considerations about the way the world is and the way it works that we use in arriving at an initial plausibility rating of a claim rarely guarantee the truth (or falsity) of the claim. Rather they give the claim a certain degree of plausibility (or implausibility). When setting out these considerations as **plausibility arguments,** we judge the arguments by a different standard than we judge arguments that are intended to be valid. The point is that the considerations are supposed to give the claim nondeductive support. The most fruitful question to ask about such an argument is not whether it is valid, because it usually will not be, but *how much* support do the premises give the claim.

Recall that we assessed the claim that Hitler is alive and living in South America. We saw that for various reasons this is an extremely implausible claim. These reasons could be set out in the form of a plausibility argument for the claim that Hitler is not alive.

Hitler would be over one hundred years old.

Hitler would have had to evade allied troops that had surrounded Berlin and were on the lookout for him.

Hitler would have had to perpetrate a hoax concerning his death and everyone party to it would have had to keep the secret all these years.

Hitler would have had to evade detection for over fifty years.

Therefore Hitler is not alive in South America.

This argument for the claim that Hitler is not alive is extremely strong. However, it is not valid. Given the truth of all the premises in the argument for the claim that Hitler is not alive, it is still possible that Hitler is alive. Even if we add suppressed premises such as that few people live to be over one hundred and that such hoaxes and evasions are very rarely successful, the argument would still not be valid.

The argument for the conclusion that Hitler is not alive could be made valid, just as any argument can be made valid, but to make it valid we would have to add suppressed premises that are false (such as "No one lives to be over one hundred"). Rather than attempting to make such an argument valid, we would be better off to think of it as a plausibility argument reflecting the considerations that we actually use in determining plausibility. These considerations amount to nondeductive support.

With a valid argument, if we accept the premises, then we must accept the conclusion. It would be self-contradictory to accept the premises of an argument and agree that it is valid and yet reject the conclusion. The Hitler argument is not valid, so it would not be *self-contradictory* to accept the premises and reject the conclusion. Yet the support for the claim that Hitler is not alive is extremely strong. What is the force of this support? The force, given that we accept all the premises of the argument and that it pretty well sets out the relevant considerations, is that it is *more rational* to believe that Hitler is not alive than that he is alive. Although the claim that Hitler is not alive has not been *deductively proven,* it is more rational to believe that Hitler is not alive because it has more support than the competing claim that he is alive. Indeed, given the evidence, I think it would be fair to say that it is *irrational* to believe that Hitler is alive in South America.

BELIEF, RATIONALITY, AND EVIDENCE

Of necessity, the discussion here of belief, rationality, and evidence is abstract and incomplete. In fact, the relationships among belief, rationality, and evidence are complex and not fully understood. The issues become even more complex when we must make decisions on the basis of nondeductive support. We may be in a situation where we must decide what to do. There are many competing possibilities. We have little or no evidence in support of a crucial claim or any of its alternatives. There may be little or no reason to decide between competitors. Nevertheless we may have to act before we can conduct further research or tests. Something of great value may depend on our making the right decision. If one of the alternatives has much more support than any of the others, then we choose that one to guide our behavior. If the two best alternatives have about equal support, then we are at an impasse. Reasoning cannot help us unless we have time for further tests and considerations.

Furthermore, the kind and amount of support we will be satisfied with depends on what is at stake. I may believe, indeed rationally believe, that I can get across the chasm on that rather old and worn-looking rope bridge. But I will not try it lightly because if I am wrong, the loss would be so great. That it was rational to believe that I could get across the bridge would be small solace if I am lying at the bottom of the chasm. Likewise if the question is whether to disgrace someone and deprive them of their freedom—in other words, convict them of a crime and send them to jail—we demand a great deal of support for the claim that they are guilty. Since so much is at stake, it should not be enough that it is more rational, given the evidence, to believe that they are guilty than that they are innocent. We require that the evidence support the claim of guilt beyond a reasonable doubt. Without knowing precisely what "beyond a reasonable doubt" means, we can say that it at least means more evidence is necessary than would be required to make guilt more likely than not.

STATISTICAL ARGUMENTS

There are several different kinds of nondeductive support besides plausibility arguments. Two of these, statistical arguments and inductive generalizations, will be discussed in this chapter. Causal and analogical arguments will be discussed in the next two chapters.

With **statistical arguments** the claim that some individual or some group of individuals has some property is supported by claims about percentages of the population to which that individual or group belongs. For example, the claim to be supported might be that my dog has fleas. The support is the fact that 98% of the dogs in my county have fleas. This can be set out as a nondeductive argument.

Ninety-eight percent of the dogs in my county have fleas.

So my dog has fleas.

The premise does not prove the conclusion to be true, but all other things being equal the premise gives a great deal of support to the conclusion. We can introduce "all other things being equal" into the argument by adding a premise: "My dog is a typical member of the dog population of my county."

Ninety-eight percent of the dogs in my county have fleas.
My dog is typical of the dog population of my county.

So my dog has fleas.

Indeed we can say exactly how much support the premises give the conclusion—98%! Given the premise that 98% of the dogs in my county have fleas and that my dog is typical, we can say that my dog has a 98% chance of having fleas. In general, a premise to the effect that n% of population p has property q means that a typical member of p has an n% chance of having q.

In practice, however, rarely are all other things equal. If I observe my dog scratching and biting its fur, that fact could be added to the premises, and the support would then be almost conclusive (but still not 100% guaranteed). On the other hand, the fact that I recently had my dog treated for fleas would substantially lower the probability that my dog has fleas.

The point is that a premise which states that a certain percentage of the members of a certain population has a property can be used to support the claim that an individual member or group of members of the population has the property.

Arguments in which the percentage is replaced by a term such as "most" can be treated as statistical arguments. For example, if instead of "98% of the dogs have fleas" we used "Most dogs have fleas" as a premise, the argument would be vaguer but not substantially changed.

> Most dogs in my county have fleas.
>
> My dog is a typical member of the dog population of my county.
>
> ---
>
> So my dog has fleas.

can be treated as substantially the same as the percentage argument. We cannot now say that the premises give the conclusion a likelihood of 98%, but we can say that the truth of the premises makes the conclusion much more likely than not. There are many terms—such as "most," "almost all," "a majority of," "few," "a few," "hardly any"—that enter into statistical arguments in fairly obvious ways. Instead of a premise about a certain percentage of the population, we can use a premise about a certain proportion of the population in a statistical argument. In evaluating such arguments, we assess, in perhaps very vague ways, the amount of support that the premises give the conclusion.

INDUCTIVE GENERALIZATIONS

Statistical arguments are nondeductive arguments that use facts about entire populations to support claims about individuals or groups within a population. **Inductive generalizations** are nondeductive arguments that use facts about individuals or groups of individuals to support claims about entire populations. For example, when we considered general claims, we saw that they are refuted by counterexamples; but if we search for a counterexample to a claim and fail to find one, our confidence in the truth of the generalization increases. The failure to find a counterexample to a generalization is especially good support for it when the search for a counterexample has been conducted in an organized fashion that uses such techniques as random sampling or when a vast number of examples of all types have been studied. For example, the argument

All turtles so far examined have been found to be voiceless.

Therefore all turtles are voiceless.

is a very strong inductive generalization. Here the sample is *turtles so far examined* and the population is *turtles*. The premise gives the conclusion a great deal of support (although again the argument is not deductively valid, because it is possible that the next turtle examined will be found to have a voice). Part of the reason that the premise—"All turtles so far examined have been found to be voiceless"—gives the conclusion—"All turtles are voiceless"—so much support is that we know that the sample is very large. Vast numbers of turtles from all over the world have been examined. This fact could be added to the argument as a premise that would further explicitly spell out the support.

Inductive generalizations can also use percentages (and all of their vaguer expressions such as "most"). We can argue from the fact that a percentage of a sample of a population has a certain property to the claim that the same percentage of the entire population has the property. The following argument is an example of an inductive generalization.

Ninety-eight percent of the dogs captured by the county dog warden have fleas.

Hence 98% of the dogs in the county have fleas.

This argument points out one of the most serious and difficult questions we have to face in assessing inductive generalizations—namely, the nature of the sample. Even though "98%" appears in both the premise and the conclusion of this argument, the premise does not give the conclusion much support because of the nature of the sample. The sample is *dogs captured by the county dog warden* and the population is *dogs in the county*. In this case, the sample is likely to be biased because the dogs captured by the dog warden may not have had as good care as other dogs. It may turn out that the dogs captured by the dog warden are not a representative sample of the population of dogs in the county.

How to judge whether a sample is representative is often a difficult and subtle problem. There are notorious cases where erroneous generalizations were made on the basis of nonrepresentative samples. (The most famous examples are telephone surveys made in the late forties. Telephone customers were not representative of the whole population.) Again, for our purposes, we can often rely on our background knowledge and common sense, being aware at the same time that it is easy to be misled when judging inductive generalizations. Clearly, for example, if a survey is taken in a big city about attitudes toward air pollution, we should be reluctant to generalize the results to the entire population of the state. We know that air pollution is worse near big cities and that people tend to be more concerned about problems in their immediate environment.

MARGINS OF ERROR

Opinion polls are a form of inductive generalization. When results of opinion polls are given in the media, they are often given with a margin of error. The pollster will say: "In a survey of four hundred randomly selected adults in Tahoma County, 78% are in favor of a reduction in county sales taxes. This survey has a margin of error of plus or minus four percentage points." When pollsters say that the survey has a margin of error of plus or minus four percentage points, what they say is intended to enable us to assess an inductive generalization.

> Seventy-eight percent of four hundred randomly selected adults in Tahoma County are in favor of a reduction in county sales taxes.
>
> ───────────────────────────
>
> Therefore 78% of all adults in Tahoma County are in favor of a reduction in county sales taxes.

Let us assume that the survey really is random (although true randomness is almost impossible to achieve) and that the population of Tahoma County is fairly large—say, over one hundred thousand. Even given these assumptions, it is not likely that *exactly* 78% of all adults in Tahoma County are in favor of a reduction in county sales taxes, nor does such exactness matter much. The survey will give us valuable information as long as the actual percentage of adults that favor a reduction in county sales taxes is close to 78%. The margin of error is how close to 78% we can confidently expect the actual percentage to be.

The margin of error can be calculated with mathematical precision. A margin of error of plus or minus four percentage points means that there is a 95% chance that the actual percentage of all adults in Tahoma County who favor a reduction in county sales taxes is between 74% and 82% (78 - 4 = 74 and 78 + 4 = 82). The 95% chance is called the confidence level. Most margins of error are given at the 95% confidence level. A 95% confidence level means we can be very confident. We should not expect a confidence level of 100%. After all it might be that by some sheer coincidence every adult in Tahoma County who is not in favor of a reduction in county sales taxes was included in the survey. The actual percentage of adults in Tahoma County who favor a reduction in county sales taxes might be 99%.[1] Given the sample this is unlikely, however. Since the sample is random we should be very confident that the survey does represent the opinions of all the adults in Tahoma County. We should be very confident that the percentage of adults in Tahoma County who favor a reduction in county sales taxes is close to the percentage in the survey. How confident and how close? To repeat, there is a 95% chance that the actual percentage of all adults in Tahoma County who favor a reduction in county sales taxes is within four percentage points of 78%. There is only a 5% chance that the survey is off by more than four percentage points.

---

[1] At different confidence levels the margin of error changes. At the 90% confidence level a smaller sample will give the same margin of error as a larger sample at the 95% confidence level. No sample size short of the entire population would be adequate to achieve a confidence level of 100%.

The margin of error depends on the size of the sample. The larger the sample (always assuming randomness) the smaller the margin of error. The following is a table of margins of error at the 95% confidence level for a survey in which 78% are in favor of a reduction in county sales taxes.

Confidence Level = 95%
Percent of Those Surveyed in Favor = 78%

Sample Size	Margin of Error
1,000	Plus or minus 2.6 percentage points
400	Plus or minus 4.1 percentage points
200	Plus or minus 5.7 percentage points
100	Plus or minus 8.1 percentage points
20	Plus or minus 18.2 percentage points

Notice that as the size of the sample decreases the margin of error increases. If a small margin of error is desired, a large sample is required.

SUMMARY

Plausibility arguments are nondeductive arguments in which a claim is supported by background knowledge and other relevant information. The strength of the support depends on the plausibility that the premises give to the conclusion.

Statistical arguments are nondeductive arguments in which a claim about an individual or group of individuals is supported by a claim about a certain percentage or proportion of an entire population. The strength of the support depends on the individual or group being typical of the population.

Inductive generalizations are nondeductive arguments in which a conclusion about an entire population is based on claims about individuals or groups of individuals. The strength of the support depends on the individual or group being representative of the entire population. The margins of error of inductive generalizations based on random surveys can be calculated with mathematical precision.

A CAUTION ABOUT STATISTICS

A great many arguments and considerations involving statistics are presented these days in the media. Statistics—that is, percents, averages, probabilities, and so on—give an air of mathematical precision to an argument. They make it seem more technical and scientific. However, statistics can be misleading in ways that are not easy for people to detect without special training.[2] For example, the term "average" when used in the media, as in "The average hourly income of workers at Humbolt Steel and Die is $24.85," can mean several different things. And the number is going to be different if the average is computed in different ways.

Graphs and charts as representations of statistics are notoriously misleading. The two accompanying graphs present precisely the same information. The only difference is the scale—and the impression they give. Although our common sense

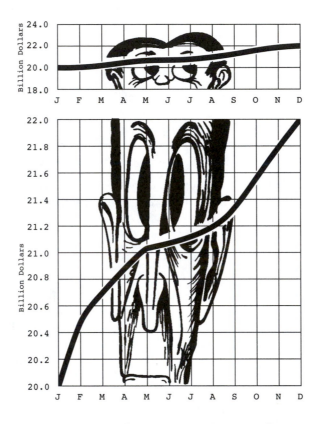

Source: Darrell Huff, *How to Lie with Statistics* (New York: W. W. Norton & Company, 1954), pp. 62-63.

and background knowledge will take us a long way, more is needed when dealing with statistical arguments. Our discussion in this text of statistical arguments and inductive generalizations barely scratches the surface. For anyone who needs to understand and evaluate arguments involving statistics, probabilities, and numerical inductions, as anyone who reads the newspapers these days must, there is no substitute for a course in statistics taught by a competent statistician.

[2] For an excellent discussion of this, see *How to Lie with Statistics* by Darrell Huff. This is a classic work on misleading uses and abuses of statistics.

DEDUCTIVE VS. NONDEDUCTIVE ARGUMENTS

When are arguments nondeductive as opposed to deductive? When do we use nondeductive as opposed to deductive reasoning? Logicians are not agreed on the answers to these questions. Clearly we have the option of treating the argument

> Ninety-eight percent of the dogs in my county have fleas.
>
> My dog is typical of the dog population of my county.
>
> ———————————————————
>
> So my dog has fleas.

as either an (invalid) deductive argument or as a (strong) nondeductive argument. Treating it as a nondeductive argument is more charitable and thus accords better with the principle of charity. On the other hand, if someone actually reasoned this way (i.e., argued that "98% of the dogs in my county have fleas and my dog is typical of the dog population of my county, therefore my dog has fleas") we would think that there is something wrong with that person's reasoning. The conclusion just is not warranted by the premises. They have inferred more from the premises than the premises imply.

In fact, if you started with the premises that 98% of the dogs have fleas and that your dog is typical, you would be reluctant to simply state that your dog has fleas. Your conclusion would be much more guarded. In fact, you would say something like "My dog probably has fleas" or "It is very likely that my dog has fleas." In other words, you would hedge the claim "My dog has fleas" by adding such hedging expressions as "probably" or "it is very likely that." Such hedging reflects the fact that you know that the premises do not validly imply the conclusion that your dog has fleas and yet at the same time you also know that they give strong support for the claim that your dog has fleas. It is best, then, to treat such expressions as "probably," "it is very likely that," "most likely," and so on as expressions of nondeductive reasoning. In setting out nondeductive reasoning we will include the hedging expressions when they seem required to avoid the misleading impression of poor deductive reasoning.

EXERCISE 11.1

For each of the following, determine whether it is a plausibility argument, a statistical argument, or an inductive generalization (for an inductive generalization state what the sample is and what the population is). Determine how much support the premises (assuming they are true) give to the conclusion. Your assessments of the support can be quite vague, such as "not very much" or "a lot."

★ 1. Eighty-nine percent of the residents of Davenport, Iowa, were born west of the Mississippi.
   Ralph is a resident of Davenport, Iowa.
   _____

   Therefore Ralph was probably born west of the Mississippi.

2. We conducted a poll of people entering the Paloma County Public Library for one month and found that they averaged reading one book a week.
   _____

   Thus the people in Paloma County are very well read—they read on average one book a week.

3. The Scranton Wombats are better coached, better prepared to play, and larger and more skilled than their opponents the Dandy Lions.
   _____

   Looks like the Wombats are going to win.

4. Harriet is articulate, intelligent, assertive, and hardworking.
   _____

   She'll make a good lawyer.

5. Most lawyers are rich.
   Ralph is a lawyer.

   _____

   So Ralph is probably rich.

★ 6. Observations of large felines (such as lions, tigers, panthers, and leopards) in major zoos have resulted in the fact that they sleep eighteen to twenty hours a day.

   _____

   Thus lions, tigers, and other big cats are only active about four to six hours a day.

7. Ninety-five percent of male children whose parents both smoke turn out themselves to be smokers.
   Both of Nathan's parents are smokers.

   _____

   So Nathan will very likely take up smoking.

8. True food allergies are extremely rare in adults.

   _____

   Therefore the hives Oswald is getting are not likely to be an allergic reaction to the clams he just ate.

9. Visitors to and residents of the Adirondack Park think the environmental quality of the park has declined over the last decade and support taking steps to improve it, according to a new survey.

    The survey of 462 people, released Thursday, was taken among visitors to the Adirondack Museum in Blue Mountain Lake this summer and fall.

    "A solid majority of respondents in all groups—full-time and part-time residents and visitors from within New York—agreed that environmental conditions have declined in the Adirondacks in the past 10 years," said Timothy P. Holmes, a Saranac-Lake-based pollster who did the survey.

    Ithaca Journal, December 1990

10. Tests we conducted this spring showed that the 1989 apple crop was essentially free of daminozide. We tested 100 fresh apples—samples of 11 varieties, purchased in Boston, Detroit, New York City, Seattle, and Washington, D.C. Only two apples (Cortlands, purchased in New York) had been treated with *Alar* ["Alar" is the trade name of daminozide]. More than three-fourths of the samples contained no detectable daminozide—less than 0.02 part per million. The rest had faint traces of the chemical, most likely residues from spraying in prior years. Those residues are too low to cause concern.

    Consumer Reports, July 1990

11. "Girls aren't popular for who they are, but for how pretty they are and what they own," says Peter Adler, the chairman of the University of Denver sociology department and author of the study [of grade-schoolers and popularity] with wife Patti, a University of Colorado sociologist. Boys join the "in" group through athletic prowess and "cool" clothes.

    The Adlers' study, the first of popularity among girls and boys in elementary school, was published last month in a journal, *Sociology of Education.* The Adlers talked to their own kids, now 10 and 14, and hundreds of their kids' friends and classmates over five years. Most were white, middle-class and from Boulder, Colo. . . .

The couple found:

- Popular girls are pretty, which kids seem to judge "intuitively."
- Popular boys excel in sports.
- The "in" kids of both sexes enjoy costly trappings like their own phones at home and "name" sneakers. . . .
- Being smart can shut a boy out of the "in" crowd; but for girls it's OK.

Joni H. Blackman, "What Makes a Kid 'In'?",
USA Weekend, August 14–16, 1992

12. As a further exercise of a different sort, analyze and criticize the following article using your common sense, background knowledge, and the skills emphasized in this text so far.

INEXPENSIVE IMPORTS ARE SLOWLY DISAPPEARING

Detroit—Low-priced cars like the old Volkswagen Bug or the original Honda Civic once dominated the import market.

But the cheap import looks like an endangered species, if current sales trends keep up.

The average import sold for $19,411 in the first three months of 1992, according to the Commerce Department.

That's 10.6 percent higher than the average for 1990.

The new figures highlight the growing price gap between imports and U.S.-built cars. The average domestic car cost $16,666 in early 1992, up 6.2 percent since 1990. . . .

Through mid-May, sales of luxury imports are up 20.5 percent. Mercedes, BMW and Infiniti all posted solid gains. By contrast, sales of imported entry-level subcompacts declined 4.6 percent, according to Ward's Automotive Reports. . . .

The Commerce Department's data define "domestic" cars as any vehicle built in North America. That includes the U.S.-built Toyota Camry and Honda Accord.

The figures count any car built outside North America as an import, including vehicles with Big Three nameplates such as the GEO Storm, Ford Festiva or Dodge Stealth. . . .

Ithaca Journal, June 13, 1992

CHAPTER 12

CAUSAL REASONING

This chapter is concerned with our reasoning about causal relationships. Causal reasoning is another important form of nondeductive reasoning.

KEY TERMS AND HEADINGS

Causal Arguments	Causes and Correlations
Causally Sufficient Conditions	Common Causes
	Control Group
Causally Necessary Conditions	Competing Causal Explanations and Mechanisms
Cause	
Effect	Specific Causal Claims
Background Assumptions	Side Effects and Traces

In the previous chapter we studied various kinds of nondeductive arguments. The key feature of a nondeductive as opposed to a deductive argument is that in a nondeductive argument the premises, even if true, do not guarantee the truth of the conclusion. Nondeductive arguments *could* be construed as invalid deductive arguments, but that approach overlooks the fact that it is often useful to consider what support there is for a claim even though the support does not establish the claim with certainty. We must be able to consider arguments whose premises do not prove their conclusions but give them some support. We do not want to be in the position of having simply to reject such arguments.

With a nondeductive argument we can accept the premises and reject the conclusion without contradicting ourselves; nevertheless, to do so may not be rational. The premises may give so much support to the conclusion, without actually proving it, that rejecting the conclusion if we accept the premises would not be rational. A great deal of natural science is broadly nondeductive in the sense that scientific theories are never proven with 100% certainty.[1] Even though no scientific

---

[1] Mathematics, on the other hand, is considered to be deductive.

theory is ever established with absolute certainty, there may be so much evidence in its support that it would not be rational to reject it.

The fact that scientific reasoning is broadly nondeductive does not mean that scientists do not need deductive methods. Quite the contrary, deductive methods are absolutely vital in natural science (as well as in every other area of study and in everyday life). For one thing, theories are tested by validly deducing conclusions from them in the form of predictions. If the predictions turn out to be false, then the theory is false. (We recall that a valid argument cannot have true premises and a false conclusion.)[2]

CAUSAL ARGUMENTS

In our scientific and everyday dealings with the world and each other we are greatly concerned with the causal relations among things. We want to know what produces or brings about what, what causes what, and what will happen as a result of our acting in a certain way. The practical value of knowing the causal nature of things is obvious—it is what enables us to make our way in the world. Furthermore, many of the great scientific breakthroughs have been about the causes of things, such as the discovery by Pasteur that many diseases are caused by germs and Darwin's discovery that speciation is caused by natural selection. Recently there have been vitally important causal discoveries, such as that smoking cigarettes causes lung cancer. Many causal claims on which our future well-being depends are still unsettled; for example, it has not yet been determined whether CO_2 emissions cause global warming or whether acid rain causes forest die back. These are the subjects of continuing research.

Despite their importance, causal claims, even the ones we consider to be discoveries, are never proven, if what we mean by "proven" is given an absolutely 100% airtight guarantee. The premises of a valid deductive argument, if true, prove the conclusion with an absolute 100% guarantee. Causal claims are never proven in this sense, because the evidence in support of them, even if correct, does not give them a 100% guarantee. It always remains a possibility, for example, that the claimed causal connections are mere coincidences. This is why causal arguments fall under the heading of nondeductive support. Even a claim such as that smoking cigarettes causes lung cancer has not been absolutely proven in the same sense as it has not been absolutely proven that Hitler is dead. This does not mean that it is a real practical possibility that Hitler is still alive or that smoking might not cause lung cancer. That these are not absolutely proven in the deductive sense should have no practical significance whatsoever. Indeed, someone who claims that it has been proven that smoking cigarettes causes lung cancer can be interpreted as saying something true and valuable. Namely, it would be irrational, given the evidence in favor of it, not to accept the claim that smoking cigarettes causes lung cancer. It is proven beyond a reasonable doubt (but not beyond any possible doubt). As we saw earlier, "prove" is an ambiguous word.

---

[2] In this connection see the section on deduction and validity at the end of Chapter 4.

CAUSALLY SUFFICIENT AND CAUSALLY NECESSARY CONDITIONS

Given the importance of causal reasoning to us, it is vital to understand how causal claims are established and refuted. To do this we must understand the nature of causal claims and how they are supported and criticized.

Causality is a matter of relations, a matter of how things, states of affairs, and events affect each other. Causality can be thought of most easily as a relation between separate events. When one event causes another, the causing event is the **cause** and the event that is caused is the **effect.** The notions of necessary and sufficient conditions, which were introduced in Chapter 5, are helpful in understanding the relations of causality, and like other types of necessary and sufficient conditions causal relations can be expressed in terms of conditional sentences. That event C is capable of causing effect E means that C is sufficient for E. When I claim that C will cause E, I am claiming that C is sufficient for E. For example, I tell a child that watching the horror movie will cause her to have nightmares. Here the cause would be her watching the horror movie. The effect would be her having nightmares. This is a familiar kind of claim, the sort that we all make frequently. What I am claiming is that her watching the horror movie is a sufficient condition for her having nightmares. If she watches the horror movie, then she will have nightmares.

If C causes E, then C is a sufficient condition for E. However, not all sufficient conditions are causes. For example, being a mare is a sufficient condition for being female but being a mare does not cause being a female. To distinguish the causal case, we will call it a **causally sufficient condition.**

We recall that sufficient conditions must be distinguished from necessary conditions. Being a mare is sufficient for being female but it is certainly not necessary. We must make the same distinction in the causal case, so we must distinguish **causally necessary conditions** from causally sufficient conditions. If C is a causally necessary condition for E, then C is causally required for E. E cannot occur without C.

When we say that C causes or will cause E, we mean that C is a causally sufficient condition for E. Clearly, C need not also be causally necessary for E. When I tell the child that watching the horror movie will cause her to have nightmares, I am not saying that if she does not watch the horror movie, she will not have nightmares. Her watching the horror movie is not a causally necessary condition for her having nightmares. Nightmares might also be caused by something else besides watching horror movies.

Interest in causally necessary conditions seems to arise mainly when we are concerned about what caused some past event, particularly when we want to assign responsibility. If we determine that pilot error caused the crash, then presumably this means that without pilot error the crash would not have occurred—there were no mechanical problems, the weather was fine, and so on. Pilot error was responsible for the crash.[3] Expressed this way, the pilot error seems to be a causally necessary condition for the crash.

---

[3] Was pilot error also causally sufficient for the crash? In other words, when we claim that pilot error caused the crash, do we mean that pilot error was causally necessary and causally sufficient for the crash? This is unclear. Consider the following technical problem: If A is causally necessary and sufficient

In a way, this difference between our interest in causally sufficient and causally necessary conditions makes sense. Our forward-looking causal claims are focused on how to produce some effect or what will happen if something else happens. Events in the past have already occurred, and we want to know what or whom to blame or praise.

BACKGROUND ASSUMPTIONS

Causal claims are made with a commonsense understanding of background conditions. When we say that flicking the switch will cause the lights to go on, we mean that flicking the switch is a causally sufficient condition for the lights to go on—if I flick the switch, the lights will go on. Of course, a number of background assumptions are being made. Flicking the switch, simply and ultimately, is not by itself causally sufficient (nor is it causally necessary) for the lights to go on. We assume and understand that the switch is hooked up to the light, the current is on, the bulb is not burned out, the laws of physics have not changed, and so forth. Likewise, if we say that watering the plants will cause them to grow, we are aware that plants also need light and soil, among other things, to grow. Even with the background assumptions, it need not be the case that the causes are causally necessary for the effects. Flicking the switch may not be the only way to turn on the light—it might be hooked up to another switch. Watering the plants may not be necessary for the plants to grow because it might rain.

Keeping unstated but assumed background conditions in mind is essential to understanding causal claims. When we say that smoking causes lung cancer, we are clearly not saying that smoking is causally necessary for getting lung cancer, because it is well known that some people get lung cancer who have never smoked. So smoking cannot be a causally necessary condition for getting lung cancer. On the other hand, smoking does not seem to be a causally sufficient condition for getting lung cancer either, because some, indeed many, people who smoke never get lung cancer. For one thing, some smokers die in automobile accidents without ever having gotten lung cancer. Other people live to be eighty-five or ninety, smoking heavily, and still do not get lung cancer. If smoking is neither causally necessary nor causally sufficient for getting lung cancer, what can be the sense in which it is correct to say that smoking causes lung cancer?

To answer this question we must consider what background assumptions are in play. Given the natural assumptions that one does not die prematurely of other causes and that one has the requisite susceptibility, smoking *is* causally sufficient for lung cancer. We do not yet know about the susceptibility to lung cancer directly, but we do know that most have it (but not everyone has it). So what we mean when we say that smoking causes lung cancer is that given the background conditions, if you

---

for *B*, then *B* is causally necessary and sufficient for *A*. But if *A* is the cause of *B*, then *B* is not the cause of *A*. (Technically, the relation of cause and effect is asymmetrical, whereas the relation of being necessary and sufficient is symmetrical.) So it seems that when we say that *A* caused *B*, we cannot mean that *A* is causally necessary and sufficient for *B*. The entire issue is cloudy, however. The nature of causality and the meaning of our talk about causality are the subject of deep and unresolved philosophical disputes.

smoke, then you will get lung cancer and, furthermore, a large number of people satisfy those background conditions.

Compare the smoking and lung cancer case to a hypothetical one. Let us suppose that some people have a fatal clam allergy. Perhaps one in a million has such an allergy. For them, eating clams will cause death. So if someone satisfies certain background conditions—namely, they have the fatal allergy to clams, then for them eating clams is causally sufficient for a fatal allergy attack. We do not say flat out "Eating clams causes death" because so few people satisfy those background conditions.

Because knowing what causes what is crucial to many decisions, causal claims have a great deal of force and are subject to misuse and misinterpretation. For example, a certain small percentage of the population is susceptible to committing sex crimes as a result of exposure to pornography. On the one hand, it is misleading to say, as some do, that pornography causes sex crimes, because the vast majority of people will not commit sex crimes no matter how much pornography they are exposed to. On the other hand, it does not seem correct to deny that pornography causes sex crimes on the basis of the fact that many people are exposed to pornography and never commit any sex crime. What is correct is that exposure to pornography causes people with a certain susceptibility to commit sex crimes and that a certain small percentage have this susceptibility.

CAUSES AND CORRELATIONS

Causal claims are always based on **correlations.** A correlation is a relation between types of events. One type of event is correlated with another when they tend to occur together.[4] For example, the occurrence of lightning is correlated with the occurrence of thunder, because when lightning occurs there is thunder shortly after. Causes are always correlated with their effects. Clearly if events of type C are causally sufficient for events of type E, they will tend to happen together. On the other hand, not all types of events that are correlated are related as cause and effect. For example, in human males a deepening voice is correlated with the appearance of facial hair but neither causes the other. Correlation is a necessary but not a sufficient condition for causality. One of the primary challenges of causal reasoning is determining when correlations are causal and when they are not. And even if we have determined that two types of events are causally related, we still have the challenge of determining which is the cause and which the effect.

If events of type A are correlated with events of type B, there are several possibilities:

    a. Events of type A cause events of type B.

    b. Events of type B cause events of type A.

---

[4] What is here being called simply "correlation" is sometimes called "positive correlation." Events are positively correlated when they tend to happen together, negatively correlated when one tends to happen in the absence of the other. When we say here that types of events are correlated, we mean positively correlated.

c. Events of some other type *C* cause both events of type *A* and events of type *B*. Events of type *A* and events of type *B* have a **common cause.**

d. The correlation between events of type *A* and events of type *B* is just coincidence.

e. Events of type *A* are events of type *B,* so the correlation is identity not causality.

Example of common cause: The correlation of deepening voice and the appearance of facial hair in human males is an example of common cause. The deepening voice does not cause the appearance of facial hair nor does the appearance of facial hair cause the deepening voice, rather both the appearance of facial hair and the deepening voice are caused by the physiological changes involved with the onset of puberty.

Example of coincidence: It was once discovered that certain events in the stock market were correlated with sunspot activity. This is pretty clearly a coincidence.

Correlations of events with other events that would have happened anyway can be considered coincidental. For example, suppose someone claimed that almost 100% of students taking SATs report feeling hungry afterward. Surely we would not be justified in concluding that the tests caused the hunger because people get hungry after a period without food anyway. The students would have gotten hungry whether or not they had taken the test. The correlation between taking the tests and the hunger is just coincidental.

Example of identity: If someone claimed that migraines caused headaches, they would be confusing causality with identity. Migraines are headaches.

Determining how correlated events are causally related or whether the correlation is just coincidence can be difficult and involves highly technical scientific expertise. Indeed, the point of scientific experiments is to make just this sort of judgment. A large number of rats in the lab who ingest substance *S* get cancer. Does ingestion of substance *S* cause cancer in rats? We cannot simply conclude from the correlation that ingestion of substance *S* causes cancer in the rats. Perhaps the cancer is caused by something else in the environment of the rats or by something else in their diets. To test the claim that substance *S* causes cancer in rats, the experimenter would separate the rats into two groups keeping everything about the groups the same except that one group would be given substance *S*. The one without *S* is called the **control group.** If the group with *S* has a much higher rate of cancer, then this is support for the claim that *S* does cause cancer in rats.

For such an experiment to work, however, everything else but what is being tested must be the same between the control group and the experimental group. This sameness is almost impossible to achieve. For example, if the experimenter knows which is the control group, that is a difference between the groups. To avoid this, experiments are conducted blind. For example, the person examining the rats for signs of cancer would not know which ones had gotten *S*.

The whole study of experimental design and the technical methods used to determine causal relations is an entire subject matter of its own. Nevertheless, without being experts, there is a great deal that we can do toward making intelligent evaluations of causal judgments. We each have a great deal of background knowledge and common sense about how the world works, and we can use this to make initial plausibility judgments about causal claims just as we do about other kinds of claims. For example, it does not seem initially plausible that sunspots cause the stock market to go up. We just have no idea how sunspots could cause such a thing. This does not mean that we have proof that it is impossible for sunspots to cause the stock market to go up or that it does not happen that way—it is just that we have absolutely no reason, other than the mere correlation, to think that sunspots cause the stock market to go up. Further investigation may show that sunspots do cause the market to go up but, at least initially, such a causal relation is highly implausible.

Likewise, we can often make sound judgments about the direction of causality. One safe principle is that the effect occurs at the same time as or after the cause. Thus we know that smoking causes lung cancer, and it is not lung cancer that causes smoking.

We have got to be careful with these sorts of judgments, however. The lung cancer case is quite obvious and many other judgments of the direction of causality are equally obvious, but not all are. Suppose there is a correlation discovered between being overweight and experiencing strong social stress. It would seem plausible that this is not just coincidence, but what is the nature of the causal relation? Our background knowledge and common sense will not guide us here. Is it that being overweight causes social stress or that people under social stress eat more as a result of the stress? Or is there some common cause? Initially each possibility seems equally plausible. To determine the causal relation between being overweight and experiencing social stress would require extremely careful research and documentation.

Perhaps in the area of causal reasoning more than in any other we must recognize the limitations of our background knowledge and common sense. This is an area in which people are prone to jump to conclusions. Often the most useful exercise of common sense in this area is to accept that there is a correlation between two types of events but recognize that a great deal more investigation would be necessary to determine what, if any, the causal relation between them is.

COMPETING CAUSAL EXPLANATIONS AND MECHANISMS

Two important components in making initial plausibility judgments of causal claims are competing causal explanations and our understanding of mechanisms. If two types of events are correlated, we should be reluctant to attribute a causal relation between them if we have a better causal explanation of the occurrence of one or the other type of event. For example, we may be reluctant to say that sunspots cause the stock market to go up, even though there is a correlation, because we have better explanations of stock market activity in terms of economic factors. Further, we are reluctant to attribute a causal relation between sunspots and the stock market, because we have no idea of any mechanism between them. If we were to find a plausible mechanism that would explain how sunspots could affect the stock market, we would find the causal claim more plausible. Compare this to the case of smoking and lung cancer. We do not have a complete idea of the mechanism here, but we do know that tobacco smoke contains carcinogens (cancer-causing substances) and that smoking involves inhaling the smoke and thus allowing the carcinogens to come in contact with the delicate tissues of the lung. Here we have at least some notion of a mechanism, of a way that smoking would produce lung cancer.

The search for competing causal explanations and mechanisms plays a key role in the fringe areas and frontiers of scientific knowledge. One of the difficulties with such alleged phenomena as telepathy and psychokinesis,[5] for example, is lack of a mechanism. We may feel that sometimes our thoughts have been guided by others in telepathic ways or that people can affect distant objects by pure thought. A great deal of effort has been put into attempting to establish correlations in this area and some have been established, but we have not the remotest idea of a mechanism that would explain telepathy or psychokinesis. Likewise, one of the things that makes astrology so highly implausible when judged against our background beliefs and common sense is that we have absolutely no idea how the planets and stars could control our fates. If someone came up with a plausible mechanism for explaining a detailed causal connection between the positions of the planets and the specific events in our lives, astrology would be a lot more plausible. As it is, where people want to believe but cannot find a mechanism to justify their beliefs, they appeal to occult forces and causes.

SPECIFIC CAUSAL CLAIMS

Although causal claims are based on correlations between types of events and we are very concerned about general causal claims such as that germs cause many diseases or that the motions of the moon cause the tides, we are also very concerned about specific causal claims. We want to know what caused a specific event, or what will happen if we act in a certain way. We want to know what caused the airplane crash, or what effect it will have if I tell my friend my true feelings. We are concerned to know what caused the important events around us and what effects our actions will produce.

Our causal claims about individual or specific events are based on correlations just as are our general causal claims. My claim that the child's watching the horror movie will cause her to have nightmares is based on past experience of such events. I know that people commonly have nightmares after watching horror movies and that in the past the child has had nightmares after watching horror movies.

Many events, however, are unique or are of a type that happens only rarely, such as airplane crashes. How can we have causal knowledge of a unique event? I have never before eaten a mushroom like the one I found in the forest, so there is no correlation between my eating this kind of mushroom and any other event such

---

[5] Telepathy and psychokinesis are forms of ESP. Telepathy is defined as direct mind to mind transfer of thoughts—mind reading. Psychokinesis is defined as direct control of objects outside one's body by thought. ESP has not been scientifically established.

as my getting sick. How, then, can we make any justified causal claims about what will happen if I eat the mushroom?

No event is totally unique. Every event is like others in many ways—it falls under various categories. We have causal knowledge, based on correlations, of the categories of events under which this event falls. We can apply this knowledge to these "unique" events. I may have never eaten this kind of mushroom before, but other people have and they have gotten sick. I know that they are physiologically similar to me, and so on, so it probably will cause me to get sick, too. Even if no one has ever eaten a mushroom like this, I may still have strong evidence that it will make me sick. It may be known to contain chemicals that are similar to other chemicals that cause sickness in humans.

Suppose a mid-air collision causes a plane to crash. We do not need to base our causal judgment that the collision caused the crash on a widespread correlation between mid-air collisions and crashes—after all, very few mid-air collisions have ever occurred—because there are surely more general correlations at work here, such as correlations between impacts on delicate machinery and damage to them, and so on. We also have a rough idea of a mechanism here. Without knowing much about aeronautics, we know that planes have delicate steering mechanisms, that they are held aloft by air passing in special ways over their surfaces, and that a hard impact would disturb these severely. In other words, we have a pretty clear idea of how a mid-air collision would bring about a crash.

Our knowledge of **side effects and traces** also plays an important role in judging and justifying specific causal claims. Causes have characteristic ways of working; they leave traces and have side effects. The presence of these traces and side effects helps us determine the cause. For example, if a person watches a horror movie and then has nightmares, the content of the nightmares would be relevant to the causal judgment that watching the horror movie caused the nightmares. If the content of the nightmares bears a striking resemblance to that of the horror movie, then that is strong support for the claim that watching the movie caused the nightmares. We know that smoking causes lung cancer, but that alone does not establish that a particular case of lung cancer was caused by smoking even if the victim was a smoker. The victim might have gotten lung cancer from a different cause. Nevertheless, we know that lung cells affected by smoking go through various changes that are precancerous and that the effect of smoking is not sudden and immediate. Presumably we could examine the victim's lungs and see whether the cells have gone through stages characteristic of lung cancer that is caused by smoking. If so, this would be very strong support for the claim that the victim's lung cancer was caused by smoking.

SUMMARY

When we claim that C causes E, we are claiming that C is causally sufficient for E. If C occurs, then, given the background assumptions, E will occur. Sometimes, especially when talking about events in the past, we mean that E would not have occurred without C—that C is causally necessary for E.

Causal claims are based on correlations. Although correlation is necessary for causality, correlation by itself does not always indicate the direction of causality nor even that any causal relation between the correlated events exists. A correlation between events of type A and events of type B can be based on any of the following:

a. Events of type A cause events of type B.

b. Events of type B cause events of type A.

c. Events of type A and events of type B have a common cause.

d. The correlation between events of type A and events of type B is just coincidence.

e. Events of type A are events of type B.

We make initial plausibility judgments of causal claims but must recognize severe limitations here. Our judgments are based in part on our understanding of a mechanism that would link cause and effect, on our ability to eliminate competing causal explanations, and the occurrence of side effects and traces.

EXERCISE 12.1

Each of the following passages contains causal claims and causal reasoning. What is the causal claim being made or considered? What is the cause and what is the effect? What mechanism, if any, is suggested to link cause and effect? Answer these and any additional questions asked about each passage.

★ 1. In adults, a thorough [dental] cleaning may cause soreness that lasts a day or two. Some adults simply have sensitive teeth. Or, if periodontal disease exists, the dentist or hygienist may need to scale teeth well below the gum line.

Consumer Reports, May 1990

2. The color patterns of butterfly wings are made up of thousands of tiny overlapping scales. Colors are produced two ways, through chemical pigment within each scale or through light hitting the surface of the scale itself.

Scales with chemical pigments absorb certain wavelengths of light and transmit what is left, giving most butterflies their beautiful color patterns.

The most brilliant colors, however, are produced by scales shaped to allow light to bounce off minute films and ridges in the scale surface. This type of scale can produce a breathtaking flash of color or an iridescent effect as the butterfly spreads its wings to fly.

Butterfly World: Official Guide

3.   Some 16 million cases of food poisoning occurred last year in the U.S. from food cooked in the home, not in restaurants. The main culprit: poorly cooked meat, poultry, and seafood that harbored bacteria.

Consumer Reports, November 1991
(slightly adapted)

Additional questions: How would they know that the cases are caused by food cooked in the home not restaurants? How could they come up with the figure 16 million?

4.   [Radon] gas, [is] said to be the second-leading cause of lung cancer in the country,. . . .

The gas itself does not cause harm, as it tends to pass out of the lungs as a person exhales. Lung cancers are actually caused by two of radon's decay products, which are solid isotopes of polonium.

Radon has a relatively short half-life of 3.8 days. When its decay products are inhaled, they can lodge deep in the lungs. The alpha radiation they emit causes cell damage that may manifest itself years or decades later.

. . . [A]n estimated 20 percent of lung cancer deaths in the country are caused by radon. Eighty percent are linked to cigarette smoking.

Ithaca Journal, November 2, 1991

Additional questions: Does the claim "The gas itself does not cause harm" contradict the other things claimed about radon in the passage (i.e., that 20 percent of the lung cancer deaths in the country are caused by radon)? Is there a charitable way to interpret this?

★ 5. **Q** I have been using Listerine mouthwash twice a day for a year. Recently I was told that my continued use of this alcohol-based product will increase my chances of getting oral cancer. Is this true?

A You're referring to a study from the National Cancer Institute that compared 850 patients who had oral or throat cancer with more than 1200 similar people who didn't. People who had habitually used mouthwashes containing more than 25 percent alcohol . . . had a significantly higher risk for these cancers.

(The writer comments as follows: But retrospective studies like this one can't prove a causal connection, and earlier, smaller studies of the same question produced mixed results.)

Consumer Reports, November 1991

Additional questions: What support is offered, if any, for the causal claim being considered? How else could the correlation of using alcohol-based mouthwashes with oral cancer be explained? Are there competing explanations?

6. Prolonged nervous and emotional disturbance of the mother during the later months of pregnancy seems to be related directly to early feeding difficulties and to an irritable and hyperactive autonomic nervous system in the infant. The autonomic nervous system of the fetus seems to become sensitized through the hyperactivity of the mother's neuro-humoral system [nervous plus endocrine systems].

Wallace A. Kennedy,
Child Psychology

Additional questions: Are there two separate effects here or is one of the effects the cause of the other? Can you think of mechanisms to link causes and effects here?

7.   Simpson (1957) reported, in a retrospective study of 7,449 patients, that heavy smokers are twice as likely to have premature babies as nonsmokers. This does not prove that the smoking causes the prematurity; it might be that the woman who smokes heavily during pregnancy smokes for reasons which in turn cause prematurity. Nevertheless, it is a highly significant finding.

Following up the Simpson study, Frazier et al. (1961) studied 2,736 pregnant black women and found a significant relationship between prematurity and smoking: the rate of premature deliveries was 11.2 percent for nonsmokers, 13.6 percent for those who became smokers during pregnancy, and 18.6 percent for smokers. Moreover, the incidence of prematurity increased with the amount smoked. Frazier et al. also found that the infants of smokers weigh less than the infants of nonsmokers regardless of the duration of the pregnancy, which suggests a fetal developmental mechanism rather than an early onset of labor.

Wallace A. Kennedy, *Child Psychology*

Additional questions: What support is given for the causal claim? When the author says "it might be that the woman who smokes heavily during pregnancy smokes for reasons which in turn cause prematurity," the author is referring to the possibility of what we would call a _____ . Do you think this possibility is plausible or is the author just being cautious? This is the second passage in which the term "retrospective study" was used. What do you suppose this means?

8.   Do you feel bloated the day after eating a big Chinese meal? If so, you're probably suffering from water retention, or edema, a buildup of bodily fluids in the tissues that results in swelling.

Although the precise physiological mechanism that causes edema isn't understood, experts know certain circumstances, such as eating high-sodium food and standing or sitting too long can cause fluids to accumulate in the body. Certain common medications, such as steroids can also promote edema.

In addition, many premenopausal women experience bloating before their periods. Why? . . . [T]he accepted theory is that higher ratios of estrogen to progesterone cause the body to store salt, which in turn leads to water retention.

Crash dieting often results in edema. When you pare off pounds quickly, much of what you lose is water. The body then compensates by conserving sodium. . . .

Jessica Sachs, "Routing Water Retention," *New Woman,* April 1991

Additional question: Notice that there is a causal chain (or chains) being described in this passage. A bunch of things cause something else, which in turn causes something else. Try to piece this chain together.

9. Severe winter depression is medically known as "seasonal affective disorder," or SAD. Caused by lack of sunlight during the winter months, the disorder visits mostly those in the north: In one survey, 10 percent of New Hampshire residents reported experiencing SAD symptoms, while only 1.4 percent of Floridians were similarly bummed. . . .

Winter depression is a reminder of an evolutionary connection to our fellow creatures. "The need for sleep and the weight gain you see with SAD look hauntingly similar to that experienced by hibernating animals," says Michael Freeman, an assistant clinical professor of psychiatry at the University of California at San Francisco. "Some authorities call SAD a 'hibernation response.'"

Michael Castleman, "Brighten Up, Lighten Up," *Sierra,* November/December 1991

Additional questions: What support is given for the causal claim? Are there competing causal explanations, especially for the difference (10% versus 1.4%) between depression sufferers in New Hampshire and Florida? How plausible is the suggested mechanism?

10.   A child formed from the union of a normal sex cell with one containing an extra chromosome by nondisjunction will carry three copies of that chromosome in each cell, instead of the normal two. This anomaly is called a trisomy.

In humans, the twenty-first chromosome suffers nondisjunction at a remarkably high frequency, unfortunately rather tragic in effect. About 1 in 600 to 1 in 1000 newborn babies carry an extra twenty-first chromosome, a condition technically known as "trisomy-21" [Down's syndrome]. These unfortunate children suffer mild to severe mental retardation and have a reduced life expectancy. They exhibit, in addition, a suite of distinctive features, including short and broad hands, a narrow high palate, rounded face and broad head, a small nose with a flattened root, and a thick and furrowed tongue. The frequency of trisomy-21 rises sharply with increasing maternal age. We know very little about the causes of trisomy-21; indeed, its chromosomal basis was not discovered until 1959. We have no idea why it occurs so often, and why other chromosomes are not nearly so subject to nondisjunction. We have no clue as to why an extra twenty-first chromosome should yield the highly specific set of abnormalities associated with trisomy-21.

Stephen Jay Gould, *The Panda's Thumb*

Additional question: Even though the author claims that specific knowledge of mechanisms is lacking, there is a background knowledge of a mechanism that allows us to go from the correlation of trisomy-21 with the physical and psychological traits characteristic of Down's syndrome to a causal claim. In other words, we find it plausible that having the extra chromosome causes the "highly specific set of abnormalities." What is this background knowledge of a general mechanism that is at work here?

11.   The excess in purchasing power can result only in price increases and an inflationary spiral; money national income will rise because of "paper" price changes, but real national product cannot go above its maximum full-employment level. Unfortunately, the upward movement of prices will continue for as long as there is an inflationary gap. (Footnote: The process does not end with higher prices. . . . On the contrary, since the higher prices received by businesses become in turn somebody's income—that of the worker or property owner—demand again shifts upward and prices will continue to rise. Attempts of labor to secure higher wages as compensation for

the soaring cost of living may only cause the inflationary spiral to zoom at a dizzier speed.)

Paul A. Samuelson, Economics, 6th ed.

Additional question: Can you flesh out in causal terms the notion of "spiral" as it is used here? Think carefully about what is causing what and how they are interacting (i.e., about the direction of causation).

★ 12.   In the animal world, fidelity is a special condition that evolves when the Darwinian advantage of cooperation in rearing offspring outweighs the advantage to either partner of seeking extra mates. Three biasing ecological conditions are known that seem to account for all of the known cases of monogamy: (1) the territory contains such a scarce and valuable resource that two adults are required to defend it against other animals; (2) the physical environment is so difficult that two adults are needed to cope with it; and (3) early breeding is so advantageous that the head start allowed by monogamous pairing is decisive.

Edward O. Wilson, Sociobiology

Additional question: Would it be fair to say that this author is claiming that the "three biasing ecological conditions" cause monogamy?

13.   "If you are a patient with heart disease, and you have neither love nor money, your prognosis is worse," said Dr. Redford B. Williams of Duke University. . . .

Williams said that people who were not married and had no one to talk to had three times the heart disease death rate of people who were not socially isolated. . . .

A number of studies have suggested that low social and economic status is associated with a poorer heart disease outlook. The new study refines the earlier work by showing that social isolation and low income are independently correlated with poor prognosis, Williams said.

The importance of the finding is that it suggests relatively simple ways to lower the heart disease death rate, he said.

"The social isolation could be a target for intervention by simply having a nurse visit once a month," Williams said.

Ithaca Journal, November 12, 1991

Additional questions: What does Williams mean when he says "that social isolation and low income are independently correlated with poor prognosis"? Does the fact that Williams suggests that having a nurse visit once a month would lower the heart disease death rate justify us in attributing to him the view that the social isolation is causing the poor prognosis? If so, does this causal judgment seem justified? What other explanations might there be for the correlation between social isolation and poor prognosis? If social isolation does cause a higher heart disease death rate, does it seem likely to you that having a nurse visit once a month would help much?

Exercise 12.2

In each of the following there is a causal judgment made on the basis of a correlation. These are fictitious examples, so the correlations are not factual in every case. Assume, however, for the sake of the exercise that the correlations are real. Is the causal judgment justified by the cited correlation? If not, (1) does it get the direction of causality wrong? (2) is there a common cause? (3) is the correlation just coincidence? (4) is the correlation just identity? It is impossible to know the answers here with any finality, but try to make an initial plausibility judgment that you can defend by appeal to background knowledge and common sense.

★ 1. In the United States almost all children were born in a hospital. Therefore we can conclude that going to the hospital causes pregnant women to give birth to children.

2. In virtually every case known to humans, night follows day, so day causes night.

3.   Biologists recently found many dead and dying fish in a local lake that is polluted. The owner of a factory that is near the lake denied that the factory was polluting the lake. The factory owner said that it was all those dead fish that were causing the pollution.

4.   The common cold causes sexual arousal! Eighty-six percent of participants in a recent survey involving young adults reported being sexually aroused sometime during a forty-eight-hour period after getting over a cold.

★   5.   Since the mid-fifties there has been an amazing negative correlation between the number of inmates in mental institutions and the number students enrolling in college. As the number of inmates in mental institutions has gone down dramatically, the number of students in college has gone up dramatically. This leads us to suppose that the decline of inmates in mental institutions has caused the rise in college enrollments.

6. Every flood in North America was caused by an inundation.

7. In an extensive survey it was found that in 89% of cases of death due to natural causes, people had lost at least some weight in the weeks or months before death. Dieters beware! The conclusion is that weight loss causes death.

8. A strong positive correlation exists between drug use and the feelings of dependency and depression and the lack of clear goals and ambition. So drug use leads to and results in these personality and character defects.

9. It was discovered in a survey that there is far more alcoholic consumption on Friday and Saturday than on Sunday and Monday. This was used as evidence to support the contention that Sunday church attendance has an important role in reducing alcohol consumption.

10. The psychological effects of colors are very interesting. It is well known that drivers of red and orange cars are stopped by the police with a higher frequency than drivers of cars of other colors. So it must be that the colors red and orange have a psychological effect on police officers that causes them to be more aggressive in enforcing the law.

CHAPTER 13

ANALOGICAL REASONING

This chapter concerns reasoning based on comparisons. Such reasoning is important in all areas but has become especially important recently in science in the form of reasoning based on such things as computer models. The final set of exercises is a collection of analogies from philosophical works.

KEY TERMS AND HEADINGS

Analogy	Analogical Arguments
Models	Analogies in Logic
Correspondence	Analogies in Philosophy
Correspondence Schema	(Exercise 13.3)

An **analogy** is based on a comparison of one thing to another. When reasoning analogically, we draw conclusions about one thing from our knowledge or understanding of another that is similar to it. Any two things are similar in some respects and different in others. Nevertheless, sometimes two apparently very different things will have striking and even surprising similarities, and we can use these similarities to extend our knowledge of the things. Although analogical reasoning is fraught with difficulties and is easily abused, it is an important source of insights in science and mathematics, as well as in everyday life.

The most useful similarities for analogical reasoning are similarities of structure. If we note a similarity of structure between two things, we can examine the structure of the one thing to discover facts about the other thing. For example, there is an analogy between an individual human being and an entire nation. Although the similarity in structure may not be apparent at first, consider that each is made up of a vast number of individual units—the cells of the individual on the one hand and the people of the nation on the other—and that each has an overall organic organization. So, for the analogy, we may say that the people of the nation are like the cells of the body. Just as cells have different functions, so people also have different functions—some are teachers, others are farmers, and so on. Just as the individual human has a brain, the nation has a government, and so on.

Someone could use this analogy between an individual human and a nation to derive conclusions. They might, for example, use the analogy to support the claim that just as for proper functioning of the individual the brain must exercise control over the rest of the body, so for the nation to function properly the government must exercise control over the rest of the population.

Even though it may be granted that there is an analogy between an individual human and a nation, the conclusions drawn may be questioned. Indeed we must consider carefully when and to what extent arguments based on such analogies are acceptable.

MODELS

Understanding the role and use of **models** in analogical reasoning will be helpful in understanding in more detail how analogical reasoning works. The central meaning of "model" in this context is that a model is an artificially constructed object that enables us to study features of the thing modeled.[1] We can, and often do, produce an artificial structure to help us reason by analogy about the things we are interested in. A model is tailor-made for the purpose of using its similarity to the thing modeled. For example, we are all familiar with the use made of scale models of cars and airplanes to study aerodynamic properties. This is a form of analogical reasoning using constructed models. Engineers examine the model to learn about the thing being modeled. They are able to do this because the model is similar in certain ways to the thing modeled.

Although the term "model" is usually restricted to things, such as scale models, that are artificially constructed for the purposes of analogy, we shall, by extension, also speak of natural models. Thus, the individual human being was used as a model of the entire nation in the analogy we just considered, even though individual human beings were not constructed for the purpose of this analogy. Given this extension of the term "model" we can say that all analogies involve using or treating one thing as a model of another. Whether we adopt some already existing thing as a model or construct one especially for the purpose makes no fundamental difference. Some analogies use natural models, others use constructed models. A model is simpler, more abstract, more easily studied, or more familiar than the thing modeled. That is why it is useful.

Although natural models are widely used in reasoning, constructed models are pervasive, and we could hardly conduct our lives without them. We have already mentioned scale models. Most of us are aware of their indispensible role in engineering and education. There are also many other types of constructed models

---

[1] It is important not to confuse this sense of model with any of the many other senses that model has. For example, the term "model" has another sense in which it means an excellent example, as in "She is a model citizen." There is also the sense in which model means someone who poses for artists or photographers. None of these should be confused with the special sense in which model is being used here.

that we use constantly. For example, maps, graphs, and charts are constructed models. A map represents a territory by being structurally similar to it. Likewise, graphs and charts can represent processes and relationships, because they share structural features with the processes or relationships being represented. To the extent that a map has the same structure as the territory being represented we can use the map to learn features of the territory. For example, by using the scale of the map we can determine distances between points in the territory by measuring distances between the corresponding points on the map.

Computer models are a kind of constructed model that has recently been playing a greater and greater role in science. Computer models are highly sophisticated mathematical models that are being used to help us understand natural and social processes. These models are so complex and vast that the calculations required to derive information from them can only be done by computers. Computer models are giving us new tools to investigate natural processes such as the weather and social processes such as economic trends. For example, a great deal of the evidence for the global warming effect of CO_2 is based on computer models of the atmosphere.

CORRESPONDENCE

When we recognize an analogy between two things, we must have in mind a **correspondence** between them. This means that the parts of the one thing can be related to the parts of the other thing. So, for example, in the analogy between a human being and a nation the cells of the body correspond to the people, the brain to the government, and so on. The intended correspondence between one thing and the other is given in a **correspondence schema.** A correspondence schema is like the key on a map. It says that the red lines stand for (or correspond to) highways, the blue lines for back roads, the dots for cities, and so on. Without a key, a map would be useless, because there would be no way to tell what the marks on the map were supposed to correspond to. One thing is a model of another under a particular correspondence schema. One thing can be a model of another only if there is some schema that determines what in the model corresponds to what in the thing modeled. The correspondence schema of an analogy need not always be given explicitly as in the key to a map. Often the intended correspondence schema is obvious or can be derived from one or two correspondences.

If an exact correspondence exists between the structure of the model and the thing modeled,[2] then whatever we know about the structure of the model will also be true of the thing modeled. We could learn everything we want to know about the structure of the thing being modeled by studying the structure of the model. Such an exact correspondence requires that for each part of the model there is a unique part of the thing being modeled (so they would have to have exactly the same number of parts), and the parts of the model would have to stand in exactly the same

---

[2] Technically this is called an isomorphism. If two things are structurally identical to each other, we say that they are isomorphic to each other.

relations to each other as the parts of the thing being modeled. An example of such an exact correspondence would be two congruent triangles.

Most interesting analogies are not exact, however. For example, there certainly is not an exact correspondence between a human being and a nation. Recall that in that analogy the cells of the body were to correspond to people of the nation, the brain to the government, and so on. Consider the differences: There are many more cells in a human body than there are people in even the largest nations; cells have no thoughts or feelings, desires or interests of their own; they do not form families, groups, and clubs; they do not have rights and duties; cells, with one important exception, cannot move around from one part of the body to another, but people can move from one part of the nation to another and even to other nations; a muscle cell cannot become a brain cell, but a worker can become part of the government, and so on. Indeed, the differences between an individual human being and a nation under the suggested schema are as great or greater than the similarities.

One reason that most interesting analogies are not exact has to do with one of the main points of using models. We use models because things are complex or unfamiliar. We study the structure of the model to get insight into the structure of the thing modeled, because the structure of the model is simpler, more familiar, or more easily studied than the thing modeled. This means that the thing modeled may have many features and parts that are not represented in the model. And a model will generally have features that do not correspond to anything in the thing modeled. A map leaves many features of a territory out, and there are many features of the map which do not represent anything about the territory. For example, the widths of the lines that represent highways will not correspond to the actual widths of the highways. If there were an exact correspondence between a map and the territory it mapped, then the map would be every bit as complex as the territory. Such a map would be unwieldy because it would contain all sorts of irrelevant detail. Every rock, gully, and mound would have to be represented; not just where the roads went, but their width and shape would be represented, and so on. A map is a simplified and abstract representation of a territory. Likewise, scientists use computer models to study the atmosphere because the atmosphere itself is so complex and vast. If the computer model had to correspond exactly to the atmosphere, then some item in the model would have to correspond to each molecule in the air. This model would be so large that no computer could handle it. Like a map, a computer model is a simplified and abstract representation.

ANALOGICAL ARGUMENTS

Given that most models share only certain features with the things modeled, how can we use models to learn about the things they model? When are we justified in drawing conclusions about a thing by studying another thing that is supposedly analogous to it?

Assuming that the model is similar in the intended ways to the thing modeled and that we correctly understand the model, the crucial point is that we must be able to go from the fact that the model and the thing modeled correspond in certain ways to the conclusion that they correspond in other ways.

In simplest outline an analogical argument would take the following form:

M is a model of *S*.

M has property *P*.

_____

So *S* has property *P*.

For such an argument to work the premises must be true and they must adequately support the conclusion (but note that such reasoning is nondeductive). That the premises are true means that the model really is similar in the intended ways to the thing modeled and that the model has the features attributed to it. That the premises adequately support the conclusion means that we can go from the fact that the model and the thing modeled are similar in some ways to the claim that they are similar in other specific ways.

Correspondingly, there are three ways such an argument could go wrong.

1.   *M* may not be a model of *S*.

2.   *M* may not have property *P*.

3.   Even though *M* is a model of *S*, and *M* has *P*, this does not support the conclusion that *S* has *P*.

   1. When one thing is used as a model of something else, there is an intended correspondence between them. However, the two things may not correspond in the ways intended. A proposed model may simply fail to be similar, in the ways intended, to what it is supposed to model.

   For example, early in the twentieth century some people believed that the solar system and an atom had a similar structure. They thought that the solar system could be used as a model for understanding the structure of the atom. The sun would correspond to the nucleus of the atom, and the planets to electrons; just as the planets revolve around the sun, so the electrons revolve around the nucleus. Physicists have now discovered that the solar system is not analogous in structure to an atom. Electrons are not single, locatable objects like planets, they do not in any ordinary sense revolve around the nucleus, and so on.

   To understand how physicists discovered this, we would have to delve into sophisticated quantum physics, but we can understand the process of discovering that a model is wrong or not a model of what we thought it was in a commonsense way if we think of how we would discover that a map is wrong or is not a map of the territory we thought it was. If the map says that there are various mountains and rivers in certain relations and locations, we can actually go and check whether the features are where the map says they are. If the map says that the territory is a certain way and when we go and actually look, the territory is not the way the map says it is, then the map is wrong. (This assumes that we are using the map properly, reading the key right, and so on.) Likewise, scientific models can be used to make predictions about how certain experiments will turn out or what will be observed under certain conditions. If the predictions turn out to be false, then the model is faulty. (Again, assuming that we are using the model correctly, we are deriving the predictions correctly, and so on.)

2. The second way an analogical argument can go wrong is if the model does not have the properties attributed to it. It is possible to make errors about a model. This would be like misreading a map. A map could be an accurate model of a territory, and we could still go wrong using it if we misread it. We think the map says that there is a village there but it does not.

Someone using an individual person as a model of a nation might say that the brain controls *every* function of the body and draw authoritarian conclusions about the government from this. However, that person is wrong about physiology. The brain does not control every function of the body—the spinal cord controls a lot.

3. Last, an analogical argument could go wrong because the model is inadequate or more limited than the use being made of it in the argument. In other words, although the model is similar in the intended ways to the thing modeled and has the properties attributed to it, we cannot extend this attribution to the thing modeled. In this case the model is being misused or overextended. The arguer is trying to derive more from the model than it is capable of giving. Overextension of a model is the most interesting and complex way for analogical reasoning to go wrong.

Clearly just from the fact that M is a model of S (that is, M is similar to S in the intended ways) and M has property P, it does not follow that S has property P. Unless there is an exact correspondence between M and S, there will be differences between them, and usually a large number of differences. P might be one of those features of the model that does not correspond to any feature of the thing being modeled. To conclude that the thing modeled has P because the model has P, we must be able to extend the correspondence schema to include P. Overextension of a model occurs when the correspondence schema cannot be extended to include P.

Consider again how a map works. Some features of the map are representative of features of the territory and others are not. For example, a perfectly good map that shows, say, airline routes might represent cities by dots. It would certainly be a mistake to conclude that the cities are circular because the dots that represent them on the map are circular. This would be an overextension of the correspondence, a faulty assumption that there is a correspondence beyond the point where the correspondence ceases.

An analogical argument can be undermined if we can give good reasons to think that it involves overextension of a model. Consider how such a criticism might work in the following analogical argument:

The human body is a model of a nation.

The human body only functions properly when the brain controls the activities of the rest of the body.

_____

So the nation only functions properly when the government controls the activities of the rest of the population.

Let us assume that we accept the premises—we agree that an individual human is a model of a nation (but this does not mean that there is an exact correspondence) and that a human only functions well when the brain controls the activities of the rest of the body. We could still reject the conclusion, because we could deny that the correspondence between an individual human and a nation can be extended that far.[3]

What reasons could we cite? As stated earlier, many differences exist between an individual human and a nation. Not all of these differences are relevant, however. For example, the fact that the body is composed of many more cells than there are people in the nation is not relevant to questions of control. On the other hand, some of the other differences cited would be relevant. The fact that citizens, unlike individual cells, have interests and desires of their own may be enough of a difference to undermine the argument. This difference raises questions about how far the correspondence between a human and a nation can be extended. We can agree that humans and nations are similar in that each is made up of a vast number of separate but interdependent "units" (cells in the one case, people in the other) and that something is needed in each case to coordinate the activities of the units (the brain and the government). But we could say that the nature of the units is so different in each case that the nature of the coordination would have to be immensely different. For example, the coordination by the government would depend (or at least should depend) on cooperation and the sharing of common goals, and on compromise and negotiation when there are conflicts. To think of cells in these ways would be absurd. Here we have given grounds for supposing that the correspondence cannot be extended to the point required for the argument. People are just too different from cells to support inferences about how they should be governed from facts about the way the brain works.

ANALOGIES IN LOGIC

In Chapter 4 on validity and soundness of arguments, two methods of determining the validity of arguments were given. Both were based on analogical reasoning using constructed models. When we are given an argument, we can determine that the argument is invalid if there is another argument of the same form whose premises are true and conclusion is false.[4] Another way to say this is: An argument is invalid if we can find a substitution instance of the argument that has true premises and a false conclusion. This substitution instance or other argument of the same form is a constructed model. The other way of determining validity was drawing

---

[3] Whether we would want to reject the conclusion is another issue. A lot depends on what is meant by "control." We would certainly agree that the government should coordinate the activities of the rest of the population. "Control" has a much more authoritarian meaning than "coordinate." I would certainly resist the contention that the government should control the population the way the brain controls the body.

[4] Recall that for an argument to be valid it must be the case that it is impossible for the premises to be true and the conclusion false.

circles. If we can draw circles accurately picturing the premises without automatically picturing the conclusion, then the argument is invalid. These pictures are constructed models of the arguments.

Let us see more formally how using substitutions works. Example 1 from exercise 4.2 was designed to show that the following argument is invalid:

A

> All shrimps are toadstools.
>
> No wallabies are shrimps.
> _____
>
> Therefore no wallabies are toadstools.

This argument was shown to be invalid by the following argument of the same form with true premises and false conclusion.

B

> All poodles are dogs. (true)
>
> No beagles are poodles. (true)
> _____
>
> Therefore no beagles are dogs. (false)

The argument labeled B is being used as a model of the argument labeled A. Our analogical reasoning is this:

> Argument B is a model of argument A.
>
> Argument B is invalid.
> _____
>
> So argument A is invalid.

Argument B is a model of argument A in that it does have the intended similarity to argument A—they both do have the same form (i.e., logical structure), and this form could be set out in detail as we did in working the exercise. Besides the similarity of form between the arguments there are many irrelevant differences—for example, the content.

This analogy works because we know that argument B is invalid (its invalidity is evident from its true premises and false conclusion) and we know that validity and invalidity depend only on form. The correspondence schema can be extended from corresponding forms to validity and invalidity.

Setting out the method of drawing circles as a formal analogical argument would be more complicated, but the idea is that the drawing captures or exhibits the form of the argument in a particularly simple and evident way. Certain features of the drawing will correspond to features of the argument, from which we can determine its validity or invalidity.

The use of analogies such as these could go wrong if the argument that is being used as a model does not have the same form as the modeled argument (i.e., they do not have the intended similarity), or the determination of the model's validity or invalidity is wrong. Furthermore, we could go wrong by overextending the model. For example, one argument could be a model of another in that it has the same form as the other, yet the model could be sound and the modeled argument unsound. The fact that two arguments have the same form and one is sound does not mean that the other is sound. Soundness depends on more than just form.

SUMMARY

Analogical reasoning is based on similarities. The most interesting and widely used similarities are similarities in structure. If one thing—the model—is similar to another—the thing modeled, we can draw conclusions about the thing modeled from our knowledge of the model. There are natural models and constructed models, but the principles of reasoning when using them are the same. An argument from analogy is based on the correspondence schema between the model and the thing modeled. For the argument to work (1) the model must actually be similar in the intended ways to the thing modeled, (2) the model must have the features attributed to it in the argument, and (3) we must be able to extend the correspondence to include the feature being attributed to the thing modeled. To criticize the argument, one of the premises must be questioned or a difference between the model and the thing modeled that is sufficient to undermine the extending of the correspondence must be found.

EXERCISE 13.1

The following exercises involve analogies. Carefully consider each analogy in terms of the concepts described in the chapter. Answer any questions.

★   1. Consider an analogy between a (living) human body and a machine—say an automobile—where the machine is a model of the human body. What would correspond to the fuel of the machine? What would correspond to the exhaust? To the carburetor? To the radiator? To the fuel filter? What about the pistons, wheels, and drive shaft? What is one interesting and important conclusion that you can draw about the human body on the basis of its analogy to a machine? What are some important disanalogies between a machine and a human body?

2. Consider an analogy between a computer and the human mind in which the computer is taken as a model of the human mind. What corresponds to the computer input? What corresponds to the output or printout? What corresponds to the program? What corresponds to the programmer? What corresponds to the computer memory? What important conclusions can we draw about the human mind on the basis of its analogy to a computer? What are some important disanalogies between a computer and a human mind?

3. Consider an analogy between chess (or any similar game with which you are familiar) and warfare where chess is taken as a model of warfare. What are some correspondences? Are there any important conclusions about the nature of warfare that can be supported by its analogy to chess? What are some important disanalogies?

4. Consider the analogy between a criminal trial and a boxing match where the boxing match is taken as a model of a criminal trial. Who in the trial corresponds to the boxers? Who or what corresponds to the referee? Are there any other interesting correspondences between a boxing match and a criminal trial? What are some important differences or disanalogies? Are there interesting or important conclusions to be drawn about criminal trials on the basis of the analogy with a boxing match?

5. Consider the analogy between the rules of a game such as football and our legal system where the rules of the game are taken as a model of the legal system. What are some interesting correspondences between the rules of a game and a legal system? Are there any important disanalogies? Does this analogy shed any light on the nature of the legal system?

★   6.   Consider the analogy between vision and knowledge where vision is taken as a model of knowledge. What are some interesting correspondences between vision and knowledge? Does this analogy shed any light on the nature of knowledge? What are some important disanalogies between vision and knowledge?

7.   There is an analogy between the operation of addition of integers (the integers include the positive and negative whole numbers and zero) and the operation of multiplication of integers. Take addition as a model of multiplication. What points of correspondence can you think of? Where does the correspondence break down?

8.   Consider an analogy between music and language where music is taken as a model of language. What are some important points of correspondence between music and language? What is the key point of divergence between music and language where the correspondence breaks down? Does using music as a model of language shed any light on the nature of language? Could this analogy be reversed—that is, could language be usefully used as model of music? If so, what light would it shed on the nature of music?

9. This drawing represents a cocktail party at a given moment in time. The boxes represent men; the circles represent women. All of the people at the party are represented (i.e., there were twelve people at the party). Married couples are numbered the same, so, for example, man 1 is married to woman 1. People connected by lines are conversational partners at this particular moment. Suppose that a person can speak to two people at once but cannot listen to two people at once. Let us also suppose that no one can listen and speak at the same time.

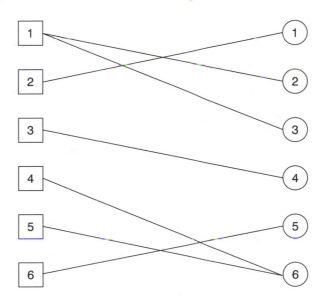

List several things about the party that you can tell from this model. List several things that you cannot tell about the party from the model.

10. This drawing represents courses and prerequisites (note that it is exactly the same drawing as in question 9). Circles represent upper-level courses; boxes represent lower-level courses. Lines connect courses with prerequisites. A lower-level course cannot require an upper-level course. Departments are numbered 1 through 6. Courses with the same number are in the same department. (These are not all the courses given by these departments, but all of the prerequisites of these twelve courses are given here.)

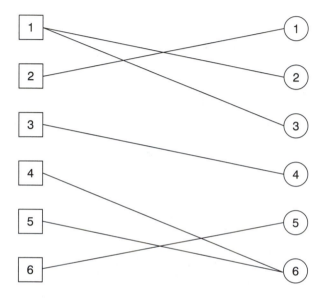

Which course has the most prerequisites? Which course is most required? What else can you tell from this model? What are some things that you cannot tell? What interesting fact about the use of models can you conclude from questions 9 and 10?

EXERCISE 13.2

Evaluate the following analogical arguments by taking the following steps: State what the model is. State what the thing modeled is. List several similarities and several differences between the model and the thing modeled. State which, if any, of the differences you listed are relevant to showing that the correspondence has been overextended. State which, if any, of the premises seem to be implausible or false. State why.

★   1.   Whenever I play my computer poker game, I win a lot of "money." So if I play real poker at the casino, I'll win a lot of money.

2.   The human mind is like a computer. And like a computer the mind can always be reprogrammed to process information in a new way.

3.   A business is like a family. So just like in a family where the father is the leader and wants what's best for all, so also in a business the CEO is the leader and wants what's best for the employees.

4. Carrying a [destination] sign when [hitchhiking] is a lot like going to college. Even though deep down inside it may not mean a thing, it's a convenient way of explaining to people what you're up to.

Ken Hicks, The Complete Hitchhiker

★　5. Learning reasoning is like learning arithmetic. All you're learning about is how to manipulate signs and symbols. You'll never get to the really important ideas that way.

6. Taking steroids is like putting horsepower-boosting additives in your gas—you get more power out of your engine. How can you lose?

7. Just like a watch requires a watchmaker, so the universe requires a maker or creator.

8. The earth including the atmosphere is like a living organism. And just as we should have special regard for living organisms, we should have special regard for the earth.

9. The earth is your mother! (Seen on a bumper sticker.)

10.   Ideas and pictures are like maps, so if maps are constructed analogies, then ideas and pictures are, too.

11.   Warfare in the nuclear age is a no-win proposition. Since I cannot say "Deal me out," I am going to join those who are working to freeze, and eventually reduce, nuclear warheads.

Time, February 21, 1983

12.   God is like Santa Claus for grown-ups. And just like Santa is a myth, so is God.

EXERCISE 13.3

ANALOGIES IN PHILOSOPHY

Each example in this exercise contains a use of analogy in philosophy. Each is brilliant in its own way and at the same time presents difficulties of interpretation and comprehension. I have suggested questions about the passages to help guide your thinking. (For other interesting analogical arguments, see exercise 15.3, question 4, and exercise 16.1, question 5.)

1.   The first passage is from *Dialogues Concerning Natural Religion* by David Hume, an eighteenth-century British philosopher.

> Look round the world: Contemplate the whole and every part of it: You will find it to be nothing but one great machine, subdivided into an infinite number of lesser machines, which again admit of subdivisions, to a degree beyond what human senses and faculties can trace and explain. All these various machines, and even their most minute parts, are adjusted to each other with an accuracy, which ravishes into admiration all men, who have ever contemplated them. The curious adapting of means to ends, throughout all nature, resembles exactly, though it much exceeds, the productions of human contrivance; of human design, thought, wisdom and intelligence. Since therefore the effects resemble each other, we are led to infer, by all the rules of analogy, that the causes also resemble; and that the Author of nature is somewhat similar to the mind of man; though possessed of much larger faculties, proportioned to the grandeur of the work, which he has executed.

Who is the "Author of nature"?

This analogy is offered by Cleanthes, one of the fictional participants in the dialogues. It is pretty clear that Hume does not accept the argument. Philo, another participant, says in reply:

> If we see a house, Cleanthes, we conclude, with the greatest certainty, that it had an architect or builder; because this is precisely that species of effect, which we have experienced to proceed from that species of cause. But surely you will not affirm, that the universe bears such a resemblance to a house, that we can with the same certainty infer a similar cause, or that the analogy is here entire and perfect. The dissimilitude is so striking, that the utmost you can here pretend to is a guess, a conjecture, a presumption concerning similar cause.

Questions: Note that Philo is basing his criticism of Cleanthes' analogy on the huge differences between a house (which we know has an intelligent maker) and the universe. In other words, he is arguing that Cleanthes has overextended the analogy. Do you think that Philo is right in his criticism of Cleanthes? Why? Why not?

★ 2.   This passage is from *Philosophical Investigations* by Ludwig Wittgenstein. Wittgenstein was a twentieth-century philosopher who was very interested in language.

> . . . [A]sk yourself whether our language is complete;—whether it was so before the symbolism of chemistry and the notation of . . . calculus were incorporated in it; for these are, so to speak, suburbs of our language. (And how many houses or streets does it take before a town begins to be a town?) Our language can be seen as an ancient city: a maze of little streets and squares, of old and new houses, and of houses with additions from various periods; and this surrounded by a multitude of new boroughs with straight regular streets and uniform houses.

Questions: What is the model here and what is the thing modeled? What is Wittgenstein's point in saying that the symbolism of chemistry and the notation of calculus are suburbs? What would the houses correspond to? What would be analogous to the downtown part of the city? What is analogous to the new sections of the city with straight streets and uniform houses? Why straight streets and uniform houses? What is the point that Wittgenstein is trying to make?

3.   This passage is from *The Republic* by Plato. Here Socrates is talking to Glaucon.

> And so, after much tossing, we have reached land, and are fairly agreed that the same principles which exist in the state exist also in the individual, and that they are three in number.
>
> Exactly.
>
> Must we not then infer that the individual is wise in the same way, and in virtue of the same quality which makes the state wise?
>
> Certainly.
>
> Also that the same quality which constitutes courage in the state constitutes courage in the individual, and that both the state and the individual bear the same relation to all the other virtues?
>
> Assuredly.
>
> And the individual will be acknowledged by us to be just in the same way in which the state is just?
>
> That follows, of course.
>
> We cannot but remember that the justice of the state consisted in each of the three classes doing the work of its own class?
>
> We are not very likely to have forgotten, he said.
>
> We must recollect that the individual in whom the several qualities of his nature do their own work will be just, and will do his own work?
>
> Yes, he said, we must remember that too.
>
> And ought not the rational principle, which is wise, and has the care of the whole soul, to rule, and the passionate or spirited principle to be the subject and ally?

Questions: Again we see the analogy between an individual person and the nation. Set out Plato's argument formally as an analogical argument. It would be premature to judge the analogy without reading the entire *Republic,* because the book is an extended analogical argument whose core is captured in this passage.

4. The following short passage is from *Word and Object* by W. V. O. Quine, a philosopher and logician who taught at Harvard for many years. Quine is using an analogy proposed by Otto Neurath, an Austrian philosopher. Many think Neurath's analogy is especially insightful and fruitful.

    > Neurath has likened science to a boat which, if we are to rebuild it, we must rebuild plank by plank while staying afloat in it.

    Questions: What is the model here and what is the thing modeled? What corresponds to the planks? What corresponds to or is meant by "staying afloat in it"? By "rebuilding it"? Why must we rebuild it while staying afloat in it?

5. The following is from a famous passage from *The Genealogy of Morals* by Friedrich Nietzsche, an important nineteenth-century German philosopher.

    > . . . [L]et us guard against the snares of such contradictory concepts as "pure reason," "absolute spirituality," "knowledge in itself": these always demand that we should think of an eye that is completely unthinkable, an eye turned in no particular direction, in which the active and interpreting forces, through which alone seeing becomes seeing *something,* are supposed to be lacking; these always demand of the eye an absurdity and a nonsense. There is *only* a perspective seeing, *only* a perspective "knowing"; and the *more* affects we allow to speak about one thing, the *more* eyes, different eyes, we can use to observe one thing, the more complete will our "concept" of this thing, our "objectivity," be.

    Question: This is the inspiration for exercise 13.1, question 6. The model is vision, the thing modeled is knowledge. What is the point that Nietzsche is trying to make about knowledge on the basis of its analogy with seeing?

6. This passage is from *The Human Use of Human Beings* published in 1950 by Norbert Wiener. Norbert Wiener was professor of mathematics at MIT and was one of the founders of the science of cybernetics.

> In the ant community, each worker performs its proper functions. There may be a separate caste of soldiers. Certain highly specialized individuals perform the functions of king and queen. If man were to adopt this community as a pattern, he would live in a fascist state, in which ideally each individual is conditioned from birth for his proper occupation: in which rulers are perpetually rulers, soldiers perpetually soldiers, the peasant is never more than a peasant, and the worker is doomed to be a worker.

Questions: The author is considering an analogy. What is it? What is the model and what is the thing modeled? He goes on to criticize the analogy:

> It is a thesis of this chapter that this aspiration of the fascist for a human state based on the model of the ant results from a profound misapprehension both of the nature of the ant and of the nature of man. I wish to point out that the very physical development of the insect conditions it to be an essentially stupid and unlearning individual, cast in a mold which cannot be modified to any great extent. . . . [Whereas] variety and possibility belong to the very structure of the human organism.

The analogy between the ant hill and the state is similar to the analogy between the human being and the state. Norbert Wiener is criticizing the ant analogy on much the same basis as our criticism of the human being analogy. The basic point that Wiener is making is that ants are too different from people to draw any conclusions about governments from the nature of ant hills. We might add as a difference between ants and citizens of a state that ants do not have rights against the ant colony but citizens do have rights against the state—but this is one of the main things that is at issue between the fascist and Wiener.

7.   The following is an interesting discussion by a contemporary philosopher, Michael Walzer, of an analogical argument having to do with nuclear deterrence. It is from his book *Just and Unjust Wars*.

> The problem [of the morality of deterrence] is often misdescribed—as in the following analogy for nuclear deterrence first suggested by Paul Ramsey and frequently repeated since:
>
>> Suppose that one Labor Day weekend no one was killed or maimed on the highways; and that the reason for the remarkable restraint placed on the recklessness of automobile drivers was that suddenly everyone of them discovered he was driving with a baby tied to his front bumper! That would be no way to regulate traffic *even if it succeeds* in regulating it perfectly, since such a system makes innocent human lives the *direct object* of attack and uses them as a mere means for restraining the drivers of automobiles.
>
> No one, of course, has ever proposed regulating traffic in this ingenious way, while the strategy of deterrence was adopted with virtually no opposition at all. That contrast should alert us to what is wrong with Ramsey's analogy. Though deterrence turns American and Russian civilians into mere means for the prevention of war, it does so without restraining any of us in any way. . . . [W]e . . . lead normal lives. It is in the nature of the new technology that we can be threatened without being held captive. . . . We have come to live with . . . [the threat of destruction] casually—as Ramsey's babies, traumatized for life in all probability, could never do. . . .

Questions: Walzer is here criticizing an analogy. What is the analogy? What is being used in the analogy as a model for what? What is Walzer claiming is the crucial difference between the model and thing modeled? Is this enough of a difference to undermine the argument? (For example, suppose the babies were drugged or in some way treated so that they were not traumatized or even discomforted by their exposure. Would this make Ramsey's analogy a better analogy? Would this undercut Walzer's objections?)

CHAPTER **14**

INFORMAL FALLACIES

Several important and well-known forms of incorrect reasoning are described in this chapter.

KEY TERMS AND HEADINGS

Fallacies	Argument from Authority
Formal Fallacies	Fallacious Appeal to
Informal Fallacies	Authority
Begging the Question	Fallacy of False Alternatives
Complex Question	*Ad Ignorantiam* Argument
Straw Man Fallacy	Slippery Slope Argument
Ad Hominem	Fallacy of Equivocation
Fallacy/Genetic Fallacy	Other Fallacies

Although most of the time most people reason correctly, there are times when each of us makes errors in reasoning. Certain kinds of errors in reasoning are so characteristic or striking that they have acquired standard names and descriptions. These characteristic or striking kinds of errors are **fallacies.** The study of fallacies goes back to the origins of the study of logic and reasoning, and many of the names of the fallacies are ancient and venerable. Being aware of these fallacies is valuable both so that we can confront them when they are committed by others and so that we can avoid them in our own reasoning.

We are already familiar with **formal fallacies** from the discussion (in Chapter 7) of patterns of inference. Two of the invalid patterns of inference were called fallacies: fallacy of denying the antecedent (FDA) and fallacy of affirming the consequent (FAC).

Formal fallacies such as FDA and FAC can be stated in terms of the forms of the arguments. The forms are clearly invalid and yet we have some sort of penchant for accepting arguments of these sorts. **Informal fallacies,** on the other hand, are not of any special invalid pattern of inference and indeed some of them may be valid (and even sound). The informal fallacies cannot be defined by patterns of inference. They involve other, informal features such as context, content, and audience.

More than one hundred informal fallacies have been named and studied. There is no need to learn all of these. Discussions of several important and interesting informal fallacies are included in this chapter. They are: begging the question and complex question, straw man, *ad hominem* and genetic fallacies, fallacious appeal to authority, false alternatives, *ad ignorantiam* fallacy, slippery slope fallacy, and equivocation.

As we study these informal fallacies, keep in mind that we must be extremely cautious when attributing a fallacy to some piece of reasoning. It is rare for anyone to flat out and in broad daylight, as it were, commit any of them. To claim that a discourse commits a fallacy is to accuse someone of doing something dishonorable or unintelligent. This is not an accusation to be made lightly. The recognition of a fallacy in the give-and-take of an actual disagreement or discussion usually comes as the result of confusion. We sense that something is wrong, troubling, confusing, but we are not quite sure what. To interpret a discourse as committing one of the fallacies is a way of helping us sort out our confusion. But keep in mind that to claim that a discourse commits a fallacy is always to make an interpretation and often a difficult and controversial one.

The naming of fallacies should not be seen just as a weapon in debate that can be used to defeat the opponent. And it goes without saying that the intentional committing of fallacies to persuade or confuse an opponent is dishonorable.

BEGGING THE QUESTION AND COMPLEX QUESTION

Some fallacious arguments are valid and even sound! How then can they be fallacious?

An atheist and a theist are arguing about the existence of God. The theist offers the following argument[1] for the existence of God:

Either God exists or 2 + 2 = 5.

2 + 2   5.

_____

So God exists.

Clearly there is something wrong with this argument, but what is wrong with it? The argument is valid; indeed it is a disjunctive syllogism. And the theist no doubt thinks it is sound. Even if *we* believe that the argument is sound, we still think that there is something wrong with it, and we would find it annoying if someone proposed such an argument as a proof of the existence of God.

Here is an analysis of what is wrong with it: It is obvious that the arithmetic is doing absolutely no work in the argument. Everyone knows that 2 + 2   5. That is not part of the issue between the theist and the atheist at all, and it has nothing to do with the existence or nonexistence of God. In this context, the arithmetic is pure

---

[1] This argument occurs in *God, Freedom, and Evil*, by Alvin Plantinga. Plantinga does not, of course, seriously propose this as an argument that proves the existence of God.

decoration and distraction. Let us clear it away! With the arithmetic removed, we have

God exists.
———————————
So God exists.

Now the premise and the conclusion are exactly the same. This is really the whole content of the theist's argument.

Any argument that has the same statement for both premise and conclusion is valid,[2] but it is not an argument that will get anyone anywhere in settling an issue. The argument

$2 + 2 = 4$
———————————
So $2 + 2 = 4$

is not worth much as a piece of reasoning, even though it is sound. So what can we say by way of criticism of this argument? We cannot say that it is invalid (because it is valid), and we cannot say that it is unsound (because it is sound). What we can say is that it **begs the question.**[3] And by the same token we can say that the argument given by the theist begs the question.

To claim that an argument begs the question is to reject the argument. It is to reject it not because the premises do not support the conclusion and not because the premises are false, but because the premises (or at least one premise) and conclusion are too similar. An argument begs the question when, in the context, it is worthless because the premise and the conclusion are, in effect, the same.

The qualifications "in the context" and "in effect" in this definition of begging the question are essential. Consider, for example, the important role of context. We could imagine a context for the theist's argument in which it no longer seemed to beg the question.[4] We can only justifiably claim that the argument begs the question in a context in which no attempt has been made to connect arithmetic facts with the existence of God.

[2] An argument in which the premise and conclusion are the same is valid in the technical sense that it is impossible for the premise to be true and the conclusion false, otherwise the same statement would have to be both true and false.

[3] The origin of the term "begging the question" is somewhat obscure. The suggestion may be that instead of answering the question (i.e., the issue at hand) the answer is taken for granted. The *Oxford English Dictionary* offers the following as one of the definitions of "beg": "To take for granted without warrant."

[4] We have to use a little imagination for this. Suppose that the theist's argument occurred after a long train of reasoning in which arithmetic facts were argued to have some sort of connection to the existence of God. Here I am supposing that "Either God exists or 2+2 = 5" is itself the conclusion of some other, perhaps very involved, theological argument. In such a context, the arithmetic would not be pure decoration. It would play a role, and we could not justifiably claim that the argument begs the question. It is not important that we be able to imagine what such a theological argument would be. After all I am not claiming that the reasoning of the theist would be good reasoning, just that in such a context the argument would not beg the question.

We need the qualification "in effect" because the premise and conclusion may be worded differently or involve irrelevant material.

All lawyers are rich.

So all attorneys are wealthy.

Here the premise is not precisely the same as the conclusion, but the argument still begs the question (depending on the context), because the premise is the same, in effect, as the conclusion. They mean basically the same thing.

The context dependence of the fallacy of begging the question is important. For example, in any transpositive argument the conclusion, in effect, says the same thing as the premise. Nevertheless, there are contexts in which such arguments can be useful. For example,

If a number is even, then it is divisible by 2 without remainder.

So if a number is not divisible by 2 without remainder, then it is not even.

This argument could be quite useful to someone trying to figure out how to test whether a given number is even. To claim that an argument begs the question is to claim that, *in the context,* the argument is useless and unenlightening because it simply consists, in effect, of repeating the premise as the conclusion. No argument except one in which the premise and conclusion are precisely, to the word, the same can be said to beg the question apart from a context. This is why begging the question is an informal fallacy. It is largely context dependent.

We can think of begging the question as circular reasoning. In practice, in the actual give-and-take of argumentation, it is rare for arguers to straightforwardly beg the question by repeating a premise as the conclusion. There might be a great deal of irrelevant material that must be cleared away before we can see the circularity of the reasoning or there might be a long train of reasoning, which on careful analysis turns out to assume the conclusion as one of the premises. The following is a fictional but more realistic example of begging the question: Someone claims that Cloudy Rivers is a great blues guitarist. What is the support for that claim? The support given is that Mat Nentoff,[5] the music critic, thinks Cloudy is terrific. But now it is fair to ask about the qualifications of Mat Nentoff. In reply we get a lengthy discussion of various music critics and other features of the music scene, together with the claim that Mat Nentoff is one of the most sensitive and insightful critics. Again we ask what is the support for the claim that Mat Nentoff is one of the most sensitive and insightful critics. The reply is that Mat Nentoff appreciates the greatness of Cloudy Rivers. Here we have circular reasoning. The conclusion that Cloudy Rivers is a great guitarist is used as a premise in the argument. But note that there is a lot of intervening and irrelevant material.

Begging the question is closely related to the somewhat devious tactic of asking a **complex question.** A complex question is a question that cannot be

---

[5] The names "Cloudy Rivers" and "Mat Nentoff" are fictitious.

answered without committing the answerer to more than one thing. For example, a parent asks a teenager, "Are you going out with that jerk again this weekend?" The teenager cannot answer this yes/no question without seeming to accept the description "jerk." The parent has asked the teenager a complex question. The connection between complex question and begging the question might be thought of this way: Something that is a matter of disagreement or contention is already assumed in the question. The words of the parent already assume that it is agreed that the teenager's date is a jerk, when in fact this may be a point of intense disagreement.

Complex questions are especially dangerous when the person being questioned is not in a position to fully explain themselves. For example, Senator Joe McCarthy used to ask witnesses at Senate hearings such questions as "How long have you known that Ralph Schmedlap[6] was a communist?" Even if the witness answers "I didn't know that Schmedlap was a communist," he seems to be accepting the claim that Ralph Schmedlap is or was a communist. Complex questions must be answered with great care. Perhaps the best response when asked a complex question that you do not want to answer is to say something like "I cannot simply answer that question," and then try to sort things out, but often it is not easy.

In summary, then, begging the question is a fallacy that occurs when someone presents an argument that is worthless, in the context, because the premise is, in effect, too similar to the conclusion. In other words, what is supposed to be argued for is instead already assumed to be true in the premises. A complex question is a question that seems to be asking for a simple answer, but where an answer commits the answerer to more than one thing. A complex question by its wording gives the impression that certain things have been settled when they in fact are still in contention.

STRAW MAN FALLACY

The **straw man fallacy** can only occur in the context of a disagreement or dialogue. It is a fallacious means of countering another's viewpoint or argument. The fallacy of setting up a straw man consists in attacking a much weaker position than the opponent's actual position. When people commit the straw man fallacy, they have surreptitiously substituted their own weaker version for their opponent's real position. This move is fallacious because one cannot refute or undermine a position by criticizing a different, weaker position.

The motivation to commit the straw man fallacy is obvious. For one thing, an arguer can discredit her opponent by attributing an obviously weak position to her. For another, criticizing weak arguments is much easier and requires less thought than criticizing strong arguments. Usually, however, the only result of a straw man is confusion and annoyance. It is a serious hindrance to productive dialogue.

The name of this fallacy is an indication of what is happening when it is committed. The metaphor of a straw man suggests something that does not have much substance or weight, that is easy to push over. The real man (i.e., the real

---

[6] This is a fictional name.

position or argument) is hard to push over (i.e., refute), but the straw man (i.e., the substituted weaker position) is easy to push over.

The straw man fallacy is a fallacy that occurs frequently. Everyone of us has been subjected to the straw man fallacy at one time or another (and perhaps used it ourselves). We have all had the experience of making a claim or argument that was quite reasonable and moderate, but that we found to be misinterpreted, often willfully, and turned into something quite unreasonable and immoderate. We then have the burden of having attributed to us some unreasonable view. It gets worse if others think that we have been refuted because the straw man is refuted.

Consider how a straw man fallacy might arise. For example, let us suppose that someone is defending legalizing marijuana because the costs of jailing so many people for a minor problem is harming the legal system without benefiting society. The opponent replies: "What you're saying is that we should just legalize drugs no matter how dangerous or addictive. Just let people destroy themselves and others— basically let the country go to ruin, without any attempt to prevent it." This is a straw man. The argument was not that all drugs be legalized, only marijuana, and the claim was not that we should let the country go to ruin but that legalizing marijuana would help prevent the country from going to ruin. This may not be a good argument, but the issues it raises have not been addressed by the straw man.

A straw man fallacy can arise simply by attributing an extreme and unreasonable position to a person who does not hold it. For example, a parent tells a teenager "You can't go out this weekend until you clean up your room." If the teenager replies "You're mean, you don't *ever* want me to go out," then this is a straw man. Certainly it would be extreme and unreasonable for a parent to want a teenager never to go out. This is quite different from the reasonable view that entertainment ought to be balanced by responsibilities.

When the straw man fallacy is committed intentionally, as it often is, it can be considered to be a willful violation of the principle of charity. The principle of charity says to interpret a discourse in the way that makes the most sense. This means that when interpreting an argument we should always attribute the strongest possible argument or position that is compatible with the words used. When people commit the fallacy of straw man, they violate the principle of charity, because they attribute a weaker position or argument to someone than they could.

To claim that someone has committed the straw man fallacy or set up a straw man is to say that that person has misinterpreted a position or argument by substituting a weaker version for the real one.

AD HOMINEM AND GENETIC FALLACIES

The *ad hominem* **fallacy** is probably the best known fallacy. It occurs when someone attacks an argument by talking about the arguer, usually in insulting ways, instead of the argument. It is a fundamental fact of reasoning that whether an argument is valid or sound has nothing to do with who is offering the argument. Objections to an argument must focus on the argument not the arguer. Suppose, for example, that someone argues that deer hunting is immoral because it is wrong to intentionally kill innocent living things just for sport. This may or may not be a good argument, but it would be an *ad hominem* fallacy if someone else replied that the person giving the antihunting argument is just a sentimental weakling who only cares about deer because they are cute, has seen *Bambi* too many times, and really cares nothing about morality. Even if all this is true, it makes no difference to whether or not the antihunting argument is sound.

An *ad hominem* fallacy can arise in many different ways and need not always be insulting. It is a version of the *ad hominem* fallacy if a person makes a special appeal to another on the basis of something in their background or circumstances. For example, it would be an *ad hominem* fallacy if the hunting advocate said "You should reject the moral argument against hunting because your parents own a hunting lodge." That one's parents own a hunting lodge may be a strong psychological reason to reject an antihunting argument, but it is not one that legitimately bears on the argument.

The **genetic fallacy** is closely allied to and in practice almost indistinguishable from the *ad hominem* fallacy. The genetic fallacy is committed when someone attacks another's argument or position by mentioning the causes of the other's holding the position or giving the argument. Like the *ad hominem* fallacy, this is fallacious because it is directed at the person rather than the argument or position. Why someone actually holds a position or gives an argument is irrelevant to whether the position is correct or the argument is sound. Claiming, for example, that people are religious because they are fearful of the unknown or are psychologically disposed to accept theistic arguments because they are afraid of a cold, purposeless universe is irrelevant to the truth or falsity of religion and religious arguments.

"*Ad hominem*" is a Latin expression that means to or about the person, and what all the *ad hominem* type fallacies have in common is that they are to or about the person holding the position or giving the argument rather than about the position or argument.

As with begging the question and straw man, a large amount of context dependence exists with *ad hominem* and genetic fallacies. In the actual give-and-take of real discussions, it may be interesting and relevant to point out why someone holds a view or is disposed to give an argument. Discussing the psychological origins of a view would be relevant if, for example, the prevalence of the view is used as support for it. People have argued for the truth of religion on the basis of the fact that a belief in some sort of deity is found among all peoples. In this context, offering a psychological explanation of religious belief would be entirely relevant and not at all fallacious.

The *ad hominem* fallacy occurs when someone attempts to attack a view or argument by talking about or appealing to the person who holds the view or is giving the argument in ways that are, in the context, irrelevant to the rational assessment of the view or argument. It would, in general, be an *ad hominem* fallacy if all that was said in opposition to a view were personal things about the holder and this was thought to refute it.

FALLACIOUS APPEAL TO AUTHORITY

In an **argument from authority** the arguer appeals to the authority or expertise of another person to support or undermine a position. In general, arguing from authority is not fallacious as long as the person who is being appealed to as the authority could reasonably be thought to be an appropriate authority or expert on the subject under discussion. Attempting to support a position by appealing to the opinions of someone who had no special expertise in the area would be a **fallacious appeal to authority.**

Someone could legitimately support the claim that, for example, Descartes is one of the most important modern philosophers by appealing to what his philosophy teacher said. A philosophy teacher's pronouncements, however, on topics on which the teacher is not an expert or is not in a position to speak with authority should carry no special weight. Simply because someone is held in high regard or has accomplished things in one area does not mean that her judgments on matters outside her areas of expertise have any special weight.

In some sense, we all rely on arguments from authority all the time, because we rely on the judgments of experts. A patient justifiably believes himself to be in good health because his physician says he is on the basis of a complete physical examination. A client follows the legal advice of her lawyer. Most of us have no way of directly verifying many of the facts that we take to be true, such as that the sun is 93 million miles from the earth, that sound travels at 740 miles per second at $0°$ C, that there is a hole in the ozone layer, that AIDS is not contagious by casual contact, and so on. We rely on experts and authorities—and rightly so. There is no fallacy in this. What is fallacious is to accept someone's judgment as support for a claim when that person has no special relevant knowledge or is in no special position to know.

The topic of appeal to authority has a close relation to some of the topics we discussed under the heading of plausibility judgments. Determining whether someone is a legitimate expert or whether that person's opinion is adequately grounded is not always easy. But again common sense and background knowledge can get us quite a long way. One thing that is vitally important is that experts' opinions can be checked against the opinions of other experts. If we have some reason to question an expert's opinion, we should consider whether it is corroborated by the views of other experts in the field. A patient can check the diagnoses of his physician by seeking a second opinion. We can check statements made in one textbook against those made in another. Expert opinion should not have to be taken on pure faith.

To claim that an argument involves a fallacious appeal to authority is to claim that the authority appealed to is not an appropriate authority on the subject matter of the argument.

FALLACY OF FALSE ALTERNATIVES

If an argument gets its persuasive power from falsely assuming that there are only two alternatives when in fact there are more, it commits the **fallacy of false alternatives.** A classic example of this fallacy is when someone argues

You're either for us or you're against us.

You aren't for us.

So you're against us.

The "us" here might be some political organization or movement. Usually the argument would not be spelled out in such detail; instead only the first premise would be stated: "You're either for us or you're against us." The rest would be left for the listener to supply.

This argument is valid because it is a disjunctive syllogism. The problem is with the first premise, however. It would certainly seem on reflection to be highly doubtful. After all, there is another alternative—you may be neither for them nor against them, but totally indifferent.

We should consider carefully exactly what is fallacious in this example. It has a false premise ("You're either for us or you're against us"), but an argument can have a false premise and not commit a special fallacy. What is characteristic of false alternatives is that the false premise has a certain kind of superficial attractiveness. False alternatives can be considered a special fallacy, because people are prone to think in terms of two mutually exclusive alternatives even when things are more complicated. Reducing a situation to two mutually exclusive alternatives may be simpler and more convenient, but if the situation is more complicated, then such oversimplified thinking will lead to error.

The disjunctive premise in an argument that commits the false alternatives fallacy appeals to a tendency to oversimplify a situation. If there really are only two alternatives, then we must accept the premise and no fallacy is committed. Nevertheless, when an argument relies on dividing a problem into two mutually exclusive alternatives, we should be on our guard. We should think about whether there are more alternatives that need to be considered.

An argument that commits the fallacy of false alternatives need not be a disjunctive syllogism, since disjunctions can also be expressed as conditionals. The following would also commit the fallacy of false alternatives:

If you're not for us, you're against us.

You're not for us.
_____

So you're against us.

This argument is a *modus ponens*.

To claim that an argument commits the fallacy of false alternatives is to claim that it relies for its persuasiveness on an oversimplification that consists in assuming that there are only two alternatives when there are in fact more.

AD IGNORANTIAM FALLACY

An *ad ignorantiam argument*[7] arises when it is claimed that since something is not disproven or there is no evidence against it, it is true, or that since it is not proven or there is no evidence for it, it is false. We must be careful not to confuse our present evidence for or against a conjecture with its truth or falsity. A conjecture could be true although we have, at present, no evidence for it. Likewise, a conjecture could be false even though we have no evidence against it. Again, with an *ad ignorantiam*

[7] "Ignorantiam" means "ignorance."

argument, context and background conditions and assumptions play a key role. In a context in which we should reasonably expect proof or evidence, the argument is not fallacious, otherwise it is.

Consider how facts about the nonexistence of evidence could be used in a misleading way. Suppose that someone is concerned about the health effects of some additive—call it "additive A." That person writes to the company that makes additive A and is told "There is no evidence that additive A has any harmful effects on health." The argument would be as follows:

> There is no evidence that additive A has any harmful health effects.
> _____
> So additive A does not have any harmful health effects.

Clearly this argument as it stands is not deductively valid, but it does not seem obviously fallacious either. We reason this way frequently, and justifiably so.

The argument can easily be made valid by adding the suppressed premise "If additive A had any harmful health effects, there would be evidence that it had harmful health effects."[8] Clearly the company's argument needs something like this suppressed premise. Whether or not this suppressed premise is true is going to depend on how much testing was done, what kind of testing, and so on. If no testing of additive A has been done, then the company's claim that there is no evidence that additive A is harmful may be *true* but carries no weight. If no testing of additive A has been done, it is highly misleading, to say the least, to claim that additive A is harmless on the grounds that there is no evidence that it is harmful.

How much weight the existence or nonexistence of evidence carries also depends on what is meant by evidence. Usually evidence means things such as traces, observations, or the results of experiments. In this sense I think that it is correct to say that there is no reliable evidence that there is life elsewhere in the universe. Nevertheless, there may be very good reasons to believe that there is life elsewhere in the universe.[9] The following argument is clearly fallacious:

> There is no reliable evidence that there is any life anywhere in the universe but on earth.
> _____
> So there is no life anywhere in the universe but on earth.

Often there is no evidence against some position or view that is absurd on its face. The lack of evidence against the view in no way supports it. For example, we have no evidence that there is not a copy of this textbook at the exact center of the moon. It would be absurd to think that the total lack of evidence in any way supports the notion that there is a copy of this textbook at the exact center of the moon.

To claim that an argument commits the fallacy of *ad ignorantiam* is to claim that the argument relies on misleading use of the nonexistence of evidence or proof to support the conclusion.

---

[8] Note also we added the suppressed conclusion "Additive A does not have any harmful health effects." Since the company's reply "There is no evidence that additive A has any harmful effects on health" was to the question about the harmfulness of additive A, this is justified.

[9] For example, general facts about the universe such as that there is life on one planet and there are trillions of stars, many of which probably have planets with conditions suitable for life.

SLIPPERY SLOPE FALLACY

A slippery slope is dangerous, because once someone starts down it, there is grave danger of slipping and falling all the way to the bottom. Some arguments rely on this metaphor for their persuasiveness. For example, some people argue against any form of zoning control on the basis that if we let the government restrict how we use our land, next the government will control all use of it, we will not have any say at all about how our own property is to be used, and finally the government will just take possession of our property and kick us off, and we will end up with communism where nobody owns anything and everybody is a slave. All because of zoning. The slippery slope here is the supposedly irresistible slide from zoning control to overall control of the use of private property to the government taking possession to kicking the owners off to communism. The arguer may even assert, on the basis of this slippery slope, that if you are in favor of zoning control, you are a Communist because you are in favor of taking property away from rightful owners and kicking them off their own land, whether you realize it or not. The slippery slope argument is used because zoning is, in the general view, legitimate. The person who is opposed to zoning tries to argue against it by connecting it via the slippery slope with something we all (or almost all) think is illegitimate—taking land from the rightful owners and kicking them off.

Not all **slippery slope arguments** are fallacious. Clearly sometimes there is a slippery slope. Each argument must be judged on its own merits. Nevertheless, there is a certain kind of questionable psychological assumption behind many slippery slope arguments. The assumption is that somehow people (or governments, or whatever) will not be able to resist going further and further. Once we weaken and give up one point, all the rest will follow inevitably. We cannot stop the slide down the slippery slope. Many notable arguments against gun control, for example, rely on this assumption. Some suggest that if we ban armor-piercing bullets, pretty soon we will lose the legal right to defend our homes and families against intruders.

The very least that we can say here is that to be successful an argument must rely on more than mere appeal to the metaphor of a slippery slope. If an argument relies for all its persuasiveness on this metaphor, then it is legitimate to claim that it commits the fallacy of slippery slope.

FALLACY OF EQUIVOCATION

An argument commits the **fallacy of equivocation** when some of the words in the argument change their meanings in a way that gives the argument an air of validity even though it is invalid. Some of the crudest examples of equivocation would fool nobody, but they are somewhat amusing. For example:

Moldy bread is better than nothing.

Nothing is better than pizza.

So moldy bread is better than pizza.

This argument appears superficially to be valid. If X is better than Y, and Y is better than Z, then it follows validly that X is better than Z. Obviously, however, this is not the real form of the argument. The first premise means that having moldy bread is better than not having anything at all to eat. The second premise means that no other food is preferable to pizza. From these two premises it certainly does not follow that moldy bread is better than pizza. The word "nothing" is used ambiguously in this argument—it has more than one meaning.

Not all examples of equivocation are this obvious, however. The most insidious form of the fallacy of equivocation is when someone defends her view against objections by shifting the meaning without changing the words. In a sense, any position can be tenaciously defended by surreptitiously changing the meanings of the terms used to state the view, even to the point of trivializing it. Such a ploy certainly contributes to confusion.

For example, suppose a struggling student goes to his advisor and asks if he should drop Organic Chemistry since he is in danger of failing it. The advisor says: "Effort is the key. All you have to do is try hard enough. If you try hard enough, you will pass the course." So, encouraged by this advice, the student stays in the course and gives it everything he has—he studies hard, gets tutoring, and so on. Still he fails. When he confronts his advisor with his failure, the advisor says: "Look, obviously you didn't try hard enough—if you had, you would have passed. That you didn't pass shows that you didn't try hard enough. I said 'If you try hard enough, you will pass' and I was right. Don't blame me."

The meaning of "try hard enough" has shifted here. In the original context it meant one thing. Later it means something else. The student had the right, originally, to take the advisor as saying that it was within the student's capacity to pass Organic Chemistry. Later, the advisor seems to mean something else, since the only evidence for the student's not trying hard enough is that he failed. The advisor has defended his claim at the cost of trivializing it. In this trivial sense *anybody* can succeed at *anything,* if the person only tries hard enough. This sense of "try hard enough" has nothing to do with anyone's capacities. The meaning of "try hard enough" has been changed to equal "succeeds." Many claims seem to get their persuasiveness from this kind of shifting of meaning. For example, "You can quit smoking if you want to bad enough" or even "If you only believe hard enough, it will come true."

To claim that an argument or position is guilty of equivocation is to claim that it gets its air of validity or truth from the shifting in meaning of some key words or phrases. Good reasoning requires that a word or phrase that appears more than once in an argument be used with the same meaning in all of its occurrences.

OTHER FALLACIES

Among the many other fallacies that have been noted and named in the past some are so obvious as not to require any extensive discussion. For example, it is fallacious to appeal to force or to make threats to support a conclusion (*ad baculum*). It is fallacious for someone to try to support a position or argument by making others feel sorry for or take pity on her (*ad misericordiam*). It is fallacious to support a position by claiming that many people believe it or that it is widely accepted (*ad populum*)[10] (although here again context will play an important role). Keep in mind as well that an argument need not commit a named fallacy to be unsound.

ONE FINAL NOTE

Trying to discern if a fallacy has been committed can be a way to focus our efforts when confronted with doubtful reasoning. The names of the fallacies give us something to say beyond "The premises don't support the conclusion" or "A premise is false." In a way, they are diagnostic tools. And like any diagnostic tool, they must be used with intelligence and discretion.

The goal is to be able to analyze and evaluate arguments intelligently, using our common sense and background knowledge. It is not important that we be able to attach a label such as "begging the question" to a particular piece of reasoning. In itself the labeling does not get us very far. What is important is that we be able to discern what is wrong with fallacious reasoning and that we be able to articulate what we discern. To the extent that the names of the fallacies help us do that they are valuable.

The principle of charity plays a key role in the evaluation of any argument. Often a piece of reasoning that seems superficially to commit some crude fallacy of reasoning can with a little charitability be interpreted as containing some intelligence (even if we disagree with it). I urge you not to use the fallacies to superciliously dismiss reasoning with which you disagree. Any reasoning must be interpreted charitably. When some reasoning is still confusing and troubling, even under the most charitable interpretation, then interpreting it as committing one of the fallacies may be helpful. Keep in mind also that simply asserting that a discourse commits a fallacy is not sufficient to undermine it. A reasonable case must be made that the accusation is correct.

SUMMARY

The following are meant merely as reminders and should not be allowed to substitute for the detailed discussions of the fallacies.

Begging the Question: Arguing in a circle.

Complex Question: Asking a question that forces the answerer to commit to more than one thing.

Straw Man: Substituting a weaker argument for the real one.

Ad Hominem/**Genetic:**   Attacking a position or argument by talking about the person who holds the position or is giving the argument.

---

[10] "*Baculum*" means "stick" or "club." "*Misericordiam*" means "pity." "*Populum*" means "people" or "population."

Appeal to Authority: Arguing on the basis of someone else's opinion.

False Alternatives: Oversimplifying a situation by reducing it to two mutually exclusive alternatives.

Ad Ignorantiam: Arguing that since there is no evidence or proof for a position, it is false, or since there is no evidence or proof against it, that it is true.

Slippery Slope: Reasoning in a way that relies on the idea that there will be an unstoppable slide to the bottom once the first step is taken.

Equivocation: Using a word in more than one sense.

EXERCISE 14.1

The following are discourses that should be discussed in terms of the informal fallacies. Answer any questions asked about each discourse.

★ 1. What fallacy is committed in the following discourse? Explain briefly.

Every time you vote you are either voting for the environment or you are voting against it. A vote for Senator Mark Mywords is a vote *for* the environment. So a vote against Senator Mark Mywords is a vote *against* the environment.

2. What fallacy does Ralph commit in the following discourse? Explain briefly.

Question: How did you get in trouble, Ralph?

Ralph: Well, my wife kept bugging me to go out and make some money. So I did what she said. Trouble is I got arrested for counterfeiting.

3. What fallacy does the author of the following discourse commit? Explain briefly.

Professor Holdforth argues that we should be kind to one another and be caring, but I don't see why I should pay any attention to what he says. He's divorced and sometimes fails students. Does that show kindness and caring?

4. The following discourse is about three gangsters, Nan, Fran, and Dan. Although Nan's ploy may have been effective, she can be accused of at least one fallacy. What is it? Briefly explain. (There may also be another. Hint: Review the fallacies that were mentioned under the heading "Other Fallacies.")

Nan was dividing their arsenal (two knives and a pistol), getting ready for a heist. She gave Fran and Dan each a knife and kept the pistol herself. Fran and Dan asked her how come she got the pistol? Nan answered: "I'm the leader." When Fran and Dan asked her how come she was the leader Nan answered: "I've got the pistol!"

5. What fallacy is illustrated in the following discourse? Explain briefly.

On the Senate floor in 1950, Joe McCarthy announced that he had penetrated "Truman's iron curtain of secrecy." He had 81 case histories of persons whom he considered to be Communists in the State Department. Of Case 40, he said, "I do not have much information on this except the general statement of the agency that there is nothing in the files to disprove his Communist connections."

Richard H. Rovere, *Senator Joe McCarthy*

★ 6. What fallacy occurs in the following discourse? Explain.

Don't believe all those doomsday pronouncements about cigarettes causing lung cancer! They're mostly made by ex-smokers who want to justify all the suffering they went through when they quit.

7. What fallacy is committed in the following discourse? Explain.

   Look, there's nothing morally wrong with abortion. I went to the clinic and the doctor there said that the unborn fetus is not a person and has no moral rights.

8. What fallacy do you think the author of the following discourse commits? Briefly explain.

   If you once indulge yourself in procrastination and incivility, you will come next to Sabbath-breaking and drinking, and from thence to robbing. Once you think little of robbing, it is but a small step to murder. Once you begin the headlong tumble downward there is little knowing where you will stop.

9. What fallacy occurs in the following discourse? Explain briefly.

   That the world is good follows from the known goodness of God; and that God is good is known from the excellence of the world he has made.

10. What fallacy does the author of the following discourse commit? Explain briefly.

Mayor Wallace is opposed to pornography and wants to close down the adult bookstore on Front Street. He claims that it is corrupting and a bad influence and could lead to sex crimes. But why should we pay any attention to him? Mayor Wallace owns the biggest liquor store in town. He obviously doesn't care that some people who buy booze in his store may become alcoholics.

11. In the following discourse, what fallacy is the restaurant owner committing? Explain briefly.

Brock Lee, local animal rights activist and vegetarian, argued that we ought not to kill animals for sport, research, or food because animals, like humans, are capable of suffering and feeling pain.

The owner of the Char Grill Restaurant replied as follows: "This shows the weakness of the animal rights argument. Brock is claiming that animals are just like humans, but we know that animals are different from humans in many ways—animals unlike humans have no religion, language, or ability to reason."

12. The following discourse seems to commit one of the fallacies. Which one? Do you think that it actually does commit that fallacy? Why or why not?

Either the universe was created by a divine, all-knowing, perfectly good being or it had its inception in chaos and randomness. The universe is not at all chaotic or random. So it was created by a wonderful, divine, intelligence that we call "God."

13. The authors of this passage certainly seem to be rather grossly committing one of the fallacies. Which one? This is from an article on chronic fatigue syndrome (CFS) (*Consumer Reports,* October 1990). Is there any way that the authors could defend themselves against the charge?

THE MYTH MACHINE

CFS is highly contagious. It isn't. Although some experts believe that CFS has a viral origin, there's little evidence that the disease can be transmitted from person to person.

CFS patients are at increased risk of cancer. They aren't. There's no evidence that people with CFS have a higher incidence of cancer than the general population.

CFS has become an epidemic. It hasn't. There's no reliable evidence of an epidemic, and no one knows whether CFS cases are increasing or decreasing at all.

EXERCISE 14.2

The following are more discourses that should be discussed in terms of the informal fallacies. Answer any questions asked about each discourse.

★   1.   Consider the following discourse from a local newspaper (*Ithaca Journal*).

> The . . . [U.S. Supreme Court] ruled Wednesday that the state of Wisconsin was not liable for the injuries of 9-year-old Joshua DeShaney, who was left permanently brain-damaged and physically disabled from beatings by his father beginning in 1983.
>
> The boy's mother, Melody DeShaney, sued the department for allegedly violating the boy's constitutional rights by failing to prevent the abuse. . . .
>
> Chief Justice William H. Rehnquist, writing for the court, said the state's awareness of the abuse did not mean it had a duty to protect him because he was not in the custody of the state at the time.
>
> "While the state may have been aware of the dangers that Joshua faced in the free world, it played no part in their creation nor did it do anything to render him any more vulnerable to them," Rehnquist said. . . .
>
> Elaine Olsen, executive director of the Wisconsin Children's Trust Fund, said the decision threatens the safety of children in abusive environments.
>
> "Essentially what they're (the court) saying is that children have no protection under the Constitution," Olsen said.

Would we be justified in claiming that Olsen has committed a straw man fallacy here? Why or why not?

2.   Consider the following discourse from the *Ithaca Journal (February 3, 1992)*.

> [Vice-President Dan] Quayle is expected to propose legislation this week aimed at lifting what he calls lawyer-made obstacles to corporate growth. He has won applause in recent political speeches by saying the United States has too many lawyers; noting that the country has 5 percent of the world's population, but 70 percent of its lawyers.
>
> In an open letter to Quayle, released Saturday at the . . . [American Bar Association] convention here, [ABA President] Talbot D'Alemberte warned that Quayle's repeated attacks are "reinforcing the image of you as a person who is not capable of careful thought and analysis. . . ."

Quayle spokesman David Beckwith returned the fire, telling reporters D'Alemberte, a Miami lawyer and former law school dean, is a "two-bit politician" and "crazy."

Both Beckwith and D'Alemberte are committing a fallacy. Which one? Is this the sort of reasoning we have a right to expect from the president of the ABA and a spokesman for the vice-president of the United States?

3. What fallacy does the following discourse appear to be committing? How could the author defend herself against the charge?

> If contraceptive intercourse is permissible, then what objection could there be after all to mutual masturbation, . . . sodomy, buggery, when normal copulation is impossible or inadvisable (or in any case, according to taste)? It can't be the mere pattern of bodily behavior in which the stimulation is procured that makes all the difference! But if such things are all right, it becomes perfectly impossible to see anything wrong with homosexual intercourse, for example.
>
> G. E. M. Anscombe,
> "Contraception and Chastity"

Be careful with this one. Do not allow your emotional reactions to cloud your reasoning. Certainly Anscombe is opposed to homosexual behavior and on that basis is arguing against allowing contraception. However, consider carefully, for example, whether a sexually permissive person might not accept Anscombe's arguments as well. Think about how the sexually permissive person might reply to Anscombe.

4. What fallacy does Muggeridge (and Reagan by citing him) commit? Briefly explain.

> Malcolm Muggeridge, the English writer, goes right to the heart of the matter: "Either life is always and in all circumstances sacred, or intrinsically of no account; it is inconceivable that it should be in some cases the one, and in some the other."
>
> Ronald Reagan, "Abortion and
the Conscience of the Nation"

Reagan is arguing against abortion on demand. Presumably he would have the reader continue "Life is not intrinsically of no account, so it is always and in all circumstances sacred."

5. Does the following passage (from the *New York Times,* 1987) indicate that there was a fallacious appeal to authority in the Spanish court? If so, why? If not, why not?

> Madrid, Aug. 1 — When the trial of 40 merchants accused of importing and selling tainted cooking oil that killed more than 600 people opened here in late March, it was expected to last six months. Court officials now estimate the trial will continue the rest of the year.
>
> The defense in the proceeding . . . contends that the cause of the deaths lies elsewhere, probably in tomatoes from Almeria in southern Spain that were sprayed with a combination of the pesticides Nemacur and Oftanol.
>
> But so far, as expected, most witnesses have attributed the casualties to denatured rapeseed oil intended for industrial use but sold as cooking oil.
>
> Attention has centered on the testimony of Sir Richard Doll, the 74-year-old British epidemiologist and discoverer of the causal link between tobacco and lung cancer. He said the oil caused the deaths.

★ 6. What about this appeal to authority found on a cigarette pack? Is it fallacious?

Warning: The Surgeon General Has Determined That Cigarette Smoking Is Dangerous To Your Health.

7. The following is a passage by Wes Jackson from an anthology titled *Ecology, Economics, Ethics,* as quoted in *The New York Review of Books,* March 26, 1992. The author pretty clearly commits one of the fallacies. Which one? Could he have made his point without committing a fallacy? If so, how?

I do not object to either saints or wilderness, but to keep the holy isolated from the rest, to treat our wilderness as a saint and to treat Kansas or East Saint Louis otherwise, is a form of schizophrenia. Either all the earth is holy, or it is not. Either every square foot deserves our respect, or none of it does.

8. The following discourse seems, at least superficially, to be committing one of the fallacies. Which one? Can it ultimately be convicted of committing the fallacy in question?

Marijuana doesn't cause physical addiction, and no clear long-term dangers from its use have been documented. Therefore, the use of marijuana is not a health concern or problem.

Stephen Worchel and George R. Goethals,
Adjustment Pathways to Personal Growth

9. The following is a highly controversial discourse. Analyze it in terms of the fallacies described in the text.

> I have seen it stated that heart disease is the nation's biggest killer—killing almost 800,000 people a year.
> This is wrong! The nation's number-one killer is abortion—one and a half million each year.

10. Sometimes people can beg the question in subtle, unintentional, and even unnoticed ways. For example, the description "slave-owner" presupposes that slaves were property owned by the master. By using the expression "slave-owner," we are already in subtle ways accepting the fact that slaves were private property. If we think that a person could no more be the property of another person than, for example, stolen items can be the property of a thief, we should not use the term "slave-owner." (We could use the term "slave-holder," which suggests that slaves were being held against their will but does not presuppose that they were property.)

Consider whether and how the following terms can be used in a question-begging way.

"Terrorism"—as in calling one's enemy's actions terrorism.

"Pornography"—as in calling a certain popular movie pornographic. There is also potential here for equivocation: "Do-gooders want to ban sexy movies because they are pornographic. Our children see murders, beatings, and assaults every night on television. Now that's pornography!"

"Discrimination" — Consider the difference between calling a practice "reverse discrimination" and "affirmative action." Is the phrase "reverse discrimination" question begging? (On the other hand, people can get too focused on language. There was an administrator in St. Louis who had the signs changed to read "Bus Go" instead of "Bus Stop." This created so much confusion that they had to change the signs back almost immediately.)

"Mother"—as when we ask whether a mother has a right to have an abortion. Does calling a pregnant woman a mother already presuppose certain things that are in contention?[11]

"Rights"—This is a tough one. For example, does the expression "animal rights advocate" beg the question? That is, does the use of the expression already presuppose that animals *do* have rights and there are people who are advocating recognition of those rights? As an exercise think of other terms that

---

[11] There is an excellent article pointing out the question-begging character of the term "mother." See "The Fetus' Mother," *Hastings Center Report*, May/June, 1990 by Frederik Kaufman.

are or can be used in a question-begging way. Try to articulate clearly how the terms are question begging. Many of these are going to be highly controversial.

11.   Consider the following discourse from *Capitalism: The Unknown Ideal* by Ayn Rand. Analyze it in terms of the fallacies.

The defense of minority rights is acclaimed today, virtually by everyone, as a moral principle of a high order. But this principle, which forbids discrimination, is applied by most of the "liberal" intellectuals in a *discriminatory* manner: it is applied only to racial or religious minorities. It is not applied to that small, exploited, denounced, defenseless minority which consists of businessmen.

Yet every ugly, brutal, aspect of injustice toward racial or religious minorities is being practiced toward businessmen. . . .

If you care about justice to minority groups, remember that businessmen are a small minority—a very *small* minority, compared to the total of all the uncivilized hordes on earth.

Hint: It would seem to be correct to attribute the following arguments to Rand: (1) "Discrimination is morally wrong, liberal intellectuals discriminate against businessmen, so liberal intellectuals are doing something that is morally wrong." (2) "Discrimination against minorities is morally wrong, businessmen are a minority, so discrimination against businessmen is morally wrong." Do these arguments involve a fallacy? Think about whether it is corret to equate the "liberal intellectuals'" antibusiness attitudes with discrimination against racial and religious minorities (which *is* morally wrong). Do the police and courts discriminate against convicted felons when they put them in jail? After all, convicted felons are a small minority. And if the police and courts do discriminate against convicted felons, is it morally wrong for them to do so? It should be possible to straighten this out in terms of the fallacies discussed in this chapter.

12. This argument is based on an April Fool's prank in which Joe Porletto impersonated Jerry Brown (then campaigning for the Democratic presidential nomination). An interview with a local radio station was set up by another prankster who pretended to be Jerry Brown's press secretary. When the hoax was uncovered, the station personnel were embarrassed, but they were also angry. They wrote an article criticizing Porletto and his associates for being dishonest and irresponsible. Here is Porletto's reply. Do you think it is effective in getting his point across? Name the fallacy.

> I will not try to defend my actions or apologize for them. The closest I'll get to apologizing will be to say that I'm sorry that the people at TV News are so incompetent to have let this happen to them.
>
> The word credibility has been thrown about a lot over the last few weeks by people who haven't the slightest concept of its definition. The credibility issue has been used as a point of attack for people with bruised egos who refuse to admit their own ineptitude.
>
> Aside from the actual interview content, how can these people talk about credibility when they fell for this prank without once checking the authenticity of the fake press secretary or Jerry Brown?
>
> Letter from Joe Porletto
> in *The Ithacan*

13. This is a very difficult item. Consider the following passage from *A Brief History of Time* by Stephen W. Hawking.

> The only answer that I can give to this problem [of how our scientific theories can progress ever closer toward the laws that govern the universe] is based on Darwin's principle of natural selection. The idea is that in any population of self-reproducing organisms, there will be variations in the genetic material and upbringing that different individuals have. These differences will mean that some individuals are better able than others to draw the right conclusions about the world around them and to act accordingly. These individuals will be more likely to survive and reproduce and so their pattern of behavior and thought will come to dominate. It has certainly been true in the past that what we call intelligence and scientific discovery has conveyed a survival advantage. . . . [W]e might expect that the reasoning abilities that natural selection has given us would be valid also in our search for a complete unified theory, and so would not lead us to the wrong conclusions.

Can Hawking's argument here be plausibly accused of a fallacy? If it can, which one? Explain briefly. Hint: He seems to be saying that we will get closer and closer to scientific truth because scientific truth has survival value; but this presupposes the truth of a major scientific theory—namely, Darwin's theory of natural selection.

CHAPTER **15**

PERSUASIVE USES AND ABUSES
OF LANGUAGE

Reasoning must be distinguished from nonrational persuasion. This chapter discusses several ways in which language can be used and misused for persuasive purposes.

KEY TERMS AND HEADINGS

Strict and Literal Truth   Weasel Words
Modal Terms   Emotional Appeals

Reasoning takes place via language, but language is used for more than just reasoning. One of the uses of language that is closely related to reasoning is persuasion. Indeed, much of reasoning can fall under the heading of persuasion. We want to get others to agree with us or conform their behavior to our wishes. One effective way is to give them reasons. But reasons, even good reasons, by themselves are not always effective, because people may not be able to appreciate the reasons. The reasons by themselves may fall flat. They need to be dressed up, made appealing, before they will have the desired effect. Language has the power to enable us not merely to state reasons but to appeal to others' imagination and emotions in order to make those reasons compelling.

Unfortunately, this sort of appeal to imagination and emotions can be made when good reasons are lacking. Besides enhancing good reasons, language can be used to persuade by creating the appearance that reasons are compelling when in fact they are not. By using emotional appeals people can mislead others into accepting things they would otherwise reject.

The ways in which language can be used to mislead are limitless. The most obvious way to use language to mislead is to tell a lie. Someone knows P to be the case and says "not P." There are, however, more subtle ways to mislead. One way to mislead without actually lying is to say something that is strictly and literally true but that will be misinterpreted by others or interpreted in a way that is beneficial to the speaker but different from the strict and literal meanings of the words.

In this chapter we will examine this and other persuasive uses and abuses of language.

STRICT AND LITERAL TRUTH

Our ordinary language is extremely complex and subtle. Often there are (at least) two ways of interpreting a statement. One way is to interpret it strictly and literally, and the other way is loosely and naturally. These two ways of interpreting can be used to mislead. Typically this is done by making a statement that is true when interpreted strictly and literally, but false when interpreted loosely and naturally. Since the loose and natural interpretation is more "natural," this is how most people will interpret it. One can mislead in this way without saying something that is strictly and literally false. Being able to do this is a useful if reprehensible skill in areas where the desire to persuade is coupled with a strong desire not to be caught in an outright lie (as in advertising, politics, and law). On the other hand, for those of us who might be victims of misleading persuasion, it is useful to be aware of such methods.

It is not difficult to imagine examples where the strict and literal truth is highly misleading. Suppose Ralph's advisor asks his philosophy teacher about how responsible Ralph has been in his philosophy class and the philosophy teacher says: "Well, Ralph made it to class on time today." Let us suppose that Ralph has never been late to class—in fact, he has always been early—then what the teacher says is strictly and literally true—he did make it to class on time today (just like every other class). Nevertheless, what the teacher said is misleading because the natural interpretation of it is that Ralph is always or almost always late. Suppose the advisor now asks about Ralph's grades in the course and the teacher says: "He passed the last test. I suppose that he will pass the course." In fact, it is late in the semester; there have been four tests, and Ralph has gotten an "A+" on each of them. Certainly what the teacher said is literally true—Ralph did pass the last test (and the teacher does suppose that Ralph will pass the course)—but, again, it is highly misleading. The teacher has managed to give a pretty grim impression of Ralph (who always comes on time and has an A+ average) even though the teacher has said nothing that is not strictly true.[1] Examples like this can be multiplied indefinitely.

It would be merely pedantic to point out that the truth can mislead (and falsity be correct) were it not for the fact that these effects are used by advertisers, politicians, and others in ways that are harmful. In earlier chapters we have seen

---

[1] It is equally possible to tell the truth by stating something that is strictly false. After a Thanksgiving dinner my mother and my aunt were in the kitchen. My mother was holding a large bowl of carrots. She asked my aunt: "Can you freeze carrots?" The strict and literal truth is, of course, that you *can* freeze carrots. Just put them in the freezer. They'll freeze. My aunt, who is a very truthful person, answered "No, you can't." I doubt that the strict truth ever even occurred to her or would to most people.

Likewise, I do not think that someone who says something like "Everyone knows that baseball is the national pastime" has lied even though they know that it is not strictly true that *everyone* knows that.

several examples of statements that are strictly and literally true but give a misleading impression. Most of these were derived from advertisements. For example, "No aspirin gets into the bloodstream faster than Zonk aspirin." Assuming that every aspirin gets into the bloodstream at the same speed (which is not all that unlikely), this statement is strictly and literally true. None is faster than Zonk because they all get in at the same speed. Nevertheless, it is misleading because it gives the impression that Zonk is faster in getting into the bloodstream than other aspirins. In fact, it takes a bit of reflection to realize that that is not what is being directly claimed. The careful wording is the result of truth-in-advertising requirements. Advertisers realize that what is true, in the sense of strictly and literally true, can be misleading in a way that is advantageous to them and at our expense, at least if we want to base our purchases on rational consideration of information.

Advertisers also say things that are incomplete. The words can be completed in one way if they are challenged for truth, but would naturally be completed in another way by the consumer. For example, printed across the box in which HomeCookin cookies are packaged we find printed in bold letters: "50% LESS SUGAR!!!" In some sense this claim is meaningless because, even assuming it is the cookies that have 50% less sugar, we are not told 50% less than what. Without a completion of the comparison, we have no idea what the claim is. If challenged, the manufacturer could assert that it did not claim anything false because the words could be completed in many ways that would make them true. For example, HomeCookin cookies do have 50% less sugar—50% less sugar than pure honey (for example). Most people reading the words "50% less sugar" will assume that the manufacturer is claiming that HomeCookin cookies have 50% less sugar than other cookies or than they used to have, but the manufacturer has never claimed this.

Not all examples of using the strict and literal truth to mislead are as simplistic as the ones we have just been considering. The following passage, written by Andrew Hacker, a highly respected social scientist, merits close scrutiny:

> Conservatives have always known that they can win only if they raise issues that will divert attention from their solicitude for the rich. During Ronald Reagan's two terms, the Edsalls point out, the real income of American workers fell by 8 percent, while the compensation of corporate chairmen grew by 76 percent.[2]

In this passage, Hacker is citing someone else's data (the Edsalls'), but not many readers will check the original, so let us consider just the claim that "During Ronald Reagan's two terms, . . . the real income of American workers fell by 8 percent, while the compensation of corporate chairmen grew by 76 percent." Even if this claim is strictly and literally true, it is far from clear what it implies. For one thing, the comparison is between "real income" of workers and "compensation" of CEOs. The least charitable, but still possible, interpretation is that workers' income is adjusted for inflation (this is the meaning of "real") but the CEOs compensation is not, in which case the real income of CEOs could have gone down more than 8% during the period. Even assuming that everything is adjusted for inflation, it is not at all

---

[2] Andrew Hacker, "Playing the Racial Card," *New York Review of Books,* October 24, 1991, p. 15.

clear that income is comparable to compensation. Compensation may include such things as benefits and options, which are not included in income. Furthermore, there are other problems with Hacker's claim. For example, there are millions of workers and only a handful of CEOs, so a few outliers such as software tycoons, who have immense compensation packages, could grossly skew the figures. Also, there may have been many increased opportunities during the Reagan era for part-time, handicapped, and retirement-age workers, all of whom may have lower incomes than other workers, thus bringing down the average income for all workers. So, at least in that case, declining average income for all workers would not reflect "solicitude for the rich," but just the opposite—solicitude for the disadvantaged by having more job opportunities for part-time, handicapped, and elderly workers. These problems mean that it is impossible to take Hacker's claim "at face value," which is not to say that it is false.

Modal terms that express possibility such as "can," "might," "may," and "possibly" can be used to make statements that strictly and literally assert very little but seem to say a lot. For example, the WildCard Widget Company blares out in its ads: "WildCard widgets are made to last and last! WildCard widgets are made of the finest materials. In fact, your WildCard widget may be the last widget you will ever need to buy!" There is a big difference between claiming that your WildCard widget *will* be the last widget you will ever need to buy and claiming that it *may* be the last widget you will ever need to buy. Clearly the impression the company is trying to give is that WildCard widgets are so durable that they do not need to be replaced during an average human life span. If they actually said this, it would indeed be an impressive claim. On the other hand, we should not be impressed by the claim "Your WildCard widget may be the last widget you will ever need to buy." The modal term "may" is equivalent in this context to "it is possible that." Certainly it is *possible* that your WildCard widget is the last widget you will ever need to buy. Many, many things are possible, for many different reasons. Your sister-in-law may go into the widget business and supply you with free widgets, you may win a contest with a prize of free widgets for life, or you may die unexpectedly before you need another widget. So certainly it is true, strictly and literally, that your WildCard widget may be the last widget you will ever need to buy, but this says absolutely nothing about the durability of WildCard widgets.

The term "may" is used as a **weasel word**[3] in the WildCard widget example. A weasel word is a word that is used to hedge a claim. The idea is to say something very narrow and cautious while seeming to say something important and impressive. Advertisements offer us the most striking examples of the use of weasel words, but weasel words are widely used in all sorts of writing. Look again at example 9 in exercise 2.5 (a passage from *Consumer Reports* about the health effects of second-hand smoke). There are four weasel words in this passage. One phrase in the passage is especially troublesome—"possible risk." In fact, the last sentence of the passage, leaving out "a nuisance to many and," says the following: "[Secondhand tobacco smoke] can be . . . a possible risk to some people with chronic illness." This

---

[3] The basis for the use of the term "weasel" is that the weasel is supposed to be a cunning, sneaky animal.

is so full of weasel words as to be almost meaningless. What a risk is is pretty clear. Something is a risk if it is likely to cause harm. But what, then, is a "possible risk"? A possible risk is something that is possibly likely to cause harm. But now meaningfulness is fast disappearing, because we have no clear idea of what it means to say that something is possibly likely to cause harm. When "can" is added, all sense disappears. To say that something can be a possible risk is to say that it has the capacity to be possibly likely to cause harm, which makes virtually no sense. And yet the statement "Secondhand tobacco smoke can be a possible risk to some people with chronic illness" seemed to be saying something important. It would certainly be misleading if we got the impression that this sentence is saying that secondhand tobacco smoke is bad for people with chronic illness. It says no such thing (which does not mean that secondhand smoke is not bad for people with chronic illness).

Modal terms have legitimate and vital uses, and statements often do need hedging in order to be accurate (recall the remarks about revising generalizations in Chapter 9). Indeed, I have used many modal terms in the explanations in this text. There is nothing wrong with attempting to be careful when everything is above board. It is far more responsible to hedge one's statements carefully than it is to make rash and unjustified claims. Being careful and responsible should, however, be contrasted with using modal terms to mislead. How would it be if I had trumpeted: "Reasoning may be the most important skill in your life. It can mean the difference between success and failure, happiness and unhappiness. This text may be the best bargain you will ever get!"? Such a use of modal terms in seemingly puffed up claims that strictly and literally say very little would be irresponsible at best.

The point of the foregoing considerations is not to hurl condemnations. We cannot always be absolutely sure that there was intent to mislead or that the statements are in fact misleading. For example, it is not clear that Hacker in the comparison between workers and CEOs intended to mislead, or even that his claim is actually misleading. Likewise, we cannot be certain that the claim "No aspirin gets into the bloodstream faster than Zonk aspirin" is misleading. After all, Zonk aspirin may get into the bloodstream faster than any other aspirin. Most of us do not know enough about economics or human physiology to judge any of these claims with finality. The point is, however, that it is important to be cautious by considering carefully what a statement is strictly and literally claiming and keeping this distinct from the loose and natural interpretation of it. That a statement is strictly and literally true is no guarantee that it is not misleading. In certain contexts, such as advertising and politics, we should cultivate the art of interpreting statements strictly and literally while holding off the natural and loose interpretation.

EMOTIONAL APPEALS

An effective aid to persuasion is to appeal to people's emotions. Much of language is loaded with emotional overtones, and these overtones can be used to present a view in a certain light. Although an appeal to people's emotions does not in itself constitute a violation of the principles of rationality, such appeals are misleading when they are used to disguise a lack of good reasoning.

Sometimes emotional loading can be as simple as the choice of a word. Such emotionally loaded terms are often used in political contexts. Calling a group of soldiers terrorists is quite different from calling them freedom fighters. The term "terrorist" has extremely frightening associations. People call their enemies terrorists because they want to use those frightening associations. The term "terrorist" brings along with it thoughts of bombings, torture, irresponsible and wanton murder, and so on. To connect these with your enemies helps to discredit them. Each side wants to brand the other as terrorists and their own as freedom fighters.

The terms "democracy" and "dictatorship" have strong emotional overtones. Communist nations described their governments as democratic, whereas we describe them as dictatorships. In turn, we describe ourselves as democratic and they described us as a dictatorship ("dictatorship of the bourgeoisie"). The supporters of a government describe it as "democratic" because of the emotional overtones of the term "democratic." We feel kindly disposed to democracies. The term "democracy" has warm and friendly associations like "mother" and "apple pie."

The use of emotionally loaded terms need not be as momentous as the political uses just described. For example, it makes a big difference whether we call a movie "erotic" or "pornographic." The term "erotic" has one sort of emotional content, whereas the term "pornographic" has quite another. We speak of a team as "rebuilding" rather than saying that they are losers. To call them losers is insulting, whereas to say that they are rebuilding is not. We describe a player as struggling rather than saying that she is incompetent. The image of a team as rebuilding or of a team member as struggling is much more positive than simple incompetence. A person who is struggling is like an underdog and deserves our sympathy and perhaps help.

As we saw in the last chapter, terms such as "terrorist," "democratic," and "pornographic" can be used in question-begging ways. This is because of their evaluative and emotional content. To label something as terrorism, pornography, or democracy is not just to classify it, it is also to evaluate it and to take a certain emotional attitude toward it. We would mislead if we claimed to be merely classifying when we use such terms. Terms such as "pornography," "terrorist," and "democratic" have many layers of evaluative and emotional content that go beyond mere classification.[4]

Emotional appeals can be much more elaborate than just using a certain word. As was mentioned earlier, sometimes reasons by themselves will not have the desired effect. They may need to be sold. And selling usually involves an appeal to emotions. For example, there are many compelling reasons not to drink and drive. We can cite statistics about how much more likely one is to be involved in an accident if one is driving drunk, how much one's abilities are impaired, how many people are injured or killed each year in accidents involving drunk drivers, and the penalties one will incur if caught. All these reasons may have very little effect on a

---

[4] The situation is further complicated by the fact that the same term or phrase can have very different emotional and evaluative content for different people. For example, for some people the label "revolutionary activist" has very positive emotional and evaluative overtones, for others it has just the opposite overtones.

particular driver until we show him pictures of accidents caused by drunk drivers, interviews with parents whose children have been killed by drunk drivers, or movies of people who have been paralyzed or brain damaged in accidents involving drunk drivers; it will also help to make emotionally real the effects an arrest for drunk driving would have. (This latter would be an appeal to the emotion of fear.)

There is nothing wrong with such an emotional appeal. Using emotional appeals to help persuade is perfectly natural and acceptable where the mere unemotional citing of reasons would be insufficient. But ultimately it is reasons that must hold sway. To substitute emotional appeal for reasons is to abandon reasoning and engage instead in manipulation and coercion. Consider an analogy. There is nothing wrong with presenting a good product in appealing packaging; a good product does not have to be presented in a drab, unattractive package. But, on the other hand, if attractive packaging is used to trick buyers into purchasing a product of inferior quality, then something is wrong. It is wrong to allow packaging to substitute for quality.

In persuasion, it is the unvarnished reasons that must sway or else we have abandoned rationality. It is the quality of the product, not the packaging, that counts. An argument must be judged on its merits—that is, by how much support the premises give the conclusion and how plausible the premises are—without allowing emotional aspects to interfere. But if an argument is a good argument (such as the argument against drunk driving), then there is nothing wrong with presenting it in the best light and the most emotionally persuasive way. What is misleading is to use emotional persuasion to make up for deficiencies in an argument.

To appreciate the extent to which emotional appeal can cloud issues consider the following passage by Ayn Rand, a popular if somewhat infamous American philosopher. She is discussing the papal encyclical *Populorum Progressio* of Pope Paul VI (1967) in which Pope Paul criticizes unbridled capitalism.

> This [encyclical] is the spectacle of religion climbing on the band-wagon of statism, in a desperate attempt to recapture the power it lost at the time of the Renaissance.
>
> The Catholic Church has never given up the hope to reestablish the medieval union of church and state, with a global state and a global *theocracy* as its ultimate goal. Since the Renaissance, it has always been cautiously last to join that political movement which could serve its purpose at the time. This time, it is too late: collectivism is dead intellectually; the band-wagon on which the Church has climbed is a hearse. But, counting on that vehicle, the Catholic Church is deserting Western civilization and calling upon the barbarian hordes to devour the achievements of man's mind. . . .
>
> [The] . . . rapprochement [of Catholicism and communism] . . . is not astonishing. Their differences pertain only to the supernatural, but here, in reality, on earth, they have three cardinal elements in common: the same morality, altruism—the same goal, global rule by force—the same enemy, man's mind.
>
> There is a precedent for their strategy. In the German election of 1933, the communists supported the Nazis, on the premise that they could fight each other for power later, but must first destroy their common enemy, capi-

talism. Today, Catholicism and communism may well cooperate, on the premise that they will fight each other for power later, but must first destroy their common enemy, the individual, by forcing mankind to unite to form one neck ready for one leash.[5]

This passage from Ayn Rand is a vicious and clever emotional attack on the Catholic church. Notice the misleading use of emotional appeal. In this short passage she manages to associate the Catholic church with both communism and nazism. (Keep in mind that this piece was written at a time when the United States was engaged in a cold war against communism worldwide and a shooting war against communism in Vietnam. Fear and hatred of communism in the United States were pervasive.) She is using people's aversion to these fearful attempts at world domination to make us scared of the Catholic church. The suggestion that there is or was a conscious conspiracy between the Catholic church and the communists to conquer the world is particularly absurd. But note that she says "Catholicism and communism may well cooperate," not quite explicitly claiming that they do. The mention of nazism is likewise misleading because Rand is not claiming explicitly that the Catholic church supported the Nazis, but it requires careful reading to notice this. Furthermore Rand uses fear tactics by accusing the Catholic church of attempting world domination while she raises images of "barbarian hordes" ready "to devour the achievements of man's mind."

If we carefully scrutinized this passage, we could distil some reasoning out of it, but we would find that the rational support Rand gives for her claims is vanishingly thin. The real work of persuasion in this passage is done by Rand's emotional appeals to fear of communism and nazism, world domination by barbarian hordes, and images of necks ready for the leash. It is extremely important that we not be taken in by such emotional appeals because to do so would be to abandon rationality and to allow ourselves to be coerced and manipulated by unreasonable fears. It is no exaggeration to say that such emotional attempts at persuasion as this one of Rand's are the real "enemies of man's mind."

The emotionalism of this passage from Ayn Rand is quite blatant, but not all emotional appeals are this obvious. Evaluating persuasive writing requires that we sift carefully through the language and meanings of the text to separate the reasoning from the emotion. It is important to be able to separate the packaging from the product.

---

[5] Ayn Rand, "Requiem for Man," *The Objectivist,* July/September 1967.

EXERCISE 15.1

Consider each of the following claims. Try to state how each could be misleading even though strictly and literally true.

★ 1. Three out of four doctors recommend the ingredients in Arthro-Sooth Pills for the minor aches and pains of arthritis.

2. Three out of four doctors surveyed recommend Arthro-Sooth Pills for the minor aches and pains of arthritis.

3. CompuQuick Lap-Top Computers outperformed by 80% three other lap-top computers tested.

4. Anyone can lose up to ten, twenty, even fifty pounds painlessly by following the simple and easy FAST DIET. [Compare this one with example 14 in exercise 10.2.]

5. Who says we're behind the Japanese? In a recent study of math skills, American kids came in second whereas Japanese children rated second to last.

★ 6.   SmartHealth Potato Chips are good for you! They contain oodles and oodles of vitamins and minerals that the body needs.

7.   The following is from a letter accompanying an official-looking notification sent by SweepStakes, Inc.

You may have already won big Big BIG!!! BUCKS. Don't miss this opportunity of a lifetime. Just think what you and your family can do with $100,000, $200,000, yes even ONE MILLION DOLLARS!!! Travel! Vacations! Homes! Education! Security! ALL THIS AND MORE!! WAITING IN A CHECK ALREADY MADE OUT TO *YOU*!! if you are winner. . . .

8.   At Gilbert's sale this week you can save and save—up to 40% off on every item.

9.   People are amazed when Bain's shoe store advertises that it is selling quality Wallingford Men's shoes for $27.50. The store across the street is selling the exact same shoes for $55 dollars a pair (the usual price). Shoppers flock to Bain's expecting a bargain only to be sadly disappointed. How could this be even though Bain's *was* really selling the shoes for $27.50? The claim to consider is

On Sale!!! Wallingford shoes at only $27.50!

10. DOCTORS AGREE!—New improved FinoSwede Saunas are the hottest new item in home health care and fitness.

11. The following is taken from a real car dealer ad as reported in *Consumer Reports* (April 1990).

BIG 1/2 PRICE SALE!! The Price You See is Half the Price
You Pay!   1987 Mustang Convertible - $4995
1985 Ford Ranger - $3995
1985 Olds Cutlass 442 - $5985
[Etc.]

12. The following is on a package of Kellogg's Raisin Bran.

NEW! MORE RAISINS!

13. The following is from a leaflet of the National Yogurt Association (quoted in *Consumer Reports*, May 1991).

Research currently underway suggests the possibility that yogurt may boost the immune system and that it may be useful in cutting serum cholesterol. Yogurt may also offer potential against certain cancers.

14.   The following is from a Skippy Peanut Butter ad. Annette Funicello says

No peanut butter has more nutritional value than Skippy. Skippy has half the added sugar. So there really is a difference between Skippy and other peanut butters.

★ 15.   The following is from an essay arguing for a law requiring bicyclists to wear helmets. The claim is that bicycle riding is clearly becoming more dangerous.

The number of bicycle fatalities went up from 203 in 1970 to 442 in 1990.

16.   This is from an Amnesty International broadcast on Swedish Television.

Since the 1950s over five hundred people have been executed in American prisons. No one knows how many of these victims of capital punishment would have been discovered to be innocent of the charges against them, and been released, if they had been allowed to remain alive.

17. In the mid-sixties a California state legislator argued that Berkeley, California, was a hotbed of homosexuality. He claimed that Berkeley had approximately 15,000 homosexuals. When the figure was challenged, he defended it by stating that according to surveys 1 in 10 people in the United States have had homosexual experiences and Berkeley has a population of 115,000.

[This one involves emotional loading ("hotbed of homosexuality") as well as a misleading use of literal truth. It was probably literally true that Berkeley had 15,000 homosexuals (based on the survey, although there may be some question about whether having had homosexual experiences means that someone is a homosexual—nevertheless, 10 percent seems to be an accepted figure for homosexuality), but despite its being literally true it is misleading in this context. Why?]

EXERCISE 15.2

Consider each of the following pairs of terms, which can be applied to the same things. Try to state what the difference is in emotional and evaluative content. For example, both "wilderness" and "wasteland" can be applied to the same tract of land. What would be conveyed by calling it "wilderness" as opposed to "wasteland" and vice-versa?

1. "Wilderness"   "Wasteland"

★   2. "Environmentalist"   "Tree-hugger"

3. "Pro-abortion"   "Pro-choice"

4. "Affirmative action"   "Reverse discrimination"

5. "Crippled"   "Handicapped"   "Differently abled"

6. "Devout"   "Fanatic"

7. "Jock"   "Athlete"

8. "Women's basketball"   "Ladies' basketball"

9. "Solid waste"   "Garbage"

10. "Swamp"   "Wetland"

EXERCISE 15.3

Consider each of the following passages. Try to state what terms are emotionally loaded, what sorts of emotional appeals are being made, and what, if any, is the reasoning involved. Answer any questions asked about the passage.

1.   The author of this passage was a leader of the Black Panther movement of the mid-sixties. The Black Panthers supported armed and violent resistance on the part of black Americans.

> The murder of Dr. Martin Luther King came as a surprise—and surprisingly it also came as a shock. . . . But that Dr. King would have to die was a certainty. For here was a man who refused to abandon the philosophy and the principle of nonviolence in the face of a hostile and racist nation which has made it indisputably clear that it has no intention and no desire to grant redress of the grievances of the black colonial subjects who are held in bondage.
>
> Eldridge Cleaver, *Post-Prison Writings and Speeches* (from a speech given in 1968)

Does Cleaver express approval of Martin Luther King?

When Cleaver talks about "a hostile and racist nation," to which nation is he referring?

Whom does he mean to be referring to when he says "the black colonial subjects who are held in bondage"?

2.   The author of this passage is a well-known psychiatrist who worked in upstate New York. His ideas were instrumental in the dismantling of many of the nation's mental institutions in the mid-seventies.

Like all ideologies, the ideology of insanity—communicated through the scientistic jargon of psychiatric "diagnoses," "prognoses," and "treatments," and embodied in the bureaucratic system of institutional psychiatry and its concentration camps called "mental hospitals"—finds its characteristic expression in what it opposes: commitment to an officially forbidden image or definition of "reality." The people we call "mad" have, for better or worse, taken a stand on the really significant issues of everyday life. In doing so they may be right or wrong, wise or stupid, saintly or sinful—but at least they are not neutral. The madman does not murmur timidly that he does not know who he is, as the "neurotic" might; instead, he asserts confidently that he is the Savior or the discoverer of a formula for world peace. Similarly, the madwoman does not accept with resignation the insignificant identity of a domestic slave, as her "normal" counterpart might; instead, she proclaims proudly that she is the Holy Virgin or the victim of a dastardly plot against her by her husband.

Thomas Szasz, *Ideology and Insanity,* 1970

What does it mean when Szasz puts certain key terms such as "diagnoses" or "normal" in quotes?

Szasz is attacking a certain group in this passage. Which group?

Szasz is attempting to evoke sympathy for a certain group. Which group?

In what ways are the examples of madness carefully chosen to evoke this sympathy?

How would other, equally possible, examples of madness tend to undermine this sympathy?

When Szasz mentions "domestic slaves," whom is he talking about?

3.   The following is from a speech made during the Great Depression by a leading American Communist.

Characteristic for the whole system of policies known as the New Deal is their nature as preparations for war. The economic contents of these measures are those of war economy. . . . Never before has there been such gigantic war preparation at a time when the "enemy" is as yet unnamed. . . .

International social-fascism has hailed the Roosevelt policies as "steps in the direction of socialism." . . .

But the fascist direction in which the Roosevelt policies are carrying the U.S. is becoming clear to the whole world.

Earl Browder, Secretary of the American
Communist Party (From a speech delivered
on January 15, 1934; reprinted in World
Communism, ed. by Sidney Hook)

It is interesting (and typical) that one side (the Left) tried to brand the New Deal as fascist, whereas the other side (the Right) tried to brand it as socialist. Is this evidence that the New Deal was probably somewhere in the middle and that both characterizations were attempts at emotional appeal?

Do you suppose that it is at all plausible that "the fascist direction" of the Roosevelt policies was "becoming clear to the whole world"?

Is this just harmless exaggeration (like saying "Everyone knows that baseball is the national pastime") or is it something more insidious?

4.   The following is from an essay on technology. It contains an extended analogy, which should also be considered according to the approach to analogies suggested in Chapter 13.

Ever since the eighteenth century, but especially in the nineteenth and twentieth centuries, scientific and technical discoveries have provoked a decline of the old religious, moral, and social values. . . .

Unfortunately, *man has made technology sacred*. Instead of being treated as a means to make life more human, it has become an end in itself. The objects created by technology—whose workings are not understood by most consumers—have become mysterious, the objects of a new cult. The occupation of a technician has a quasi-religious attraction. Like the priests of the ancient civilizations, the technocrats, physicists, engineers, and economists constitute a ruling class which dominates the ignorant masses by its mysterious knowledge, its power, and its high rewards.

The development of technology has given rise to a new morality. Useful research, submission to the needs of production and output, concern with quantity and efficiency have become the *virtues* of the new morality, the *technological morality*. On the other hand, disinterested research, art, poetry, philosophical thought, etc., have become the new mortal sins. . . .

As Jaques Ellul has shown very well, the technological totalitarianism which already exercises such a strong religious and moral influence is insinuating itself into our family life, leisure, and education. Technological totalitarianism dominates political life itself and threatens the liberty of the citizen. . . .

The combination of *technology-state-ideology* constitutes a *super-Absolute* which aims to dominate the world and eliminate its opponents. It is in the name of this collective super-Absolute, raised to a tyrannical god, and disregarding the profound needs of individuals, that the state formulates its plans for expansion. Like other religions, technology promises a paradise for the individual, a paradise which is no longer in heaven, but on earth, in the future.

Mathilde Niel, "The Phenomenon of
Technology: Liberation or Alienation of Man?"
in *Socialist Humanism,* ed. by Erich Fromm

In some ways this passage from Niel's essay is similar to the passage from Rand discussed in the chapter. Although Niel is attacking something quite different from what Rand is attacking, the persuasive techniques are similar. Mention some uses of emotional appeal and misleading uses of language that are common to this passage and Rand's.

5. The following is from a speech given before the U.S. Senate by Senator Bill Bradley.

The future of urban America will take one of three paths: abandonment, encirclement, or conversion. Abandonment means recognizing that with the investment of billions of dollars in the national highway system—which led to suburbia, corporate parks, and the malling of America—and with communications technology advancing so fast that the economic advantages of urban proximity are being replaced by the computer screen, in those circumstances the city has outlived its usefulness. Like the small town whose industry leaves, the city will wither and disappear. Massive investment in urban America would be throwing money away, so the argument goes, and to try to prevent the decline will be futile.

Encirclement means that people in cities will live in enclaves. The class lines will be manned by ever-increasing security forces, and communal life will disappear. It will be a kind of "Clockwork Orange" society in which the rich will pay for their security; the middle class will continue to flee as they confront violence; and the poor—the poor will be preyed upon at will or will join the army of violent predators. What will be lost for everyone will be freedom, civility, and the chance to build a common future.

Conversion means winning over all segments of urban life to a new politics of change, empowerment, and common effort. Conversion is as different from the politics of dependency as it is from the politics of greed. Its optimism relates to the belief that every person can realize his or her potential in an atmosphere of nurturing liberty. Its morality is grounded in the conviction that each of us has an obligation to another human being simply because that person is another human being.

There will not be "a charismatic leader" here but many "leaders of awareness" who champion integrity and humility over self-promotion and command performances. Conversion requires listening to the disaffected as well as the powerful. The core of conversion begins with a recognition that all of us advance together or each of us is diminished, that American diversity is not our weakness but our strength.

> Bill Bradley, "The Future of America's Cities,"
> *The Christian Science Monitor,* June 8, 1992

Bradley is clearly in favor of one of the alternatives—abandonment, encirclement, or conversion. Which one? How can you tell (he never states it)?

List some of the many examples of subtle (e.g., the pun in the second sentence "the malling of America") and not so subtle emotional appeal and loading in this discourse.

CHAPTER 16

EXTENDED AND COMPLEX DISCOURSES

In this chapter we consider extended arguments that require all the techniques, concepts, and skills developed so far.

KEY TERMS AND HEADINGS

Parenthetical Elements   Holistic Analysis
Reported Arguments

The analysis and evaluation of extended discourses that contain reasoning involves no fundamentally new concepts or methods. We use the skills we have developed so far: distinguishing premises from conclusions, supplying suppressed premises, recognizing patterns of inference, determining validity, and making initial judgments of plausibility. The main difference between extended argumentative discourses and the ones we have diagrammed earlier is that the extended ones have a great deal more nonargumentative material. The primary challenge in dealing with extended discourses that contain reasoning is to distill the arguments they contain. To do this we must be able to distinguish argumentative elements (premises and conclusions) from other elements such as descriptions, examples, remarks, and asides. Writers and speakers decorate or enhance their arguments with all sorts of comments, observations, jokes, and examples that are not strictly speaking relevant to evaluation of the arguments. There is nothing wrong with decorating arguments to make them more interesting or even more persuasive (as we saw in Chapter 15), or with offering examples for clarification, but we want to be able to distinguish the argument from the other elements. As was emphasized in Chapter 15, it is the argument alone that must ultimately carry the weight of persuasion. We do not want to be distracted from the process of rational argument evaluation by decorations or other irrelevant elements.

PARENTHETICAL ELEMENTS

Often a discourse contains expressions of the author's attitude toward what is being stated or comments on the matter at hand. For example, premises or conclusions are often preceded by confidence or other attitude indicators, such as "I think that," "I believe that," "I'm afraid that," or "obviously," (see Chapter 1). Such attitude indicators are not part of the premises or conclusions; they are not part of the arguments at all and should not be included in the argument diagrams. Likewise, comments and remarks that are not directly part of the premises or conclusions of the arguments should be left out of the diagram. We will call such attitude indicators and comments and remarks that are tangential to the argument **parenthetical elements.** When bracketing, we should simply cross out parenthetical elements, because they are not part of the argument. For example, consider the following discourse:

> Because of their[1] lower metabolic rate after dieting, people with a tendency toward obesity must maintain lowered caloric intake in order to stay thin; their excess nutrients will not be 'burned off' efficiently and will, instead, be stored as fat. On the brighter side, exercise increases the metabolic rate. So to keep trim, the obese person who has successfully slimmed down must exercise regularly while counting calories carefully—easier said than done.

Clifford Morgan,
Introduction to Psychology

In this discourse the two expressions, "on the brighter side" and "easier said than done," are parenthetical elements and should be left out of the diagram. The bracketing and numbering of this fairly complex discourse is as follows:

BRACKETING AND NUMBERING

Because of ⟨their lower metabolic rate after dieting,⟩[1]

⟨people with a tendency toward obesity must maintain lowered[2]

caloric intake in order to stay thin,⟩⟨their excess nutrients[3]

will not be 'burned off' efficiently and will, instead, be

stored as fat.⟩ On the brighter side, ⟨exercise increases the metabolic rate.⟩ So ⟨to[4] [5]

keep trim, the obsese person who has successfully slimmed down must exercise

regularly while counting calories carefully⟩—easier said than done.

---

[1] Note that the antecedent of "their" is "people with a tendency to obesity."

DIAGRAM

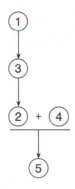

Almost any passage that contains reasoning will also contain some parenthetical elements. Although eliminating these is important when considering the argument, we should not go overboard in crossing things out. When diagramming the preceding passage, crossing out "to keep trim," "instead," "efficiently," or anything else but the two indicated parenthetical elements would be an error. Diagrammers must also exercise care not to cross out such expressions as "I know that," "I think that," or "I believe that" without considering how they are being used in the discourse. Sometimes an author is using a claim about knowledge or belief as a premise or conclusion, in which case the phrases "I know that," "I think that," or "I believe that" would not be parenthetical. For example, in the following argument, based on an argument of Descartes, the expression "I think that" plays an essential role.

I think that I exist, therefore I exist.

If we crossed out "I think that," then the argument would be

I exist, therefore I exist.

which would certainly be guilty of begging the question and would miss the point of the argument. The point is not that I am concluding that I exist from the fact that I exist, but from the fact that *I think* that I exist. To think that one exists one must exist.

Not infrequently an extended passage contains entire sentences that are not directly part of the argument and should be treated as parenthetical. Consider the following discourse:

Written histories, like science itself, are constantly in need of revision. Erroneous interpretations of an earlier author eventually become myths, accepted without question and carried forward from generation to generation. A particular endeavor of mine has been to expose and eliminate as many of these myths as possible—without, I hope, creating too many new ones. The main reason, however, why histories are in constant need of revision is that at any given time they merely reflect the present state of understanding; they depend on how the author interpreted the current *zeitgeist* . . . and on his own conceptual framework and background. Thus, by necessity the writing of history is subjective and ephemeral.

Ernst Mayr,
The Growth of Biological Thought

The conclusion that the author is arguing for is that written histories are in constant need of revision. (This conclusion is stated twice in slightly different words—in the first sentence and then later in the discourse. The second occurrence gets the same number (1) as the first, because it is the same statement.) The entire third sentence—"A particular endeavor of mine has been to expose and eliminate as many of these myths as possible—without, I hope, creating too many new ones"—should be left out of the diagram. It is neither a premise nor a conclusion, but a personal statement about the author himself.

This discourse presents interesting problems in argument analysis.

BRACKETING AND NUMBERING

⟨Written histories, like science itself, are constantly in need of revision.⟩¹ ⟨Erroneous interpretations of an² earlier author eventually become myths, accepted without question and carried forward from generation to generation⟩ ⟨A particular endeavor of mine has been to expose and³ eliminate as many as these myths as possible–without, I hope, creating too many new ones⟩ The main reason, however, why ⟨histories are in constant need of revision⟩¹ is that ⟨at⁴ any given time they merely reflect the present state of understanding;⟩ ⟨they depend on how the author interpreted the⁵ current *zeitgeist* . . . and on his own conceptual framework and background.⟩ Thus, ⟨by necessity the writing of⁶ history is subjective and ephemeral.⟩

DIAGRAM

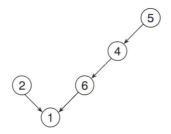

Note that number 3 is left out of the diagram because the statement it represents is neither a premise nor a conclusion (it would also be acceptable not to number it at all or just cross it out). To do a complete job of analysis and evaluation of this discourse we would also have to add suppressed premises. For example, 6 is a premise for 1 (the final conclusion), but this argument requires the suppressed premise "Things that are subjective and ephemeral are in constant need of revision."

In crossing out parenthetical elements, we are not criticizing the writing style of the author. Quite the contrary, we are not at all interested in writing style here. The parenthetical elements that we are crossing out may be interesting, charming, or essential to good writing, but that is irrelevant to our purposes when we analyze and evaluate reasoning. In crossing out parenthetical elements we are not editing the prose of the discourses being analyzed. Our task is to discern, understand, and evaluate reasoning. To do this effectively we must have the reasoning presented in its purest, clearest form. The parenthetical elements play no role in the analysis or evaluation of the reasoning, so we set them aside.

REPORTED ARGUMENTS

One serious problem in understanding complex passages that involve reasoning arises when an author presents another's argument in order to criticize it. To criticize or attack a position or argument, an author must state it or at least outline it. Unless the author is very clear, readers can become confused about what the author's position is. The reader is prone to attribute an argument to the author that the author has merely reported for the purpose of criticism. Philosophers are particularly subject to this sort of misinterpretation, and not infrequently guilty of provoking it. It is not rare for a philosophical essay to begin with page after page of elaboration of a complex line of argument that the author is opposed to and intends to attack. Only the most careful reader will understand that this is a line of argument that the author rejects.

There are many phrases that indicate that a line of argument is being reported and not actually proposed, such as "My opponents argue that . . . ," "According to my opponents . . . ," "The following argument has been given for . . . ," "Let us consider the argument offered by . . . ," or "It has been argued that. . . ." There is no limit to the ways in which an author can indicate that an argument is being reported. Unfortunately some authors give no indication, and the reader cannot tell that the author is reporting, not asserting, an argument until the author begins to criticize it. Fortunately, careful and charitable reading will usually enable one to figure out what is going on.

Note in the following passage by Douglas Hofstadter and Daniel Dennett how an argument is being reported, not asserted.

> Dualists maintain . . . that mind and matter are separate *substances*. That is, there are (at least) two kinds of stuff: physical stuff and mental stuff. The stuff our minds are made of has no mass, no physical energy—perhaps not even a location in space. This view is so mysterious, so *systematically* immune to clarification, that one may well wonder what attracts anyone to it. One broad highway leading to dualism goes through the following (bad) argument:
>
>> Some facts are not about the properties, circumstances, and relations of physical objects. Therefore some facts are about the properties, circumstances, and relations of nonphysical objects.
>
> What's wrong with this argument?
>
> Douglas R. Hofstadter and
> Daniel C. Dennett, *The Mind's I*

Hofstadter and Dennett then go on in the passage to say what they think is wrong with the argument.

The authors give us many indications in this passage that they are citing not asserting an argument. They say at the beginning "Dualists maintain . . ." This by itself would not be decisive unless the reader knows that the authors are not themselves dualists. Nevertheless, an expression such as "Dualists maintain . . ." should lead the reader to question whether the authors are describing someone else's position or asserting their own. (Precise attention to wording is important. A phrase such as "We dualists maintain . . ." would indicate that it is the author's own view that is about to be given.)

It becomes clearer that Hofstadter and Dennett are going to attack dualism when they say "This view is so mysterious." They describe "one broad highway leading to dualism" as a bad argument and present it separated from the rest of the text. Finally, they ask "What's wrong with this argument?" All these are indications that Hofstadter and Dennett are not dualists and do not hold the views (such as that "the stuff our minds are made of has no mass, no physical energy—perhaps not even a location in space") that they attribute to the dualists.

Unfortunately not all authors are as clear as Hofstadter and Dennett in indicating when they are citing rather than asserting an argument. If readers are not careful, they may end up attributing a position or argument to an author that is the opposite of what the author is actually asserting.

HOLISTIC ANALYSIS

Sometimes an argument is not stated in a discrete passage involving argument indicators, but is embedded in a diffused way in an entire essay. In such discourses, which require **holistic analysis,** it is not possible to locate the premises and conclusions in single discrete statements. The entire essay must be considered in order to appreciate what the premises and conclusion are. The conclusion (or conclusions) may only be hinted at, suggested, or offered in the form of rhetorical questions. The premises, likewise, may only be suggested, mostly left suppressed, or hinted at ironically or metaphorically. With such discourses we must step back, consider the essay as a whole, and ask "What, ultimately, is the author arguing for?" and "What, basically, is the support given?" And we must try to find answers to these questions even if they are not explicitly given in the discourse.

To demonstrate holistic analysis, we will consider in its entirety the following essay by Jeff Riggenbach. This essay requires extensive analysis that will involve virtually all the methods we have used in this text.

NEW LAWS NOT NEEDED; THEY ARE INEFFECTIVE

Houston—You'd never know it to hear the hysterical ranting of the anti-drunken driving lobby, but the gravest danger we all confront every time that we venture out on our roads and highways is not drunken driving. It is reckless driving. And the two are not the same.

It is undeniable that drinking causes deteriorations in driving skills, but it is equally undeniable that we all don't start out with equal driving skills when we are cold sober. Even if my driving is off by, say, 19%, after I've had a few drinks, I still may be able to drive more skillfully and more safely than you do, even when you don't have a single drink under your belt.

Nor are alcoholic beverages the only things that can transform a basically cautious and courteous driver into a reckless madman. Anger can do the same thing. Take a man who has just been in a knockdown, drag-out argument with his wife or girlfriend—this man is a time bomb waiting to go off, waiting for the slightest offense, or imagined offense, to send him careening across lanes, tailgating, even deliberately attempting to run others off the road.

Fatigue is another thing that can cause reckless driving.

Still another is plain inattentiveness. I have seen drivers weaving from lane to lane on freeways in both southern Texas and southern California while trying simultaneously to shave, apply makeup, tie their neckties, or brush away the crumbs they've dropped from their Egg McMuffins onto their shirt fronts.

We don't have laws penalizing angry driving, or tired driving, or absent-minded driving. We don't have field tests that measure how far drivers can hurl cups or saucers or how open their eyes are or how many grease stains they have on their clothes. So why do we have laws penalizing drunken driving? And field tests that measure blood-alcohol content?

Why don't we deal with drunken drivers just as we do with angry, tired and inattentive drivers—by moving against them only if and when they begin driving in such a way as to endanger others on the road? If we're sincerely interested in reducing the role alcohol plays in traffic accidents, there are better ways than passing draconian laws and imposing penalties on drivers who have harmed and endangered no one.

Drunken driving laws have been notoriously ineffective so far when it comes to reducing the role of alcoholic beverages in major accidents. By contrast, public-education campaigns have been extremely effective. According to the Advertising Council, it was such campaigns that were mainly responsible for a 22% drop in the number of intoxicated drivers killed in traffic accidents between 1980 and 1988.

Informing the public works better, it would seem, than "cracking down" on scapegoats.

Jeff Riggenbach, *USA Today,*
December 28, 1990

What Is the Final Conclusion Riggenbach Is Arguing For?

Notice that this essay contains only one argument indicator ("so" contained in a question) and yet it is full of interesting and difficult argumentation.

The first question we must try to answer is "What ultimately is Riggenbach trying to argue for?" Unfortunately, the answer to this question is nowhere clearly given. The title suggests that the final conclusion Riggenbach is arguing for is that new laws against drunk driving are not needed (and the title also gives a premise for this conclusion—"they are ineffective"). That they are ineffective, however, is not the main support used by Riggenbach in the body of the text, and the conclusion that he is arguing for in the text seems to be more extreme than the one indicated in the title. Indeed he seems to be arguing that we ought not to have any laws penalizing drunken driving at all. This is suggested by the question "So why do we have laws penalizing drunken driving?" Given what has just come before it, it seems he wants the reader to answer—"No reason. We shouldn't have them!"

What Are the Premises Riggenbach Has for This Conclusion?

One of the premises for this extreme conclusion—that we ought not to have any laws penalizing drunken driving—is that we do not have laws against anger, fatigue, or inattention. Set out explicitly the premise and conclusion are

We do not have laws that penalize driving while angry, fatigued, or inattentive.

[Therefore we ought not to have laws that penalize drunken driving.][2]

The conclusion depends also on the premise suggested in the question "Why don't we deal with drunken drivers just as we do with angry, tired and inattentive drivers?" On this basis, I think it is fair to attribute the following premise to Riggenbach:

> Drunken driving ought to be treated by the law like other things that impair driving ability, such as anger, fatigue, and inattention.

Then, his argument fully set out is

> [Drunken driving ought to be treated by the law like other things that impair driving ability, such as anger, fatigue, and inattention.]
>
> We do not have laws that penalize driving while angry, fatigued, or inattentive.
>
> ---
>
> [Therefore we ought not to have laws that penalize drunken driving.]

This is not the only argument in the essay, however. There is also a difficult argument suggested by the phrase "passing draconian laws and imposing penalties on drivers who have harmed and endangered no one." Together with the sentence just before the one containing this phrase and some of the material in the first two paragraphs we can distill the following argument:

> [We ought not to have laws that penalize drivers who are harming or endangering no one.]
>
> [Drunken drivers who are not driving recklessly are harming or endangering no one.]
>
> ---
>
> [Therefore we ought not to have laws that penalize drunken drivers who are not driving recklessly.]

A Suppressed Intermediate Conclusion

Although it is never explicitly stated in the essay, the main point on which the conclusions of these two arguments rest is that laws that penalize drunken driving are unfair. The claim that drunken driving laws are unfair rests in turn on the claims that drunken driving laws treat some things differently that are the same in the way they affect driving ability—that is, they treat anger, fatigue, and inattention differently from drunkenness—and that drunken driving laws penalize drivers who have harmed or endangered no one. Thus the conclusion that laws that penalize drunken driving are unfair is a suppressed intermediate conclusion supported by these premises and which in turn is support for the claim that we ought not to have such laws.

---

[2] I have put the conclusion in brackets because it is not explicitly stated in the discourse.

Another Argument Against Drunken Driving Laws

Riggenbach does, toward the end of his essay, also make the claim, mentioned in the title, that drunken driving laws are ineffective. Specifically, he states that drunken driving laws are ineffective in reducing the role of alcohol in major accidents. Now Riggenbach needs a suppressed premise to validly support the conclusion that we ought not to have drunken driving laws, but it is not clear what the suppressed premise is supposed to be. Perhaps Riggenbach's ineffectiveness argument could be set out most charitably and concisely as follows:

[Drunken driving laws are ineffective at achieving their intended purpose.]

[We ought not to have laws that are ineffective at achieving their intended purpose.]

[Therefore we ought not to have drunken driving laws.]

The only support Riggenbach gives for the claim that drunken driving laws are ineffective is some figures relating to the effectiveness of public-education campaigns. Without some sort of further argumentation, however, it is hard to see how the figures from the Advertising Council about public-education campaigns have any bearing on the question of the effectiveness or ineffectiveness of drunken driving laws. After all, the fact that public-education campaigns are effective does not show that drunken driving laws are ineffective. Consider an analogy. The fact that one medicine is effective does not show that another medicine is ineffective. Perhaps the figures from the Advertising Council show that drunken driving laws are unnecessary, but even this is questionable. I am afraid that we have to strain charitability to the breaking point to find reasonable support in this essay for the claim that drunken driving laws are ineffective. It seems that Riggenbach is just asserting it along with some distracting decoration. In any case, let us leave this issue for now and return to it later when we attempt to evaluate the argument.

What Is Riggenbach's Main Line of Reasoning?

After having gone through this rather elaborate dissection, let us step back a moment now and consider what Riggenbach's main line of reasoning is. Considered holistically, the main argument of this essay is that *we ought not to have laws penalizing drunken driving because such laws are unfair and ineffective.* Support is also given for the claim that drunken driving laws are unfair (they treat similar cases differently and punish those who have not harmed or endangered anyone), but there is no support that they are ineffective. It would not be possible to exhibit effectively this line of argumentation by circling argument indicators and bracketing and numbering statements in the essay. Nevertheless the argumentation when distilled and clarified from the whole essay is quite clear and can be set out in an organized fashion.

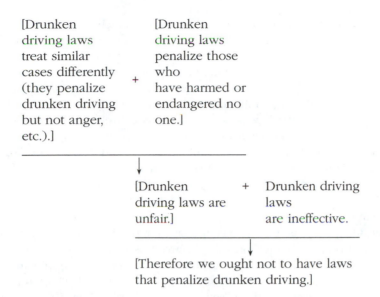

The argument also requires the two suppressed premises: "Laws that treat similar cases differently or penalize those who have harmed or endangered no one are unfair" and "We ought not to have laws that are unfair or ineffective." Notice that in our final analysis only one statement ("Drunken driving laws are ineffective") was explicitly given in the essay. The rest occur implicitly in it.

Evaluation of Riggenbach's Arguments

Riggenbach's argument with all the suppressed premises included is valid, but it is far from evident that all the premises are plausible.

The suppressed premises are initially plausible. At least initially, it seems correct to say that laws that treat similar cases differently or penalize those who have harmed or endangered no one are unfair. Also it seems quite plausible that we ought not to have laws that are unfair; indeed, this is close to a conceptual truth. Likewise, it seems that we ought not to have laws that are ineffective, although this is more questionable.

On the other hand, a key question is whether drunken driving laws penalize those who have harmed or endangered no one. Riggenbach never supports the claim that drunken driving is not in itself dangerous, although he does claim that reckless driving is more dangerous. One does not have to be a safety expert, however, to see that it is plausible that drunken driving is in itself dangerous. For example, drivers whose reaction times are seriously slowed by alcohol endanger themselves and others because of their inability to avoid accidents, even though they may not be creating them by driving recklessly. This issue is complicated, however, by the fact that anger, fatigue, and inattention behind the wheel may also be in themselves dangerous.

To examine the issue further we would have to investigate whether there are relevant differences between drunken driving on the one hand, and driving while angry, fatigued, or inattentive on the other. It seems at least initially plausible that there are. (For example, drunken driving may be much more likely to cause auto accidents, injuries, and deaths than anger, fatigue, or inattention.) If so, then Riggenbach's argument is unsound because both of the basic premises are false. Drunken drivers would be endangering others even when they are not driving recklessly merely by driving drunk, and there would be relevant differences between drunk driving and driving while angry, fatigued, or inattentive.

Unfortunately the process of evaluation is complicated by the fact that this essay contains so many fallacies and misleading uses of language. The *ad hominem* in the first sentence ("the hysterical rantings of the anti-drunken driving lobby") is particularly glaring. There is also the suspicion of a false alternatives fallacy when Riggenbach contrasts drunken driving laws with public-education campaigns, as though we can have one or the other but not both. It seems plausible that both laws and education are needed to eliminate drunk driving, not one rather than the other. More seriously, there is a fallacious appeal to authority when the author cites the Advertising Council's figures on the effectiveness of public-education campaigns. The Advertising Council is hardly a neutral, trustworthy authority in this area as would be the National Safety Council, for example. The Advertising Council obviously has a great deal of self-interest in promoting the effectiveness of public-education campaigns (i.e., advertising).

One particularly serious example of misleading use of language is when Riggenbach states that drunken driving laws "have been notoriously ineffective." The use of the term "notoriously" is highly questionable here. Although drunken driving laws may indeed be ineffective, this is certainly not as widely believed by the public as "notoriously" would indicate. Furthermore, "notoriously" has strong negative overtones that are inappropriate and perhaps question begging in this context (question begging because Riggenbach is arguing against drunken driving laws and "notoriously" already assumes something negative about them). It seems that the use of the term "notoriously" is meant to cover up the real lack of support for the claim that drunken driving laws are ineffective.

However, despite all the distracting and confusing elements, it should be clear that there is an organized and interesting line of reasoning in this essay. For the purposes of evaluation it is invaluable to be able to set out the argument clearly and straightforwardly. Riggenbach is arguing about an important and pressing issue, and we must be able to use all the tools at our disposal to advance as far as we can toward a resolution of it.

Although it is often no easy task, we must in grappling with an essay such as Riggenbach's be able to discern and articulate—and evaluate (even if in only a preliminary way)—the main line of reasoning.

SUMMARY

Extended and complex discourses that contain reasoning require careful and attentive analysis. Parenthetical elements should be eliminated. The arguments should be distilled from the discourse by separating them from irrelevant elements.

Often key premises or conclusions are not explicitly stated and, thus, a holistic approach to the discourse is required. We attempt to discern the key premises and conclusions by considering the essay as a whole. We also must consider whether arguments in extended passages are being reported or asserted. Reported arguments are not expressions of the author's own views but are arguments that the author intends to criticize.

EXERCISE 16.1

Consider each of the following passages. Attempt to distill and state the main arguments. Add any suppressed premises that are required. After each passage there are questions and comments that should be helpful in guiding analysis.

1.   The following is from an essay "The Assault on Integrity" by Alan Greenspan.

> Protection of the consumer against "dishonest and unscrupulous business practices" has become a cardinal ingredient of welfare statism. Left to their own devices, it is alleged, businessmen would attempt to sell unsafe food and drugs, fraudulent securities, and shoddy buildings. Thus, it is argued, the Pure Food and Drug Administration, the Securities and Exchange Commission, and the numerous building regulatory agencies are indispensable if the consumer is to be protected from the "greed" of the businessman.
>
> But it is precisely the "greed" of the businessman or, more appropriately, his profit-seeking, which is the unexcelled protector of the consumer.
>
> What collectivists refuse to recognize is that it is in the self-interest of every businessman to have a reputation for honest dealings and a quality product. Since the market value of a going business is measured by its money-making potential, reputation or "good will" is as much an asset as its plant and equipment. For many a drug company, the value of its reputation, as reflected in the salability of its brand name, is often its major asset. The loss of reputation through the sale of a shoddy or dangerous product would sharply reduce the market value of the drug company, though its physical resources would remain intact. The market value of a brokerage firm is even more closely tied to its good-will assets. Securities worth hundreds of millions of dollars are traded every day over the telephone. The slightest doubt as to the trustworthiness of a broker's word or commitment would put him out of business overnight.
>
> Reputation in an unregulated economy, is thus a major competitive tool. . . .
>
> Government regulation is not an alternative means of protecting the consumer. It does not build quality into goods, or accuracy into information. Its sole "contribution" is to substitute force and fear for incentive as the "protector" of the consumer. The euphemisms of government press releases to the contrary notwithstanding, the basis of regulation is armed force. At the bottom of the endless pile of paperwork which characterizes all regulation lies a gun.
>
> Alan Greenspan, "The Assault on Integrity,"
> *The Objectivist Newsletter,* August 1963

Greenspan reports an argument in order to criticize it in this passage. What is the argument? How do you know that it is being reported rather than asserted? That is, what indicators does Greenspan use to show that he is citing not asserting?

What is the main conclusion Greenspan is arguing for? What are his premises? What suppressed premises is he presupposing?

2.   The following is from a newspaper column by Elizabeth Kristol.

VIOLENCE AND VIDEO

In the past two months, I have witnessed five women being beaten and raped. In the past couple of years, I have seen a dozen or more similar incidents. I don't live in a particularly bad neighborhood, I just watch TV.

Sexploitation on television is nothing new. Nor are TV serials and after-school specials that deal with Difficult Subjects like rape and domestic violence. In an unfortunate turn of events, these have become a staple of the made-for-TV movie ("The Burning Bed" starring Farrah Fawcett, is a classic of this type). These movies are often promoted as representing the interests of women, and many networks follow the broadcast with phone numbers of social service agencies, hot lines and counseling groups. Public-interest packaging aside, these movies are easily recognized for the ratings-chasing TV fare they really are.

There is nothing wrong with trying to boost ratings, and it is certainly no sin to insult viewers' intelligence; it is quite another matter to bombard them with degrading and exploitative material. There are a few TV critics—most recently Martha Bayles of The Wall Street Journal and Tom Shales of The Washington Post—who have criticized this trend of sensationalizing rape, but the glut of movies on the subject continues.

There are two convincing pieces of evidence that the makers of these movies haven't the slightest interest in dealing with issues and have a very large interest in titillation:

- The victim is always gorgeous. Since, in truth, many homely women are sexually assaulted, and most abused wives do not resemble Farrah Fawcett, one must assume that producers feel it will be more "pleasing" to watch a beautiful woman be beaten or raped.
- The actual assault scene is usually slowly and graphically—I am tempted to say lovingly—depicted, even though these crude details have absolutely no bearing on the larger issues that are allegedly being addressed. . . .

[The author goes on to discuss and describe several specific examples of made-for-TV movies that she considers to be sexploitative.]

What compounds the inherent offensiveness of these movies is the veneer of public respectability they have managed to achieve in the media—as if to depict brutality in a realistic manner is, in and of itself, a public good.

There are real social and legal issues surrounding the abuse of women. These issues are dealt with, competently and responsibly, in women's magazines. The tremendous range of magazines ensures that articles on these subjects are read by women of all ages, races and economic groups. As opposed to TV, these articles are reaching those who have a genuine need to know—as opposed to a prurient desire to watch.

To posit, for a fleeting moment, that any of these movies bears a useful public message, just what would that message be? That it is wrong to rape, brutalize or commit incest. Is such a message really edifying? Are there really competing forces out there who are arguing the virtues of such behavior?

Only in Hollywood, it would seem.

Elizabeth Kristol, "Violence and Video,"
Washington Post National Weekly Edition,
November 20, 1989

There is a great deal of parenthetical material in this essay, but there is a central and important argument. What is the main conclusion that Kristol is arguing for? What are her premises? What suppressed premises is she presupposing? What other subsidiary arguments does she give?

3.   The following is a passage written by Mahatma Gandhi.

I see that there is an instinctive horror of killing living beings under any circumstances whatever. For instance, an alternative has been suggested in the shape of confining even rabid dogs in a certain place and allowing them to die a slow death. Now my idea of compassion makes this thing impossible for me. I cannot for a moment bear to see a dog, or for that matter any other living being, helplessly suffering the torture of a slow death. I do not kill a human being thus circumstanced because I have hopeful remedies. I should kill a dog similarly situated because in its case I am without a remedy. Should my child be attacked with rabies and there was no helpful remedy to relieve his agony, I should consider it my duty to take his life. Fatalism has its limits. We leave things to fate after exhausting all the remedies. One of the remedies and the final one to relieve the agony of a tortured child is to take his life.

Mahatma Gandhi, *Selections from Gandhi,*
reprinted in *All Men Are Brothers*

The first sentence suggests that Gandhi will argue in opposition to any killing whatsoever. Actually his position is quite different. What is it? How does he support his position? What indications are there in the passage that Gandhi is not just telling us how he feels but making a general moral claim? The final three sentences contain a very difficult argument involving fatalism. (I think it would be fair to define "fatalism," as it is used here, as "passively accepting whatever happens.") Try to state the premises and conclusion of this argument.

4.   The following is a passage from a well-known book on moral issues.

The Reverend Jerry Falwell, founder of the Moral Majority, said in a television interview: "Homosexuality is immoral. The so-called 'gay rights' are not rights at all, because immorality is not right. . . ."

Is Falwell right? . . .

If we consider the relevant reasons, what do we find? In opposition to Falwell, it may be said that homosexuals are pursuing the only way of life that affords them a chance of happiness. Sex is a particularly strong urge—it isn't hard to understand why—and few people are able to fashion a happy life without satisfying their sexual needs. Moreover, individuals do not choose their sexual orientation; both homosexuals and heterosexuals find themselves to be what they are without having exercised any option in the matter. Thus to say that people should not express their homosexuality is, more often than not, to condemn them to unhappy lives.

If it could be shown that in pursuing their way of life homosexuals pose some sort of threat to the rest of society, that would be a powerful argument for the other side. And in fact, people who share Falwell's view have often claimed as much. But when examined dispassionately, those claims have always turned out to have no factual basis. Apart from the nature of their sexual relationships, there is no known difference between homosexuals and heterosexuals in their moral characters or in their contributions to society. The idea that homosexuals are somehow sinister characters proves to be a myth similar to the myth that black people are lazy, or that Jews are avaricious.

The case against homosexuality thus reduces to the familiar claim that it is "unnatural," or to the claim—often made by followers of Falwell—that it is a threat to "family values." As for the first argument, it is hard to know what to make of it because the notion of "unnaturalness" is so vague. What exactly does it mean? It might be taken as a statistical notion—in this sense, a human quality is unnatural if it is not shared by most people. Homosexuality would be unnatural in this sense, but so would left-handedness. Clearly, this is no reason to judge it bad; rare qualities might even be good.

If "unnatural" is not a statistical notion, what other sense might it have? The word has a sinister sound to it, so perhaps it should be understood as a term of evaluation. Perhaps in this context "unnatural" means something like "contrary to what a person ought to be." But in this sense, to say that something is wrong because it is unnatural is utterly vacuous; it is to say that one ought not to be thus-and-so because one ought not to be thus-and-so! If no better understanding of "unnatural" can be found, this argument will have to be rejected.

But what of the claim, often heard from religious fundamentalists, that homosexuality is contrary to "family values"? . . . But how, exactly, is homosexuality opposed to family values? . . . [T]he existence of a minority of homosexuals in society hardly poses a danger to families, because homosexuals, as a group, are no greater threat to the lives and institutions of other people than are the members of any other group. (There have always been homosexuals; but has there ever been a society in which the institution of the family was brought down or even seriously damaged by them? No.)

Perhaps there are other arguments in support of Falwell's point of view, but I do not know what they could be. The evidence at hand, however, suggests that his view, no matter how firmly held, is not supported by reason.

James Rachels, *The Elements of Moral Philosophy*

Be careful to sort out what Rachels is attacking and what he is supporting—that is, what arguments he is reporting and what arguments he is asserting.

Try to piece together the entire main line of reasoning as we did for Riggenbach's essay.

At one point, Rachels accuses the argument he is criticizing of committing one of the fallacies named in Chapter 14. At which point? Which fallacy? Is Rachels correct?

5.   The following is a letter to the editor. It concerns gun control.

To the Editor:

Re "Treat Guns Like Cars" (editorial, May 16):

For you to disparage as "a simplistic view of safety" those Los Angeles citizens who, in the absence of effective police protection, arm themselves against the potential of mob violence to person and property is disturbingly elitist and out of touch.

Your proposal for universal gun licensing is equally so. How could universal licensing, for example, stop the black market, from which the vast majority of criminals get their guns? And how would it prevent gun smuggling from other countries? . . .

The tired old analogy of auto registration as a model for gun control is patently false. Vehicle operation is a governmentally dispensed privilege, not a constitutionally protected right. A better analogy would be the requirement of tests for sanity, criminal history, drugs, American history and literacy before one could exercise the right to vote.

Besides, in crimes where cars are concerned, we don't impose drug tests, waiting periods and bans on models used; nor do we allow the police absolute and arbitrary control over who can and cannot get licenses to drive.

Perhaps most illuminating of the bankruptcy of your views is this: despite all of the registration, screening, testing and insurance requirements, automobile drivers still kill and injure many times more people each year than gun owners do.

Where, finally, is your credibility when your own hometown, which has since the turn of the century had very strict gun registration and licensing of the type you propose, is consistently among the top crime cities in the country?

New York Times, June 8, 1992

The writer is attacking an analogy. What is the analogy? What is the basis of the writer's attack?

Attempt to analyze the letter holistically. What is the main point the writer is trying to argue for? What are the premises, intermediate conclusions, etc.?

This argument should present interesting exercises in evaluation. Among other things, you should certainly think about the cogency of the comparison of the number of people killed or injured by drivers with the number of people killed or injured by gun owners.

ANSWERS TO SELECTED EXERCISES

EXERCISE 1.1

1. Yes, it contains an argument. Circle "so." The conclusion is "Industrial growth must be slowed."

5. Yes, it contains an argument. Circle "because." The conclusion is "Greek olympians probably never envisioned winter games."

10. Yes, it contains an argument. Circle "hence." The conclusion is "It is also a study of those relations in virtue of which one thing may be said to follow from . . . another."

14. Yes, it contains an argument. Circle "show." There are really two related conclusions. One is that evolution is hopelessly improbable. The other is that bacteria are not the result of evolution.

15. No, it is not an argument. This is an if/then statement.

EXERCISE 2.1

1.   **BRACKETING AND NUMBERING**

    ⟨Marijuana is classified as an hallucinogen⟩ (because) ⟨in sufficient dosages its active ingredient, THC, causes hallucinations.⟩

    The brackets are numbered 1 and 2 respectively.

DIAGRAM

5.   **BRACKETING AND NUMBERING**

(Because) ⟨¹people with AIDS can become incapacitated without warning⟩ ⟨²they expose themselves to possible disappointment whenever they make long–or even short–range plans.⟩

DIAGRAM

10.   **BRACKETING AND NUMBERING**

(Because) ⟨¹pain and suffering are undesirable,⟩ and (because) ⟨²both human and nonhuman animals are capable of pain and suffering,⟩ ⟨³there is at least a *prima facie* case for treating all animals (both human and non-human) similarly when the infliction of pain and suffering is involved.⟩

DIAGRAM

EXERCISE 2.2

1.   **BRACKETING AND NUMBERING**

⟨¹It is important to save the earth.⟩ ⟨²It is the only one we've got.⟩

DIAGRAM

5.   **BRACKETING AND NUMBERING**

⟨¹In many ways, the Supreme Court is the worst place to win a human rights case—⟩*parenthetical (optional in this case)* ~~even when an Earl Warren is sitting as Chief Justice.~~ ⟨²It takes a large amount of money and a long time to get a case to the Court.⟩ ⟨³Even when a party wins, he may not come out with a clear victory.⟩ ⟨⁴The decisions are seldom unanimous, and a five-to-four or six-to-three split tends to weaken the impact of a majority opinion.⟩ ⟨⁵A Supreme Court decision may have a tremendous effect in the long run, but it seldom brings about immediate major changes.⟩

DIAGRAM

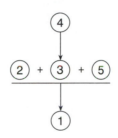

EXERCISE 2.3

1.   **BRACKETING AND NUMBERING**

(Since)⟨¹three-syllable words are harder to read than one- or two-syllable words,⟩and(since)⟨²simple ideas are more easily transferred from one human being to another than complex ideas,⟩⟨³advertising copy tends to use ever simpler language all the time.⟩

DIAGRAM

5.   **BRACKETING AND NUMBERING**

⟨¹Aerobic exercise is an integral part of the Pritikin program.⟩⟨²This contin-

uous, submaximal exercise (at training heart rate) aids in weight control⟩

(because)⟨³it enables you to burn an increased number of calories during

exercise.⟩

DIAGRAM

The antecedent of "it" is "This continuous, submaximal exercise (at training
heart rate)" or, in other words, "aerobic exercise."

10.   **BRACKETING AND NUMBERING**

⟨¹Very small babies suffer from many potentially fatal complications.⟩(Be-

cause)²⟨they have less fat to insulate them and to generate heat,⟩³⟨they have

more trouble maintaining normal body temperature.⟩ . . . (Because)⁴⟨their

immune systems are not fully developed,⟩⁵⟨they are more vulnerable to

infections.⟩⁶⟨Their reflexes are not mature enough to perform functions

basic to survival;⟩⁷⟨they may, for example, be unable to suck and have to

be fed intravenously.⟩

DIAGRAM

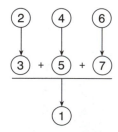

The antecedent of "they" and "their" is "very small babies."

EXERCISE 2.4

1.   BRACKETING AND NUMBERING

(Since) ⟨¹trials are often characterized by extensive court delays,⟩ ⟨²going to trial is both costly and time consuming.⟩

DIAGRAM

5.   BRACKETING AND NUMBERING

⟨¹The moral right thing to do, on any occasion, is whatever would bring about the greatest balance of happiness over unhappiness.⟩ (Therefore,) ⟨²on at least some occasions, mercy killing may be morally right.⟩

DIAGRAM

EXERCISE 2.5

1.   BRACKETING AND NUMBERING

⟨¹We need not be ashamed of our defense mechanisms.⟩ ⟨²They are a part of our nature,⟩ ⟨³they are necessary to our survival⟩ and ⟨⁴there is no one who is completely free of them.⟩ ⟨¹We do not have to be "defensive" about our defense mechanisms.⟩ ⟨⁴We all have them.⟩ (Note that 1 and 4 appear twice.)

DIAGRAM

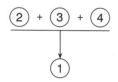

5.   BRACKETING AND NUMBERING

<Women (who perform household labor, including child care) are a group who work outside the money economy.>¹ <Their work is not worth² money,>³ <is (therefore) valueless,>⁴ <is (therefore) not even real work.> And (then) <women themselves who do this valueless work, can hardly be expected⁵ to be worth as much as men who work for money.>

DIAGRAM

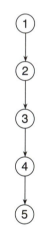

The antecedent of "their" is "Women (who perform household labor, including child care)."

10.   BRACKETING AND NUMBERING

(Since) <~~I know now that~~ <my nature is very weak and limited,>¹ but that <the² nature of God is immense, incomprehensible, and infinite,> (therefore,) <~~I also know with sufficient evidence that~~ <he can make innumerable things³ whose causes escape me.>

optional   *optional*

DIAGRAM

EXERCISE 3.1

5. A and C are knaves and B is a knight. B cannot be a knave. If B is a knave, then what he says is false. In other words, it is not the case that at most two of them are knights. The negation of "at most two" is "three or more." In other words, for B to be lying, all three of them are knights, in which case B would have to be a lying knight, which is impossible. So B is not lying in which case B is a knight. So A is lying, and C is lying. It is true that at most two of them are knights.

EXERCISE 3.2

1. A cannot be determined, but B is a knave.

    Case 1: A is a knight. B is different from A. So B is a knave.
    Case 2: A is a knave. B is the same as A (because A is lying!). So, again, B is a knave.

    These are the only two cases. We do not have enough information to determine A, but B must be a knave.

EXERCISE 3.3

1. True
5. False
10. My car is neither red nor green.

EXERCISE 3.4

1. Yes, false.
5. Yes, false. ("Neither P nor Q" is the negation of P and the negation of Q. So P must be false when "Neither P nor Q" is true.)

EXERCISE 3.5

1.   A is a knave. B is a knave. C is a knave. Here is the reasoning: Suppose A is a knight. Then what A says is true. A is asserting a conjunctive sentence, so the whole thing must be true. That means that both conjuncts are true. "I am a knave" is one of the conjuncts, so it would have to be true. But then A is a knave. So A is both a knight and a knave. This is impossible. So A cannot be a knight. Thus A is a knave. (Note that we are not supposing that A is a knave. We have now definitely proven that A is a knave.) Since A is a knave, B is lying (B says that A is a knight). So B is also a knave. If C is a knight, then what A says would be true because both conjuncts of what A says would be true: A is a knave and there is at least one knight (namely C). We have already established that A is a knave, so what A says cannot be true. So C cannot be a knight.

5.   A cannot be determined. B and C are knights.

   Case 1:   A is a knight. They must all be knights.

   Case 2:   A is a knave. What A says is false. So they cannot all be knights or all be knaves. If B is a knave, then C is a knave. So they would all be knaves. This is impossible. So B is a knight and C is a knight.

EXERCISE 3.6

1.   C must be a normal, because no knight or knave could say "I am a knave." So B is a knave and A is a knight.

5.   A is a knight. B is a knave. C is a normal.

EXERCISE 4.1

1.   At least one is false.

5.   Nothing.

10.   Nothing.

EXERCISE 4.2

1.   Form:

   All *A* are *B*.

   No *C* are *A*.
   _____

   No *C* are *B*.

The argument is invalid as is demonstrated by the following argument of the same form.

All poodles are dogs. (True)
No beagles are poodles. (True)

No beagles are dogs. (False)

This argument has true premises and a false conclusion.
Drawing to demonstrate invalidity:

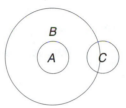

Note that the premises have been drawn without drawing the conclusion. "No B are C" would have to be B C.

5. Form:

All *A* are *B*.
All *B* are *C*.

All *C* are *A*.

This is invalid.
Substitutions to demonstrate invalidity:

All zebras are mammals. (True)
All mammals are animals. (True)

So all animals are zebras. (False)

Drawing to demonstrate invalidity:

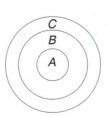

10.   Form:

No *A* are *B*.

Some *C* are not *B*.

Some *C* are not *A*.

This is invalid.
Substitution to demonstrate invalidity:

No horses are cows. (True)

Some mares are not cows. (True; at least one mare is not a cow)

So some mares are not horses. (False)

Drawing to demonstrate invalidity:

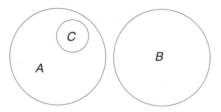

EXERCISE 4.3

1.   Valid.
5.   This depends. If we add that Harriet's printer needs the ribbon to print, then it is valid. It could also be considered to be invalid, if we are imaginative. It is possible that Harriet's printer is a dual mode printer with a ribbon and a cartridge. So it could still print even though the ribbon is used up. We have to have more information in the premises about the printer for it to be valid.
10.   Invalid. If there are both males and females in the room, as there certainly could be, then the premise is true and the conclusion is false.

EXERCISE 4.4

1.   Valid.
5.   Invalid. In fact, the premise contradicts the conclusion.
10.   Invalid. This one is similar to arguments used to show that Oswald could not have acted alone. The gun starts out loaded and aimed. It takes six seconds to get off three shots.
15.   Invalid. The market might have started out very low on Monday morning.

EXERCISE 5.1

1. Being male. Having a sibling.
6. N
9. S
14. 0
19. N

EXERCISE 5.2

3. Owning a chair. Other possible answers: Owning a table, owning a couch, owning a bed.
   If you own a chair (table, couch, bed, etc.), then you own a piece of furniture. The antecedent is "you own a chair."
   The consequent is "you own a piece of furniture." (Remember that the sufficient condition goes in the antecedent and the necessary condition goes in the consequent. So "If you own a chair, then you own a piece of furniture" also expresses the fact that owning a piece of furniture is necessary for owning a chair.)
6. Being male and having a nephew. (Note that simply having a nephew is not sufficient for being an uncle. Someone could have a nephew and be an aunt.)
   If you are male and have a nephew, then you are an uncle.
11. Being later than 2:17 P.M., January 2, 1987.

   If it is later than 2:17 P.M., January 2, 1987, then it is later than 2:16 P.M. January 2, 1987.

EXERCISE 5.3

1. Something is a knife if and only if it is a bladed, straight-handled tool used for cutting or scraping. (Note that it is very difficult or impossible to give totally adequate answers in this exercise. For example, this answer might still include some saws, which should be distinguished from knives.)
6. X commits suicide if and only if X is a person and X intentionally kills X, and X wanted to die as a result of X's intentional killing of X, or Y is a person and X intentionally has Y kill X. (This is very difficult as well. Notice that this definition implies that animals cannot commit suicide. More importantly it implies that "assisted suicide" is indeed a form of suicide. Both of these claims are controversial.)

EXERCISE 5.4

1. 0 (Someone could have a niece and be an uncle.)
5. N
9. 0

EXERCISE 5.5

2. Being a college sophomore.
5. Owning a scissors.
10. Being male and having a grandchild.

EXERCISE 6.1

1. S is sufficient for N = if S, then N = S only if N.
6. Items b, c, and d should be underlined.
9. Only item m should be underlined.

EXERCISE 6.2

1. Items b, c, and d should be underlined.
6. Items a, b, and e should be underlined.

EXERCISE 7.1

1.

BRACKETING AND NUMBERING

⟨This computer can do word processing.⟩ And ⟨if it can do word processing, then it can probably do spread sheets.⟩ So ⟨this computer can probably do spread sheets.⟩

DIAGRAM

Pattern of inference: *modus ponens*. It is valid.

6.   **BRACKETING AND NUMBERING**

$\langle$^1 If Harry owns adog, then Harry owns an animal.$\rangle$ $\langle$^2 Harry does not own
an animal.$\rangle$ (So) $\langle$^3 Harry does not own a dog.$\rangle$

DIAGRAM

Pattern of inference: *modus tollens*. It is valid.

EXERCISE 7.2

1.   Conclusion: It was the duke.

BRACKETING AND NUMBERING

$\langle$^1 We have previously established that it was either the butler or the duke.$\rangle$
$\langle$^2 We now know it could not have been the butler,$\rangle$ $\langle$^3 It was the duke.$\rangle$

DIAGRAM

Pattern of inference: disjunctive syllogism. It is valid.

6.   **BRACKETING AND NUMBERING**

$\langle$^1 If an argument is sound, then it is valid.$\rangle$ (So) $\langle$^2 if it is invalid, it is unsound.$\rangle$

DIAGRAM

6. Pattern of inference: transposition. It is valid.

EXERCISE 7.3

1. **BRACKETING AND NUMBERING**

[1] Either the moon goes around the earth or the earth goes around the moon. [2] The moon does not go around the earth. Hence [3] the earth goes around the moon.

DIAGRAM

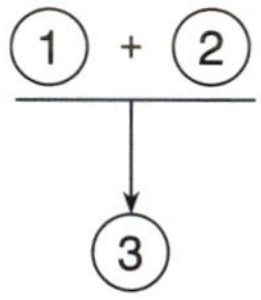

Pattern of inference: disjunctive syllogism. It is valid.

5. **BRACKETING AND NUMBERING**

[1] If I won the lottery, then I would have an obligation to donate some of my income to charity. [2] I have not won the lottery. So [3] I have no obligation to donate some of my income to charity.

DIAGRAM

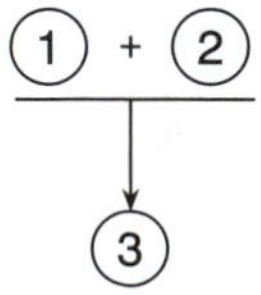

Pattern of inference: fallacy of denying the antecedent. It is invalid (there are many other ways you could incur an obligation to donate some income to charity besides winning the lottery).

10.   **BRACKETING AND NUMBERING**

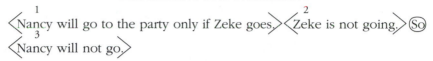

1
⟨Nancy will go to the party only if Zeke goes,⟩ 2 ⟨Zeke is not going.⟩ So
3
⟨Nancy will not go.⟩

DIAGRAM

Pattern of inference: *modus tollens*. It is valid.

EXERCISE 7.4

1.   **BRACKETING AND NUMBERING**

1
⟨If abortion is murder, then the fetus is a person.⟩ 2 ⟨If the fetus is a person,
then it has all the essential charactereristics of persons.⟩ But 3 ⟨the fetus does
not have all the essential characteristics of persons,⟩ So 4 ⟨abortion is not
murder.⟩

DIAGRAM

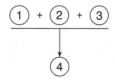

Suppressed intermediate conclusion: "If abortion is murder, then the fetus has all the essential characteristics of persons."
Pattern of inference: pure hypothetical syllogism plus *modus tollens*. It is valid.

DIAGRAM WITH SUPPRESSED PREMISE

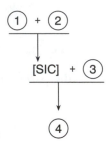

Alternatively it could be a combination of *modus tollens* and *modus tollens* with a suppressed intermediate conclusion: "The fetus is not a person."

5.   **BRACKETING AND NUMBERING**

⟨Dallas will make the playoffs only if Detroit loses or Buffalo wins.⟩¹ ⟨Pitts-
burgh is eliminated, if Detroit loses or Buffalo wins.⟩² ⟨So⟩ ⟨Dallas will not
make the playoffs unless Pittsburgh is eliminated.⟩³

DIAGRAM

Pattern of inference: pure hypothetical syllogism. It is valid.

11.   **BRACKETING AND NUMBERING**

⟨If something is worthy of desire, then it is good.⟩¹ ⟨If something is impossible to achieve, then it is unworthy of desire.⟩² ⟨So⟩ ⟨if something is good,
then it is possible to achieve.⟩³

DIAGRAM

By transposition, "If something is impossible to achieve, then it is unworthy of desire" equals "If something is worthy of desire, then it is possible to achieve." Form of argument:

If A, then B.

If A, then C.

If B, then C.

It is invalid.

If you own a collie, then you own an animal. (True)

If you own a collie, then you own a dog. (True)

So if you own an animal, then you own a dog. (False; you could own a cat)

EXERCISE 8.1

1. I'm going out tonight.
5. All people should have rights.
12. Some English majors are not athletes.

EXERCISE 8.2

1. Ghosts are not material things.
5. Teachers who work with the youngest children are the most important teachers of all.
10. Maynard is not authorized to prescribe medical treatment. We must interpret the given premise as "[All and] only doctors are authorized to prescribe medical treatment" or the argument is not valid.

EXERCISE 8.3

3. God is perfect.
7. Things that are not socially perceived as human and that cannot communicate with others are not members of society.

EXERCISE 9.1

1. All basketball players are tall.
5. All poetry is boring.

EXERCISE 9.2

1. Class: States in the United States
    Property: Being on the North American mainland
    Counterexample: Hawaii

7. Class: Great scientists
    Property: Being a man
    Counterexample: Madame Curie

14. Class: Morally right things to do.
    Property: Whatever would bring about the greatest balance of happiness over unhappiness.
    Counterexample: Turning in a fellow student who cheats on a test. It does not bring about the most happiness (in fact, it makes everybody unhappy, which is why it is so difficult to do), but it is the morally right thing to do.

EXERCISE 10.1

1. General

6. Limited (Most times you are skipping you have both feet on the ground.)

11. Specific (About the Supreme Court.)

EXERCISE 10.2

1. Very plausible. People get exited when they win the lottery. Such excitement can cause heart failure. Reliable source. Perform autopsy.

7. Not very plausible. Tobacco smoke contains carcinogens and other irritants. Biased source.

13. Very plausible. Most 100-watt bulbs are probably about equally bright and last about the same length of time. There are truth in advertising laws. (Note that the claim is not that GZ bulbs are brighter and last longer. That would be quite implausible.)

EXERCISE 10.3

4. Pretty good source. People have the ability to recognize each other. A friend should not be tempted to lie about such a thing (after all, just walking with someone else downtown does not amount to much).

EXERCISE 10.4

1. Truck going by. Airplane flying over. Earthquake. Giant gorilla climbing building. Construction nearby.

Truck, airplane, and construction are about equally plausible and head the list. They are easy to check by observation. Earthquake is the next most plausible of these explanations. Check readings on local seismograph. Giant Gorilla is very implausible.

EXERCISE 11.1

1. Statistical argument. 89% support.

6. Inductive generalization. Very low support. The sample is big cats in zoos. The population is big cats (lions, tigers, etc.). The behavior of big cats in zoos is not a good indication of their natural behavior in the wild.

EXERCISE 12.1

1. The causal claim is: A thorough dental cleaning causes soreness that lasts a day or two. The cause is a thorough dental cleaning. The effect is soreness that lasts a day or two. The mechanisms are sensitive teeth and deep scaling (irritates delicate tissues, etc.).

5. The causal claim being considered is that habitual use of mouthwashes with more 25% alcohol causes oral cancer. Cause is habitual use of mouthwashes with more than 25% alcohol. The effect is oral cancer. The support is the two cited studies. No mechanism is suggested (alcohol is not a carcinogen). There are several possibilities for competing causal explanations. One is that people who are heavy smokers or who eat large amounts of spicy food might be more likely to use an alcohol-based mouthwash and are more likely to have oral cancer. In this case, there would be a common cause. Another is that the correlation is simply coincidence. This possibility is suggested by the fact that some studies found a correlation whereas others did not.

12. In this case the causal claim is that the three biasing ecological conditions cause monogamy. The mechanism is that the Darwinian advantage of cooperation in rearing offspring outweighs the advantage to either partner of seeking extra mates when those ecological conditions occur. Yes, it would be fair to say that the author is claiming a causal relationship. He says the three ecological conditions "account for" all known cases of monogamy. Such "accounting for" in biology can only be causal.

EXERCISE 12.2

1. Clearly this causal judgment is not justified. Either of two alternatives are possible here. One is that it has got the direction of causality wrong. It is the birth, or at least the birth process, that causes pregnant women to go to the hospital. Or it could be coincidence: the women would have had the babies anyway whether or not they went to the hospital. Either answer is correct.

5. Not justified. This is clearly a coincidence. The two processes are not causally related.

EXERCISE 13.1

1. Food would correspond to fuel. Feces, urine, and exhaled breath would correspond to the exhaust. The gas tank would correspond to the stomach; headlights, to eyes; pistons to muscles. (I will leave the rest of the correspondences for the reader to figure out.) One important conclusion is that just as you must take good care of your car (keep it in good running condition, tuned up, clean fuel, change oil, etc.) if it is to run well, you must take good care of your body (do not feed it junk, get lots of exercise, etc.) if you expect it to keep running well.

6. I will not give a complete answer here, but some interesting analogies between vision and knowledge are that both vision and knowledge require proper conditions. We can only see something when there is light, our eyes are open, and our eyes are focused on the object. Likewise knowledge requires that our minds be open, that we be receptive and focused, and that nothing is interfering with our thoughts. There are many other analogies between vision and knowledge. Many have suggested that just as vision is always from a point of view or perspective so also is knowledge.

EXERCISE 13.2

1. Model: computer poker.
Thing modeled: real poker at the casino.
Similarities: Numbers, suits, and so on in both; winning and losing; ranking of hands; random distribution of cards to hands (presumably).
Differences: One big difference—no human opponent in the computer game. Another is that you play your computer game at home. The real poker game is in a public place.
These differences are crucial. Human opponents can use psychological tricks to distract you or bluff you. The atmosphere of a casino is calculated to provoke risk taking and to cloud thought (lots of noise and alcohol).

5. Among other things, the premise is wrong in this analogy. Arithmetic is clearly more than just manipulating signs and symbols. Arithmetic involves understanding and using important relationships that are crucial to our way of life. The same is true of reasoning.

EXERCISE 13.3

2. I will answer just some of these questions: The model is a city. The thing modeled is language. Wittgenstein's point in saying that the symbolism of

chemistry and the notation of calculus are suburbs is that the symbolism of chemistry and the notation of calculus are fairly recent additions, are not quite part of the language (just as the suburbs are outside of the city), are artificial and contrived, planned and carefully laid out. His deeper point is that just as some politicians and city planners have been misled into thinking that all urban areas should be rebuilt to be like suburbs, some philosophers have been misled into thinking that natural languages should be reformed to be more like scientific and mathematical notations. It would be possible to write an entire book just devoted to exploring this analogy.

EXERCISE 14.1

1. Fallacy: false alternatives. Many votes have nothing to do with the environment (e.g., when I vote for someone for school board).

6. Fallacy: *ad hominem*/genetic. The discourse is talking about the people giving the arguments and what causes them to do it. This is irrelevant to the soundness of the arguments against smoking.

EXERCISE 14.2

1. This is very difficult. The passage must be read very closely. Olsen does *not* say "The court is saying that children have no rights under the constitution," which would be a straw man. She is saying "The court is saying that children have no *protection* under the constitution." This may be a bit exaggerated, but it is not clearly a straw man. After all, at least from the article's contents this seems to be what the court is saying. I think the problem is that "protection" is somewhat ambiguous. What the court seems to be saying is that children have no special right to demand protection from the state. Children still have all those protections afforded to any citizens under the constitution. Charitably interpreted, I do not think Olsen has committed a straw man, but others may differ about this.

6. Clearly, this is not a fallacious appeal to authority. The Surgeon General is an appropriate authority on health. There is plenty of research to back her up and lots of other experts and doctors agree that smoking is bad for your health.

EXERCISE 15.1

1. The doctors recommend the ingredients (which are probably in most arthritis pills) *not* Arthro-Sooth Pills themselves.

6. How much is an oodle?

15. We would have to know the number of people riding bicycles. It could have much more than doubled in twenty years. This is just the sort of figure that can

be used (and abused) in many ways. For example, someone could use the same figures to argue that helmets should not be required. After all, the number of bicycle fatalities more than doubled during a period of increased use of helmets.

EXERCISE 15.2

2.   Environmentalist: Someone who holds a solid, clear-headed, scientific, and politically respectable position on the environment.
     Tree-hugger: A nut who likes plants more than people.

Index